5/11

D0397881

YELLOW DIRT

*An American Story of
a Poisoned Land
and
a People Betrayed*

Judy Pasternak

Free Press

New York London Toronto Sydney

*f*P
Free Press
A Division of Simon & Schuster, Inc.
1230 Avenue of the Americas
New York, NY 10020

Copyright © 2010 by Judy Pasternak

First Free Press hardcover edition September 2010

FREE PRESS and colophon are trademarks of Simon & Schuster, Inc.

For information about special discounts for bulk purchases, please contact Simon & Schuster Special Sales at 1-866-506-1949 or business@simonandschuster.com

The Simon & Schuster Speakers Bureau can bring authors to your live event. For more information or to book an event contact the Simon & Schuster Speakers Bureau at 1-866-248-3049 or visit our website at www.simonspeakers.com.

Manufactured in the United States of America

3   5   7   9   10   8   6   4   2

Library of Congress Cataloging-in-Publication Data

Pasternak, Judy
Yellow dirt : an American story of a poisoned land and a people betrayed / Judy Pasternak.—1st Free Press hardcover ed.
p.   cm.
Includes bibliographical references.
1. Navajo Indians—Government relations—History—20th century.
2. Navajo Indians—Health and hygiene—History—20th century.   3. Navajo Indians—Biography.   4. Uranium mines and mining—Political aspects—Southwest, New—History—20th century.   5. Uranium mines and mining—Social aspects—Southwest, New—History—20th century.   6. Radiation—Health aspects—Southwest, New—History—20th century.   7. Navajo Indian Reservation—History—20th century.   8. Southwest, New—Ethnic relations—History—20th century.   I. Title.
E99.N3P378   2010
979.1004'9726—dc22   2010005546

ISBN: 978-1-4165-9482-6
ISBN: 978-1-4391-0046-2 (ebook)

Los Angeles Times photos by Gail Fisher, © 2006.
Los Angeles Times graphic by Doug Stevens, © 2006.
Reprinted with permission.

Front matter photo copyright © Gail Fisher/*Los Angeles Times*

For Steve and Isaac, of course

CONTENTS

TOXIC LEGACY

PART III: THE GRANDCHILDREN
Aftermath

PART IV: THE GREAT-GRANDCHILDREN
Death and Awakening

PRINCIPAL CHARACTERS

CANE VALLEY (in Arizona and Utah, east of Monument Valley)

Adakai Son of Woman With the Stone House and Man With the Red Hair. Also known as the Gambler or John Adakai.

Anna Sling Adakai's younger wife.

John Holiday Adakai's nephew and a sheepherder. Also known as Little John Holiday.

Luke Yazzie Adakai's son (by his younger wife).

June Yazzie Luke's wife.

Mary Lou Yazzie Luke's daughter.

Lewis Yazzie Luke's son.

Lillie Sloan Adakai's daughter.

Oscar Sloan Lillie's husband.

Hoskey Sloan Their son.

Anna Adakai Cly Adakai's daughter (by his older wife).

Ben Stanley Son of Anna Adakai Cly.

Mary Stanley Ben's wife.

Adakai's Daughter Adakai's daughter (by his younger wife).

Juanita Jackson Adakai's granddaughter, child of Adakai's daughter.

Eunice Jackson Juanita's daughter.

Lorissa Jackson Juanita's daughter.

Patricia Seltzer The principal at Monument Valley High School, where Lorissa Jackson teaches business and technology.

Trent Harris A movie director based in Salt Lake City, hired by the Utah Arts Council to serve as a consultant for Lorissa Jackson's student film crew.

TRADING POSTS

John Wetherill The trader at Kayenta, south of Monument Valley, also known as Old John.

Louisa Wade Wetherill John's wife, also known as Slim Woman.

Preston Redd John Wetherill's former employee.

Harry Goulding The trader at Monument Valley.

John Ford Movie director who made legendary Westerns in Monument Valley.

VANADIUM CORPORATION OF AMERICA

Denny Viles Vanadium Corporation of America (VCA) vice president for mining and field manager. He lived in Monticello, Utah, when the company operated a vanadium mill there, and later in Durango, Colorado.

Page Edwards Worked during the war for the government's Metals Reserve program as the liaison to VCA's Monticello plant. Later, an executive at VCA.

Mary Elizabeth Edwards Page Edwards's wife.

Bob Anderson The regional manager in charge of VCA's Navajo mines.

Carl Bell Foreman at VCA's Monument No. 2.

U.S. GOVERNMENT

In Washington:

Harold Ickes U.S. secretary of the interior from 1933 to 1946.

Gen. Leslie Groves Chief of the supersecret Manhattan Project.

Jesse C. Johnson A former Metals Reserve official who became director of Raw Materials for the Atomic Energy Commission, the civilian successor to the Manhattan Project.

Henry Waxman A powerful U.S. congressman from California.

In the West:

Ralph V. Batie AEC health and safety chief in Colorado.

Duncan Holaday Public Health Service chemist based in Salt Lake City.

Howard B. Nickelson A geologist for the U.S. Geological Survey who was detailed to the reservation as an inspector of uranium mines.

Charles Reaux Environmental official in the Navajo region of Indian Health Service from 1983 to 1988.

Joseph Hans A radiation expert for the Environmental Protection Agency, based in Las Vegas.

Richard Auld Indian Health Service doctor on the reservation with suspicions about the prevalence of gastric cancer.

Donald Payne Environmental health officer for the Indian Health Service, based in the Navajo region.

Glynn Alsup A toxics specialist with the U.S. Army Corps of Engineers, he was based in Los Angeles but spent the better part of 1998–2000 collecting water samples on the reservation.

NAVAJO TRIBAL OFFICIALS

Sam Ahkeah Navajo tribal council chairman from 1946 to 1954.

Paul Jones Ahkeah's successor as tribal chairman, Jones served from 1955 to 1963.

Peter MacDonald Tribal chairman from 1970 to 1982.

Peterson Zah Tribal chairman from 1982 to 1987 and the first Navajo Nation president, from 1991 to 1994.

Harold Tso Director of the Navajo Environmental Protection Commission from 1974 to 1980.

Sadie Hoskie Director, Navajo Nation Environmental Protection Agency, from 1991 to July of 1994.

Derrith Watchman-Moore Director of the Navajo Nation EPA, she left in 2003 to join the administration of the governor of New Mexico Bill Richardson.

Diane Malone Superfund manager for the Navajo Nation EPA.

Cassandra Bloede Solid waste manager for the Navajo Nation EPA.

David Taylor An attorney in the Navajo Nation Department of Justice.

John Hueston A former federal prosecutor most famed for leading the U.S. government's team in the Enron fraud case, he was retained by the tribe in 2007.

OLJATO (in Utah, west of Monument Valley)

Mary and Billy Boy Holiday A Navajo couple who purchased a *hooghan* in Oljato.

Elsie Begay Mary's niece.

Leonard Begay Elsie's son.

Sarah Begay Leonard's wife.

Jeff Spitz A movie director from Chicago, he filmed the story of Elsie and her family.

CAMERON and TAH-CHEE (in Arizona)

Lois Neztsosie A Navajo shepherd who grazed her flocks in the Cameron area, near the Grand Canyon.

David Neztsosie, Sr. Lois's husband.

Laura Neztsosie The Neztsosies' second youngest child, who was diagnosed with Navajo neuropathy.

Arlinda "Linnie" Neztsosie The Neztsosies' youngest daughter, who was diagnosed with Navajo neuropathy.

Cherie Daut A lawyer for former uranium miners seeking compensation under the federal program set up for payments, she later filed suit for Navajo neuropathy plaintiffs.

Helen and Leonard Nez A couple who lost six children to Navajo neuropathy.

Steve Helgerson An Indian Health Service epidemiologist, he led a study of Navajo neuropathy.

James Justice A former Indian Health Service epidemiologist who was hired as an expert by the Navajo neuropathy plaintiffs.

Salvatore DiMauro A Columbia University scientist, he specializes in mitochondrial disorders.

RED VALLEY including Oaksprings and Cove (at the New Mexico–Arizona line)

Paul Shorty A Navajo who partnered with his friend, King Tutt, to stake uranium claims.

Clifford Frank A miner and resident of Oaksprings.

Mae John A mining widow who became a leader in the fight for compensation.

Harry Tome A tribal council delegate from Red Valley.

Stewart Udall A former U.S. congressman, he served as secretary of the interior from 1961 to 1969. He became the lawyer for Navajo uranium miners seeking compensation.

Tom Udall Stewart Udall's son. He worked as an investigator on the case and then went on to win public office, serving as New Mexico's attorney general and later as a member of the U.S. House of Representatives and U.S. Senate.

Marshall Tome Harry's brother and a Red Valley leader.

Franz Geiger Northwestern University chemist recruited by a group from Red Valley to take samples of water and soil in 2004.

BLACK FALLS (in Arizona, outside of the border town of Flagstaff)

Milton Yazzie A Black Falls resident who grew concerned about the illnesses that had developed in his absence.

Jani Ingram A chemist at Northern Arizona University who came to Black Falls to sample the water.

CHURCH ROCK/CROWNPOINT (in New Mexico, outside of Gallup)

Mitchell Capitan A founder of Eastern Navajo Diné Against Uranium Mining.

Larry King A rancher and board member of ENDAUM.

Chris Shuey A researcher, community organizer, and environmental activist from the Southwest Research and Information Center. He is based in Albuquerque.

YELLOW DIRT

Prologue

S-37, SOM, and SOQ

The white men first showed up in the summer of 1943. They came from the north, from Colorado, in teams of half a dozen each, hunkered down in trucks until the roads ran out. Then they switched to horses, riding into the silent reaches of the Navajo reservation, leaving their own country behind though they were still within its borders. They entered a place that seemed mystical and wild, where the residents spoke little or no English and only a few could write their names, where medicine men chanted and sifted colored sand, and witches were said to haunt the deep night along with coyotes and bears.

But, of course, to the *Diné*—The People, as the Navajos called themselves—it was the white men who were the curiosities. As summer became fall, and then the year turned, the white men kept showing up, staying for weeks at a time. The *Diné* kept an eye on the intruders, watching as one group took over a vacant cabin near a trading post. The whites lugged in bedrolls (why not soft, light sheepskins?) so they could sleep comfortably on the floor. The quarters had a stove, but no venting system, so the white men struggled to install a pipe inside to channel the smoke away. (Why not simply build a campfire out of doors?) Their makeshift flue was too short to reach the ceiling, so they jammed rocks under the stove to jack it up. Whoever was cook for the day had to stand on a chair to prepare the meals.[1]

The white men never, ever lacked for food. They brought with them fresh eggs, and all manner of meat and sugar and cheese, in large amounts

1

that would cost a goodly sum at any trading post. This was wartime, and supplies like these were supposed to be strictly rationed, even for the wealthiest people in the outside world. For these crews, apparently, someone would provide.

They needed their strength, after all. At daybreak, they donned khaki work clothes, pulled on boots—snakes were a constant concern—and secured their brimmed helmets to keep the sun's glare at bay. They saddled up, crossing dry washes and galloping over brushy plains until rough terrain forced them to dismount. Carefully, methodically, they paced along the bases of layered sandstone cliffs. From leather cases they brought forth fine-tipped pens and from cardboard tubes they unfurled high-quality paper. They set up a flat table on a tripod and equipped it with a telescope device that they repeatedly looked through. The Indians had seen surveyors before and recognized that the white men were calibrating distances, fixing their location.

They scaled hulking buttes, stopping wherever they could to put pen to paper again. They climbed into mountain ranges—the Carrizos, the Chuskas, and the Lukachukais—up past scrubby pinyons and junipers, until they reached tall cool stands of ponderosa pine. From the mesa ridges and the highest peaks, the bleak beauty of the Navajo homeland unspooled clear and still beneath them, while hawks and eagles wheeled through the wide blue skies. The San Juan River glistened as it wound its way north. Shiprock Pinnacle, the stone colossus that sailed the valley floor, stood massed against the southeast horizon.

On the scrolls the white men carried, a different version of the landscape, inked and flat and monochrome, began taking shape. Craggy heights and vast sand flats were reduced to dotted lines and points, each one numbered and labeled in cramped, meticulous print. Dirt roads and horse trails were reproduced, and surface drainage noted, and the prehistoric ages of rock strata upon which dinosaurs once lumbered were duly calculated and recorded.[2]

What were these illustrators up to? One Navajo in particular let the explorers know he was scrutinizing them just as they were scrutinizing his range. From a short remove, he observed them for hours every day. Finally, he approached the one who seemed to be the leader and, through gestures, made it known that he would like to be their host. Perhaps his wife would cook some mutton and grind some corn for kneel-down bread. The leader understood but shook his head. No. No.

The Indian never watched them work again.[3]

How could he know that the white men were afraid, not of him but of themselves? They feared that they might slip and reveal their purpose.

If asked, the white men had been told, they should explain that they worked for an international mining concern. They were given a name for this company, Union Mines Development Corp., and ample care had been taken to create proof of its existence. The firm had a real headquarters on the eighteenth floor of a real building, at 50 East Forty-second Street in far-off New York City.[4] Union Mines even set up a regional office, in the First National Bank Building, suite 404, in the Colorado peach town of Grand Junction.[5] The men were based there.

Union Mines, they were to say, was scouring all of Planet Earth for tungsten, molybdenum, and vanadium. The last mineral on the list, at least, was familiar to the Navajos. They knew that vanadium was helping to win World War II where many of their sons and grandsons were serving. This vanadium, mixed into steel, could harden the armor that protected Navy warships. They knew, too, that vanadium did lie under the soil of *Diné bikeyah*, the Home of the People.

Navajos had a complicated history with white men who wanted to exploit their resources. During the uninvited march of European and American pioneers across the continent, they had endured much for their territory: fierce canyon fighting, defeat, and bitter exile, only winning return in 1868. They'd been expelled, in part, to stop their merciless raids on settlers and neighbor tribes. But they'd also been removed so covetous outsiders, who suspected that the *Diné* lived atop vast stores of oil and gold, could try their luck with the land. Yet, alone of all the Indian tribes forced from their homes, the Navajos had come back to the one place where they belong. They could abide once more in their holy land, granted to them by their Creators, with a treaty that made the United States their guardian and protector in exchange for peace. Yet the grab for what lay underneath their reservation continued.

Prospectors kept appearing, and individual Navajos felt free to show their displeasure in the old fierce way; some trespassers never got back out. More than once, the federal Guardian tried to take decision making over minerals out of Navajo hands, but during the 1930s, the tribal council made clear, first off, that the delegates should have the last word, and next, that they rejected new exploration on the *Dinétah* in no uncertain terms.

It was a madman in Germany who changed their minds. In 1940, as the great conflict with the Nazis cast its shadow beyond Europe, the tribal council voted to express full support for the United States. The delegates took their treaty seriously. "Be it resolved," the council promised, "that the Navajo Indians stand ready . . . to aid and defend our government and institutions, and pledge our loyalty . . ."[6]

After the Japanese bombed Pearl Harbor and America jumped into a two-front war, the Navajos backed their sentiments with concrete sacrifice. They offered up their young men, and they offered up their language. Navajo Code Talkers passed important messages back and forth in the Pacific, their words inexplicable to the enemy listening in.

And if vanadium could help, then vanadium the Guardian would get. In 1941, the tribe reversed its longtime anti-mining stance and authorized the secretary of the interior to issue leases to the highest bidder on the Navajos' behalf.[7] When the men of Union Mines showed up, vanadium mining had just begun on the reservation. Another white-man-New-York company, the Vanadium Corp. of America, had contracted the previous year for several Navajo properties and was already hiring locals to dig out the ore.

So the Union Mines story was plausible. It should be easy to accept that a second business wanted to get in on this patriotic market.

But if the Navajos had been able to read and understand the reports compiled by this newest group of white men, they would have realized that vanadium was not the object of the hunt. The prize the white men sought was something else—and it might be located alongside the vanadium, in the same channels of rock. Union Mines employed code talkers, too. ". . . *31 ft. long outcrop, avg thickness 3.2 ft. of vanadium with some weakly disseminated S-37 . . .*" They wrote not just of S-37, which was an indicator that the treasure was close at hand, but of SOM, the thing itself, and SOQ, the product that could be fashioned from it.[8]

The white men stood at the outermost ring of a concentric system of secrets. They knew more than the tribal council and more even than the Indian Commissioner's superintendent on scene. They knew who was truly behind Union Mines. They knew exactly what they were looking for, and finding.

But they didn't know why. They didn't know that S-37 and SOM and SOQ fit into the plans of the most brilliant physicists, the highest-ranking generals, and even the president. They didn't know that they were changing history's course, laying groundwork for a gigantic push, a frenzy that would last for decades. They didn't know they were helping to unleash a primal force that could consume enemy cities in an instant with a towering cloud. Or that, in another form, it would emerge from hiding once the soil that blocked it had been stripped away, and in the decades following the war, it would silently, slowly, needlessly destroy American communities and lives

More than sixty years later, in June of 2005, I traveled from my home near Washington, D.C., to the Navajo Nation, which is now the formal name of the sovereign tribe. Another white interloper was coming to call. I too brought pens, but instead of cartography paper, I had stocked up on reporter's notebooks. And I carried a tool that had not been available to the men of Union Mines: a rented radiation detector.

With the passage of so much time, the reservation was in many ways a very different place. Yet I couldn't help but feel, as had those who came before me, that I had crossed an invisible checkpoint and should hold my passport close. Paved highways crossed the length and width of the twenty-first century *Dinétah*, which spans three states and is about the size of West Virginia. But in most places, it was still necessary to "make your own road," as I was so often instructed, by bumping over the path of least resistance in rock-strewn fields of tumbleweed and greasewood. (My city-slicker driving never failed to amuse.) You could admire the Code

Talker exhibit at Burger King, buy a Navajo taco at KFC, and hit up the one Chinese restaurant for a passable *moo goo gai pan*. Subdivisions of identical stucco homes with roofs of cheery blue or green had recently sprung up; the locals referred to them as "Smurf villages." This tribal-subsidized housing was not popular; many of the 180,000 people on the reservation still preferred to live, if they could, in remote enclaves of extended family, miles from any neighbors. A sizeable number still hauled their own water from wells and passed their evenings under the soft glow of a kerosene lamp. The children learned English in school, but I needed an interpreter with the elders and even with the middle-aged, who were more comfortable with the sonorous cadence of their native tongue. Navajo culture, against all odds, remained vital and strong.

Yet along with fast food and tract housing, modern-day troubles had infiltrated The Home of The People. Alcohol was banned in theory, but was easily smuggled in from border towns like Farmington, New Mexico, and Flagstaff, Arizona—as the roadside empties on the ground could readily attest. Gang graffiti decorated walls and fences. Tales of domestic violence were startlingly common, and statistics about poverty levels and life expectancy painted calamities by number.

There was something else holding these people back. Both their land and their lives were scarred deeply by SOM and SOQ, the substance that the Navajos called *ƚeetso*—"yellow dirt."

The great revelation had come in 1945: it was the Manhattan Project that had bankrolled the men of Union Mines, and uranium was their Holy Grail. Their country desperately needed it to make atomic bombs. After two superdetonations ended World War II, nations chose up sides once more, this time between Communism and Capitalism, and America worked feverishly to stockpile more of the most deadly weapons ever known. Through the most anxious Cold War years of the 1940s and '50s and '60s, mining companies swarmed *Diné bikeyah*, using maps from Union Mines; some even continued through the '80s. All that time, the Navajos dug up uranium, happy for the blessing of steady jobs and all that their new wages could buy: Plenty of food. A pickup truck. Clothing for the kids. They had little concept of its capacity to wreck their health until too late, when "yellow dirt" had crept into every aspect of their daily lives: their homes, their drinking water, their playgrounds, even their garbage dumps. Their Guardian elected not to warn them.

They certainly knew the hazards by the time that I arrived. The tribe had once been famous for low rates of cancer, but there was no more talk of a miraculous Navajo immunity. Though I thought I was prepared, I was horrified when I witnessed what had come to pass.

Below mountains once mapped by furtive scouts, I visited Cove, a hamlet of widows, where husband after husband had lost weight, felt a lump on the neck, coughed up blood, and died. Near Haystack Mountain, a man poured out his memories on liquor-sweetened breath: he described howls of pain rising from many relatives and friends suffering from cancer of the stomach. "That's why we drink," he said, excusing his condition. "We think we won't live long."

I toured Happy Valley, where every house had dangerous levels of radon—a colorless, odorless gas that "yellow dirt" gives off, escorting radioactive particles deep into the lungs. In one of Happy Valley's most unhappy bedrooms, I sat with a once-hale shepherd tethered to an oxygen tank by thin translucent tubes. While the sound of his labored breathing competed with the whirring machine, he tried to joke in Navajo. His daughter translated his halting, merry words; her voice was clogged with tears.

Later, I stood in a rural cemetery to watch a pair of neighbors dig a fresh grave. The deceased was dear friend to one, stepfather to the other. After half a day's drive, I reached a second burial ground, where I listened to a young widow talk out loud to an unmarked mound, vowing that she would raise funds for a headstone. Both of these victims died by simply trying to stay alive; for years, one unwittingly inhaled the fumes from "yellow dirt" at work, and the other did so while he slept at home.

My journey also took me to an abandoned mine that was once so confidential that even the covert crews sent by Union Mines never got close. The Vanadium Corporation of America had held the lease on Yazzie Mesa and adjoining property near the Arizona-Utah line, and VCA insisted, for competition's sake, that the entire region remain off limits. The government had a reason to placate VCA.

The area around Yazzie Mesa went on to become the biggest, richest, most productive source of "yellow dirt" in all the *Dinétah*. Hundreds labored, drilling, blasting, hammering, shipping off tons of ore that would be ground into more than five million pounds of precious yellowcake. In the process, low-level radiation, heavy metals, and radon were loosed from the dirt and rock.

To the Navajos who have dwelled for generations at its bottom, the mesa is the wounded center of their world. My detector revealed contamination that they had suspected all along. Many among them believe that the mining should never have been allowed in the first place, that the gouging of the mesa raped their Mother Earth. They say they were warned by one of their own not to intertwine their fates with *łeetso*. But they chose to do so anyway, and set in motion a slow environmental catastrophe, a fatal lesson in the perils of delay, a grand drama of betrayal and persistence, an American tragedy that has yet to play out to its end.

THE
URANIUM
RUSH

Part I

THE PATRIARCH

Discovery

Chapter 1

The Special Rocks

A dakai walked in beauty, as the Navajos say, and everyone could see that he reaped the blessings of a sacred life. He owned thousands of cattle and sheep. He had an older wife and a younger wife, sisters of the Red House clan. He could well afford two households, having settled a rare sanctuary in the harsh desert of the reservation's northern reaches, a lush plain amid the angled buttes and ocher sands. The swath of green marked the presence of springs that nurtured livestock and brought forth ample crops of melons, corn, and squash.

The extraordinary place had caught Adakai's eye from the high reaches of Comb Ridge, a rocky rise so tall and long that it was thought to be the Backbone of the World. He had been raised up there in the huge rock-walled *hooghan* of his formidable mother, who was called, appropriately enough, Woman With the Stone House. She rode an ornery mount known as Donkey Who Bites, owned a small white-handled pistol inlaid with turquoise, and carried a sagebrush branch that she kept sharpened to a point.[1] She applied cooked pine gum to this stick until it glistened like a sword, and even the bulls were afraid of her. Yet, tough as she was, she was known far and wide for her skill at healing with herbs. She traveled long miles to fetch the proper plants when a patient needed her assistance, and then she would travel even farther to administer her potion. She was as busy as Adakai's father, Man With the Red Hair, who sewed moccasins and leggings. But it was Woman With the Stone House who took charge of rearing Adakai with a characteristic mix of strict discipline and kindness. When she issued orders—and she worked her children hard—she always asked politely: "My baby, fetch some wood." "My baby, kill that lizard with a stone." Adakai helped shear the sheep, and stuffed wool into burlap bags to carry to the trading post. He helped sow crops at the family's farm on the far side of Comb Ridge, near the settlement of Dennehotso. After the harvest, he spread corn to dry and cut cantaloupe into thin strips for curing.

Yet when he grew to manhood, Adakai proved to have a mind of his own and a will as strong as his mother's. He obeyed Woman With the Stone House when she chose a bride for him and he moved to his wife's home camp several miles to the south, as dictated by Navajo custom. But after a few years, once the first three children had arrived, his wife asked her little sister to come help take care of the family and the flock, and Adakai liked what he saw. One day when the sister was out herding, Adakai approached and took her arm. From then on, he was married to her, too.[2] Then, as he reached middle age, he moved his expanding family away from all of the grandparents to the green place and made it his own.

He called his new home Dłeeshbi'tó, Tsé dich'iizhdees'ah, which means "Clay Springs, A Rough Rock."[3] Though the traditional language is still widely spoken in the Navajo Nation, few call the valley by that name anymore. On the white men's maps it is labeled Cane Valley, for the reeds, growing tall as a man, that still choke the water in two hand-dug ponds fed by the springs. Indeed, some of the Navajos also called Dłeeshbi'tó by the word Lók'aa'haagái, White Streak of Reed Coming Out.[4] Yet another name came into widespread use soon after Adakai died. The Navajos began referring to this locale as VCA, after the mining company that by then was transforming the land and the people.

But all of that came later. In the days of Dłeeshbi'tó, Tsé dich'iizhdees'ah, from sometime in the 1920s through the beginning of the 1940s, the valley belonged to Adakai and he, in turn, belonged to the valley. He was free to partake of its fruits, but he was also charged with protecting it. This was the Navajo Way, the binding pact that wraps the whole world into one interconnected force—spirits, humans, animals, plants, trees, water, rocks, and sky, all meant to bless and sustain one another.

Adakai liked a good time. His favorite diversion, in fact, gave him his name, which was derived from the Navajo word for "gambler." He was expert at a card game known as "Navajo 10," and he had an uncanny knack for drawing the high card in face-offs, similar to the white man's dice-throwing contests. He raced horses too, and seemed to always take the prize. He also enjoyed singing at squaw dances, where the women picked their partners. And he had a puckish side; after he left a relative's *hooghan,* a toddler might notice that one of his little red moccasins—just one— had disappeared with Adakai.[5]

Yet he took life very seriously. He seldom spoke, but was heeded when he did. He was, after all, the head of the community that had taken root. His two wives bore at least ten children between them, and the children married outsiders who joined them, and then most of the couples had ten or twelve children of their own. The people called him *Hostiin Adíka'í*— the respected Adakai, Mr. Gambler. Indeed, some said that he was like a god, that he had the power to point to a cloud and pull the rain down over the fields.[6] He was the one who passed along the commandments in the valley, just as his mother had up on the ridge: Build your *hooghan* facing east, toward sunrise. Get up early and run as fast and as far as you can, to guard against laziness and ensure that you grow strong. Always, always, show your gratitude for the bounty of this world, whether it comes in the form of a deer that must be sacrificed for dinner, or a secret place by the willows where you can gather salt. The proper prayers must be said, the holy corn pollen must be sprinkled. Show reverence in everything you do.

Each spring, scores of people gathered at a cedar shade house about a mile north of the springs that first drew Adakai's attention. On the appointed day, they carried dried fruits and corn from their winter stores, and heaped them all together, their voices blending too in a chant of joy that they'd survived the freezing season. They would sing their way up the valley again in the fall with offerings from summer vegetable gardens.[7]

Whenever he crossed paths with his oldest grandson from his oldest wife, Adakai proposed with delight a rejuvenating sweat bath. But as soon as the boy reached the age of six, even this respite proved an opportunity for instruction. Adakai, by this time in his fifties or sixties, enlisted the child's help in building the small rounded structure. Once you have that up, he told the boy, collect firewood. Heat stones in the fire. Use several blankets for a door. Pour the water and make steam. Take off your clothes, duck under the blanket for as long as you can, then go out and cool off, then go back inside, as many as eight times in all. The whole time, through the building, the preparing, the sweat, Adakai would break his habitual silence to recite stories nonstop, and of course all of them had morals. In the cozy darkness, the disembodied voice of the patriarch rang through the hot mist. The boy's skin soaked up the cleansing steam while his mind and heart absorbed the legends of The People: the four worlds of creation, the Monster Slayers, Coyote the Trickster, Spider Woman. "If you are wise and can understand the teachings," Adakai told his grandson, "it will take you through life." More directly, Adakai preached the virtues of raising many kinds of livestock. "That will take you a long way," he said.[8]

Treasure was counted in the throngs of lambs, horses, cattle, and goats roaming across *Dłeeshbi'tó, Tsé dich'iizhdees'ah.* They ambled past the *hooghan*s in the morning and evenings. They quenched their thirst in spring-fed pools famed both for the reeds that grew there and a large population of frogs croaking in the shade. The herds grazed their way across the sage-studded plain of the valley and up to the hill on the valley's western flank, where junipers and cedars rose high, and the saltbrush and yucca flourished low.

This good fortune, though, was relative. The rest of America thought it was suffering through the Great Depression at the time, yet most in the society outside the reservation enjoyed unimaginable luxury compared to Adakai's people. *Hostiin Adíka'í* himself dressed humbly, in thin slacks and a faded collared shirt. He always wore moccasins, never store-bought shoes, and he wrapped his long hair in the customary male bun, tied with rope. He generally added a headband. He kept a felt hat for formal occasions, but it was old and worn. The only sign of wealth and status was his silver concho belt.[9]

The Indians traveled not by car, but on foot, on horseback, or astride a donkey. They lived by season in their cozy rounded *hooghan*s made of earth, or in white canvas tents, or in open-sided structures topped with boughs—their "summer shade," they called these. They illuminated night not with the flip of a switch, but with a fire built of wood that they had collected or chopped themselves. When it was time for bed, they curled up on the dirt floor or unrolled a sheepskin, taking moccasins off feet and tucking them under heads to serve as pillows. They hauled drinking water home in buckets or barrels from the springs.

Hard labor ruled in this closed and austere realm, and Adakai demanded as much from himself as he did from the others. He employed helpers to herd his magnificent flock, but each day he too guided sheep, reserving for himself the mesa on the west, directly opposite Comb Ridge. This butte was worth the difficult climb for the banquet of shrubs that grew where it leveled off at the top.

Adakai foraged, too. He had not received the many years of training required of a medicine man, but like his mother, he knew his herbs and the prayers for special places. He made separate trips to this mesa for specific plants. These expeditions began early, as required by the Navajo Way; his slight figure could be seen trudging up the slope as black night paled into dawn. His first act upon reaching the summit was always to reach for the small deerskin sack that he kept close, grabbing a pinch of the corn pollen stored inside. He would let the light, fine grains fall through his hands upon the ground to thank the Holy Ones for the coming day. Only after blessings would he pluck tiny orange sumac berries, twist off sprigs of fragrant sage, or seek out feathery lime-green rabbit brush, according to his needs.

Looking east across his valley, he could watch the swollen, scarlet sun soar rapidly from behind Comb Ridge. Turning to the west, his gaze fell on the stark, twisted silhouettes of rock formations in the true desert miles away, the domain of movie men who'd set up shop to film their paeans to the cowboy frontier.

Unlike the Hollywood outsiders playing with six-shooters, Adakai could name all the sandstone spires, massive buttes, and whorled arches, bathed in reflected red: the Right Mitten and the Left, Gray Whiskers, Three Sisters, Bear and Rabbit, King on His Throne, arrayed in an ancient skyline that could have passed for Mars. The sun moved higher, melting into yellow, and the buttery new morning lit up the Gambler as he moved around atop the mesa.

So many excursions, such close inspection, turned every inch of the terrain into familiar ground. Occasionally he noticed a special kind of rock: chunks of grayish stone, stippled with powdery yellow veins, as if they were living beings with a circulatory system. He had never seen these up on Comb Ridge.

One day, it is said, white prospectors came to Adakai's valley and set up camp. Adakai went over to meet them. Over the course of several days, he returned again and again, making friendly overtures in order to divine their purpose. When they described what they were seeking, he immediately thought, They are looking for the special yellow rocks.[10]

He could not let them go up on the mesa. He did not trust any outsiders, least of all white men. He had his reasons, many of them, sound ones.

The first was the bitter memory of the Long Walk, still rehashed around the fires during the long hours inside the *hooghans* every winter. Through fighting, coercion, and persuasion, Col. Kit Carson, aided by old tribal enemies like the Comanches, Utes, and Mexicans, had rounded up the *Diné*, destroying their fields and stock animals, and every pot and vessel that could carry food. At the forbidding Canyon de Chelly, one of the resisters' last redoubts, Carson had ordered his men to chop down every last peach tree in a sizeable orchard that was a source of local pride as well as nourishment.[11] Throughout 1864 and 1865, the army had marched nearly nine thousand starving Navajos away from their home between the four sacred peaks. Outside these boundaries, they'd been taught, the healing ceremonies lost their powers. And the teachings appeared to be correct, for nature certainly careened out of balance in the four long years they spent hundreds of miles to the east at Fort Sumner. Under the army's supervision—the first superintendent was Carson himself—they were supposed to lean more heavily on farming than on nomadic ranching, and to live close together the "civilized" way. Instead, they were soon plagued by dysentery from bad water and besieged by cutworms in the corn, famished to the point that they let the soldiers have their way with the women and even some young girls, with a price exacted in the form of rations.[12]

And what lay at the root of all this carnage? Non-Indians and other tribes had legitimate complaints against repeated theft by Navajo raiding parties, but Carson's military commander, Gen. James Henry Carleton, was also fixated upon some special rocks. Absent much evidence, the general was certain that somewhere in Navajo country there simply must be a trove of gold for the taking. Removing the Navajos would make the taking more convenient.[13]

Like most Navajo families, Adakai's had its own Long Walk stories. His grandmother, Woman With the Four Horns, spent time in Fort Sumner. His mother, Woman With the Stone House, avoided the roundup but had a violent encounter with white outsiders, stoking the family's rage. Just before the Long Walk, when Adakai's mother was a young girl, she had journeyed with relatives who wanted to sell some wool at a distant trading post. Tensions were rising with the newcomers. When her party stopped for the night along the way, she was sent to scout for danger. The only peril, it turned out, lay back in camp. As she approached, she saw two Mexicans and three Anglo men holding her companions at gunpoint. Ferocious even then, she surprised the captors, wielding her bow and loosing arrow after arrow. She killed them all.[14]

Her brother, Adakai's uncle Metal Belt, grew up to clank and ping as he walked because of the ornaments and bells hanging from his fringed leather traveling pouch. But he too had spent his youth as a stealthy warrior. He could fire an arrow while hanging from beneath a cantering horse and he rode many times to Fort Sumner. Clad in uniforms he stole from the soldiers he'd killed, he would sneak in to visit the prisoners and listen to their tales of woe.[15]

The week after Carson died, Gen. William Tecumseh Sherman arrived from Washington amid rumors that the Navajos would be relocated again, this time to Oklahoma. Instead, moved by the eloquence of the leader who spoke on the *Diné*'s behalf, Sherman drew up an agreement that would allow them to return to the holy land where they were meant to be. The Navajos paid a price: Sherman insisted on firm borders that were much smaller than the original Navajo hunting grounds. He also insisted they continue the "civilizing." His captives, desperate, acquiesced. Under this Treaty of 1868, signed on June 1, the *Diné* foreswore raiding and the U.S. government assumed the role of guardian, promising to look out for the Navajos' welfare. The *Diné* happily retraced the Long Walk in reverse, joining those who had hidden all those years, and a delegation traveled to Washington to finish the business of making peace.

Adakai was born a few years after the exiled Navajos returned to their rightful home. Nonetheless, he grew up during a time of turmoil. Though a string of presidential executive orders from the 1880s through 1901 extended Sherman's tight boundaries, life was not the same as it had been before the Long Walk. Before Carson's arrival in their homeland, the Navajos had existed only as a loose confederation of clans, with extended families living together on their own in remote camps like the Comb Ridge *hooghan* of Man With the Red Hair and Woman With the Stone House. No leaders could truly represent them all. For the next fifty years or so after the return, the U.S. government was the boss, sometimes neglectful and at other times ham-handed. In 1923, around the same time that Adakai brought his family to Clay Springs, A Rough Rock—the future Cane Valley—a central tribal government was established, but in truth, the occupiers continued to rule. The federal bureaucrats changed everything, even names, and what is more basic than a name? *Diné bikeyah,* the Home of the People, became the Navajo reservation. Whenever one of the People first came in contact with someone official, the agents doled out an English first name and often some type of surname, which had never been necessary in a society where everyone made introductions by reciting their maternal and paternal clans (Adakai, for example, was born to Bitter Water on his mother's side and to the Salt clan on his father's). The new system was haphazard, to say the least. The authorities, who couldn't be bothered to keep track, often bestowed different last names on members of the same family, yet sometimes they gave two brothers or sisters the same first name. Adakai, for instance, was John Adakai to them.[16] His youngest wife, inexplicably, was christened Anna Sling. Anna was such a good name in the white man's estimation that two of Adakai's daughters also got it; they were each reborn in U.S. records as Anna Adakai. Adakai had one son by each of his wives. The boys received yet another surname altogether: Yazzie, which is Navajo for "little."[17]

At least they all managed to avoid being branded with the last name Bia, which is common on the reservation to this day. Some wit among the federals would conjure that one up from the acronym for Bureau of Indian Affairs.

These indignities stung. But worse, the Indian Office (as it was known at the time) was soon striking at the sheep. The bureaucrats were trying to develop an "appropriate" work ethic among the Navajos, urging men to earn wages though paying jobs were few and far between, while women wove blankets and rugs that they sold at trading posts. They still had burgeoning flocks who devoured the plants that grew in the constrained borders of the post-treaty *Dinétah*. By 1930, about forty thousand Navajos shared their country with 760,000 sheep.[18] When drought, the same parching that created the Dust Bowl to the north and east, arrived in force, the combination of the crowding and weather thinned the brush, balding the grazing lands.

The solution to this problem was obvious, the government overseers concluded, and in 1933 they dictated a new program to the puppet tribal council. Their euphemism was "livestock reduction." This involved corralling the animals deemed "extra" into gullies, slaughtering them, then burning the carcasses. The stench barreled through the junipers and pinyons and hung in the air for days. Only a few corpses were provided to the owners for meat; these had to be butchered on the spot rather than brought home for a more careful, thorough job. Owners caught concealing their animals saw them shot dead right at their feet. Navajos pleaded for mercy; they could not feed their many children with the number of livestock they were being allotted.

One of Adakai's herders, a nephew named Little John Holiday, drove thirty-seven of the family horses and more than six hundred sheep to the culling station, as ordered. He was allowed to keep only thirteen horses and 354 sheep, for which he was given a permit. The rest were killed in the ravines. Holiday was so angry that later, in separate incidents, he shot the ground at the heels of three Navajo police helping with the reduction efforts, whipped a pair of white men helping themselves to horses, and led a crowd at a midnight ceremony in overturning three tribal police cars. He knew each time, he said, that he was being "naughty," but he just couldn't help himself.[19]

The white men were coming around to take away children, too, and put them in boarding schools. At least the children came back for vacations. But Adakai's grandchildren were hidden away whenever the government agents showed up. One of them, a small girl named Juanita, piped up in protest. She wanted to go and learn even if that meant leaving home. Adakai was displeased. He needed her help with his sheep, even though their ranks had decreased. Like Little John and her cousins, she stayed in the valley.[20]

As if all this weren't enough, Adakai was still irritated by the presence of a lanky white man named Harry Goulding who was a sheepherder too. He and his young bride arrived from Aztec, New Mexico, back in 1925, and opened a trading post in a pair of tents. They leased land reserved by the state of Utah to provide income for Utah's public school systems. Near the end of the second year, a half-dozen Navajos showed up wondering how long Goulding was planning to stay. He touched the wall of canvas that enclosed them all, replying with his limited Navajo vocabulary that he would leave "when my hair gets as white as that tent."[21] The delegation laughed, but its members were not happy that he was on their range. He was less than thirty miles west of Adakai's valley, and he was building up his own herd to compete with theirs for scarce greasewood and mountain brush. The locals were even more upset when the trader managed to find a loophole that allowed him to buy his entire township section of land in 1938, creating a private enclave on the reservation. Because of livestock reduction, Goulding had to move his sheep north, but unlike the Navajos, he got to keep them. Even the federal government objected to the transaction, sending a telegram to the state asking Utah to hold off while the United States prepared a bid. But the wire didn't arrive until the sale date, and the trader clinched his deal. He would never be dislodged.[22]

Against this ominous backdrop, Adakai was especially alarmed by the campers seeking yellow rock. The trader had moved too close and was changing too much nearby; now these men had actually penetrated his home base. If they found the special rocks that he knew were there to find, they too would settle in. Mr. Gambler saw a risk he did not want to take. White men meant trouble, always. He couldn't lose the valley.

So like his mother had before him, and like his uncle Metal Belt, Adakai simply did what he had to do. No one knows what weapon he used. No one knows where he buried the bodies, or what he did with the corpses of their horses, though one of his great-grandchildren did happen upon an old saddle many years later up on Comb Ridge. No one much likes to talk about the incident at all.[23]

Afterward, Adakai realized that in order to keep the white men from finding the yellow rocks, he had to keep his youngsters quiet. In particular, he had to rein in his favorite, Luke Yazzie, the son of his younger wife.[24] Luke was forever exploring trails and trees on the mesa and collecting stones that caught his eye. The boy, like his father, recognized the yellow rocks as special; they felt heavy, he said. He used them as crayons to draw animals on the cliffs, just like the hieroglyphs of the ancients.

Adakai invoked his authority with all of his children.

Do not ever, ever show these to the white man.[25]

Little Luke Yazzie squirreled away two of these rocks in a cave on the mesa, but he did not forget them. He checked on his cache every few weeks for many years, even into his twenties, after he left his boyhood behind.[26]

Chapter 2

The Secret Quest

To Adakai, no fan of any white man, prospectors were the worst of a bad lot. They didn't understand the world at all. The Navajo Way centered on a give-and-take relationship with Mother Earth, but these American mining men had the strange notion that they could take and never give. No matter what substance they sought, their motive was always the same. Loot the ground and move along. And the mineral-rich Southwest was attracting droves of them.

He had seen plenty of them in action just across the San Juan River, the Navajos' northern boundary in Utah. There, by a rickety bridge, lived a group of adventurers who were searching for wealth they could wring from the land. They had settled at the forbidding edge of white man's territory, where even the Mormon pioneers had feared to tread.

The hamlet was originally called Goodridge, for its founder, and then Mexican Hat, for the huge sombrero-shaped red rock outside of town. The first draw was oil. Emery Goodridge and his first companions had appeared, beginning in the late 1800s, more than a decade after the Long Walk and about the time of Adakai's birth.[1] They discovered leaks of slick black liquid from the sandstone cliffs along the San Juan. The newcomers all expected to find a gusher. One of the most colorful characters was a promoter who drove a fancy car (and who knows how he got it there), built a fancy house, and so impressed the Navajos with his rich and vivid language that they called him *"Hostiin* God Damn."[2] As it happened, *Hostiin* God Damn's profanities were a natural response to the disappointing results from the rigs. By the 1930s, the local oil deposits were pronounced to be "pockety."[3]

A new crop of hopefuls showed up with the intention of panning gold dust from the river. A second set of dreams was soon dashed; the fantasy of billions in bullion gave way to a much lesser reality. One gold hunter discovered just enough flecks of raw material to forge a ring for his wife. Another extremely lucky soul reaped a harvest worth $1,500. That haul, the biggest ever in those parts, came from a sandbar that was promptly covered over by water that was never to recede again. On a boulder near Comb Ridge, where the Backbone jutted out of the Navajo country toward Mormon territory, one anonymous seeker scratched his cry of disenchantment: "100.00 reward for the damned fool who started the gold boom."[4]

Adakai, as a traditional Navajo, thought it only right that the would-be pillagers were so frustrated by the fates. How could they be rewarded for piercing deep into Mother Earth, for treating her so differently from the way the Creators had intended?

He had plenty of opportunities to observe them whenever he visited Mexican Hat on business. Despite his suspicions, he did not hesitate to barter with the whites when it suited his needs. One couple had set up a trading post by the bridge that connected Mexican Hat to the reservation. Until the traders moved in 1928,[5] Adakai regularly sold them livestock and with the proceeds bought coffee, clothing, and flour. At least once, he had so many fat, fine lambs for sale that it took an expedition of five on horseback to drive the flock across the river. He sprang for a pair of fine $8 boots for a cousin who helped out. At the trading post, Adakai no doubt heard plenty of gossip about oil and gold.

Yearning eyes, of course, turned south to the Navajo homeland. Just as gold fever had helped to launch the Long Walk, oil was behind the sudden determination of the United States to form a Navajo government nearly six decades later. The whole point of having a tribal council was to pass a resolution, written in Washington, giving consent to oil and gas leases on the reservation and ceding authority for all approvals to the U.S. Indian Commissioner. The minutes didn't mention the vote, but the lost resolution of July 7, 1923, surfaced ten years afterward, during a lunch recess of an autumn council meeting in the Navajo capital of Window Rock, Arizona. The delegates made their feelings clear about its contents; they promptly rescinded it.[6]

Nonetheless, a few hardy prospectors decided to venture across the San Juan into the reservation. Soon enough, tales circulated of two white men who set off in search of a mysterious gold deposit they'd heard of, only to be shot dead by Indians. Their horses and shoes disappeared.[7] Was this an apocryphal story or were these characters Adakai's visitors? They met a strikingly similar fate, but there is no way to be sure.

All the gold lust in the region had apparently convinced Adakai that this must be the mineral in the yellow seams of the rocks that he often passed on the mesa. But as it turned out, even Adakai could be wrong.

There was a white man who already knew much more about the special rocks than Adakai did, and he knew exactly where they were.

John Wetherill was a trader, too, but he had been at it a long time, since 1900, and he had always worked carefully on the reservation proper. His wife Louisa Wade Wetherill, called Slim Woman by the Indians, was honored for her knowledge of Navajo culture. Wetherill himself was quiet and a Quaker, but he was no stay-behind-the-counter merchant. He roamed widely both south and north of the San Juan. In 1909, he was on the first expedition of Anglos to reach Rainbow Bridge, a natural arch that connects two canyon rims, at a height so great that the U.S. Capitol could fit easily underneath.

During World War I, promoters had approached Wetherill with a question. He was a natural person to contact, the rare white man who was favorably looked upon by many Navajos and at home in the Indian lands. Did he happen to know where they might find an ore called carnotite? The buyers described the object of their hunt as unremarkable in appearance save for streaks of bright canary yellow and sometimes black, green, or red. The Navajos did not permit mining on the reservation at that time, but Wetherill, going through a rough financial patch, was game to look around. He found two spots that looked promising. One was in the breathtaking desolation of Monument Valley, home to the most spectacular rock formations in all of Navajo country. Yet it was so close to a dirt road that you could practically drive right up to it. It wasn't far from the place where Goulding would later pitch his tents. Atop a bluff there, Wetherill erected a marker. He heaped a low mound of stones together and drove an iron stake into the ground.[8]

The other outcrop was farther east in a more remote locale on the other side of Monument Valley. This second prospect was on the very mesa where Adakai would soon be herding sheep, though Wetherill had beaten even the Gambler to this spot.

Sometime around 1917, presumably illegally, he loaded up a wagon with ore and hauled it to Flagstaff, Arizona. He was told that the rocks were bound for far-off France, where Madame Curie and her husband would extract specks of their new discovery, radium, from this ore. None of that meant much to the trader, who was interested only in getting paid. But he never got a cent, so he resolved to have nothing to do with carnotite in the future.[9]

At the time, this wasn't much of a sacrifice. There didn't seem to be much call for the stuff. Two years after Wetherill's fling with the radium trade, in 1919, Congress opened the Navajo reservation to prospecting and mining claims. His brother-in-law and two partners did stake out a reservation claim, in the pine-covered Carrizo Mountains farther to the east, near the Arizona–New Mexico line. But the discovery in 1924 of a large pitchblende deposit in the Belgian Congo provided a more dependable radium supply and the interest in American carnotite fizzled.

As Luke Yazzie grew into adolescence, Adakai often ordered his son and three other teens to take buckets up to the mesa in the springtime after the rains. Their task was to collect water that had gathered in depressions in the rock and bring it back down to the valley. But he never said they had to come back right away. On one water-hauling expedition, the frolicsome four began a game of hide-and-seek. Luke told his cousin, John Holiday, that he knew the perfect place to elude the others. He beckoned John to follow him into a crevice. It was narrow at the top but it widened into a comfortable space at the bottom. And it seemed strangely perfect, almost too squared off.[10]

Down there, embedded in the wall, a layer of rock stood out with a distinctly different texture and color. This layer, streaked with red and black, was disturbed, as if someone had been digging. Luke and John kept looking. They happened upon a pillar of the same substance where some-one had excavated quite deeply. The other two boys found Luke and John, and the four of them wondered what had happened there. They thought it must be the work of the Old Ones who had lived in the *Dinétah* be-fore them, or maybe the Spaniards, though it's more likely the digger was John Wetherill. The boys laughed at how much the brightly colored rocks looked like candy; they licked at the rock but were less than impressed by the taste. Luke didn't mention his own stash of special rocks to his friends. He didn't mention his father's instructions. Maybe he didn't con-nect the red and black with his own buried treasure, his gold. Or maybe he was keeping mum, as Adakai demanded. The boys got the water and scrambled back home.[11]

Ores are a mixture of many minerals. As it happened, in addition to ra-dium, carnotite rock also contained much larger quantities of a metal called vanadium, which proved to be a hardening agent when blended into steel. This was a very valuable trait to a nation preparing for war. The Navy bought vanadium to make hulls for its ships during the Great War, as the First World War was known at the time. Most vanadium was imported from Peru, where llamas ferried ore from a remote mine to the nearest railroad. Still, control of that mine was in American hands. The owner was a company headquartered on Lexington Avenue in New York, with a blue-blood board of directors (for more than a decade, one of them was the banker Prescott Bush; he resigned in 1952 to take a seat in the U.S. Senate. He would be father to one U.S. president, grandfather to another).

The business was called the Vanadium Corporation of America, VCA for short. By 1931, the Peruvian deposit was nearly played out, a competitor opened a new mine in Canada, and VCA started losing money. But eight years later, circumstances changed again. World War II broke out in Europe. Fearsome Germany was on the march, menacing the entire continent. The United States did not send soldiers overseas, but President Franklin Delano Roosevelt declared that America would support the Allies with materiel, assuming the role of "the arsenal of democracy."

VCA smelled opportunity. The arsenal of democracy would need armor plate and thus it would need vanadium. A competitor, a subsidiary of Union Carbide called U.S. Vanadium, had begun mining carnotite in Colorado and processing it to get the vanadium out. VCA followed suit, acquiring some mineral rights in Colorado and building a mill in nearby Utah, but the company had sniffed out an even bigger prize nearby. In 1938, Congress had once again addressed the issue of mining on the reservation, passing a law that this time gave the tribal council the authority to issue leases as long as the secretary of the interior approved. VCA wanted to get in there so badly that a pair of executives traveled to the nation's capital to lock in the lode.

On an October Sunday in 1941, Interior Secretary Harold Ickes noted in his diary that during the previous week, "E.D. Bransome, President, and P.J. Gibbons, Secretary-Treasurer, of the Vanadium Corporation of America, came in to talk about the possibility of developing some vanadium ore in the Navajo reservation." [12]

By this time, a very small, very quiet cadre within the U.S. government had a new reason to value carnotite. In addition to the radium and the vanadium, there was yet another ingredient in the ore. For every six parts of vanadium, the rock also contained one part of a heavy metal called uranium. The uranium content, in fact, was the best way to identify carnotite with the naked eye: it was uranium that formed those brightly-hued slashes. For years, VCA and U.S. Vanadium had considered uranium a nuisance, waste created when their mills ground the ore to dust and sifted out their main product. They tried peddling uranium as a coloring agent for ceramics, but this was a niche market at best.

Like radium, uranium was an unstable substance throwing off energy as it decayed into different elements—some taking more than a thousand years, others as little as a few minutes—on the way to reaching a stable state as lead. Uranium's emissions were weaker than radium's, but 0.7 percent of uranium existed as an isotope known as U-235 with a special property: it was as unsteady as a reeling drunk.

By 1939, scientists knew they could shoot a stream of neutrons at U-235 to crack the wobbly atom into two lighter atoms. When the original atom was split, it would spew out energy and liberate two or three more neutrons. If a cluster of uranium atoms were packed together in a correctly calculated mass, in precisely the right circumstances, these freed neutrons might collide with neighboring atoms. It was like a game of billiards, atoms colliding into each other and setting off more splitting, which could then set off more and on and on. Theoretically at least, this chain reaction could generate intense bursts of energy capable of wreaking more destruction than any weapon known to man.

When the Americans learned that German scientists at the Kaiser Wilhelm Institute in Berlin were working on a rush uranium research project, they knew exactly what that meant. The Nazis were actively trying to build an atomic bomb that would put to horrific use a forced cascade of dividing uranium. Nine days after the attack on Pearl Harbor propelled the United States into the war, the government turned responsibility for the atomic bomb project over to the U.S. Army Corps of Engineers. No more lollygagging. The corps got things done.

The initial uranium for the American research program had come from the Eldorado mine in Canada near the Arctic Circle. More came from a Congolese stash that a Belgian mining executive took with him when he fled the Nazis, serendipitously storing it in a Staten Island warehouse. But the military hoped for a big find of grade-A American uranium, a reliable source that would leave the United States beholden to no one. They cast their eyes westward, to the vanadium processing plants sprouting in the Four Corners, where Colorado, Utah, New Mexico, and Arizona met at a single point, with the Navajo homeland spread across state borders like a blanket.

John Wetherill was always glad to receive visitors at his trading post. He'd taken the great Western writer Zane Grey out to Rainbow Bridge. He'd swapped stories with famous cartoonists, like George Herriman, creator of "Krazy Kat," and Jimmy Swinerton, who drew "Little Jimmy."[13]

In the summer of 1942, an old friend from up in Mormon country came by Wetherill's with his father. He was a twenty-seven-year-old rancher by the name of Preston Redd, known to all as Pep. Pep had previously spent two years in Wetherill's employ, fetching groceries from the white towns for the trading post. The young man and his dad had been having a talk about the craze for carnotite up in Colorado and they were determined to get into the business. The son recalled hearing Wetherill talk about the ore. Pep, true to his name, had plenty of energy and he urged his father into a car. The Redds headed south, kicking up dust on the rutted-dirt Navajo roads, to pump the old trader for advice.

Wetherill was happy to oblige. He told them about his disappointing experience from decades before. He offered to tell them where he had found the ore, but said he had soured enough on mining that he wasn't interested in being their partner.

He gave them directions to the first site, the one close to the road, and the Redds drove off. They found it without much difficulty and walked up close. The rock certainly had plenty of *something* in it, Pep remarked.

Before the next session of the Navajo tribal council, the Redds set out again from their home in Blanding, Utah, to pick up Old John and Slim Woman at their lodge in Arizona. The car traversed the unpaved roads to the south end of the reservation and crossed the line to the border town of Gallup, New Mexico, where they checked into the Harvey House hotel. The four travelers spent a week commuting from the Harvey House to the Navajo capital of Window Rock, waiting for the council to take up their request for permission to mine carnotite at the site by the road and at the more distant spot they hadn't visited.

Finally, the question rose to the top of the agenda. The Wetherills did the Redds a favor and presented the case. They knew the local Navajo council delegate well. They also had a close friend in John Collier, the head of the BIA. They'd known him for nearly twenty years. He'd stopped to visit at their trading post and Slim Woman had kept in touch ever since, informing him when the local BIA agents were abusive to the Navajos.[14]

At the end of the meeting, Collier approached the group. He put his arm around Slim Woman and assured her, "When this comes up, you folks will be taken care of. You don't need to worry. If they lease it, why, you'll get it."[15]

Although Collier, the architect of livestock reduction, was hardly popular with the Navajos, the four of them drove back to the Harvey House, brimming with confidence. But even with the potent backing of the Wetherills, the Redds were too late.

Adakai's son, Luke, a grown man now, had disobeyed his father, breaking his decades of silence to speak at last about the *leetso*—the yellow dirt—that he possessed.

Chapter 3

Jumping on the King

L ike his father, Luke had no objection to trading with the enemy. The closest merchant to Cane Valley was Harry Goulding, and Luke loved to loiter at his outpost on the other side of Adakai's mesa. On a mount or seated in a horse-drawn wagon, it was a beautiful ride past the legendary towers of rock in Monument Valley. At Goulding's, the scenery was no less exotic. By the time Luke was a young married man, the trader had long since abandoned his tents in favor of the first two-story building that the Indians had ever seen. The trading post was fashioned of stone and mortar, with living quarters upstairs and a pawn-and-purchase shop below. Goulding had carefully planned the store's layout, installing an elevated floor behind his high counter. On the other side, his Navajo customers—the "Navvies" as he called them—stood on lower ground, in an area he referred to as the bullpen, forcing them to crane their necks to look up at the proprietor.[1] He didn't need to do that to seem imposing. Like the stone spindles you could see from his doorway, Goulding was skinny and tall, his features creased and sculpted by the elements. He stood six-foot-four.

Reservation traders like Wetherill were required by the federal government to shut down for the Sabbath, but because Goulding's was on private property, the merchant could and did operate seven days a week. In fact, every Sunday, while other trading posts were closed, Goulding's sponsored a horse race, with bets on the side, or perhaps a chicken pull—

stick the bird in a hole in the ground and see who can gallop past, lean down to snatch the prize and yank off the chicken's head.

In fact, there was no such thing as a slow day at Goulding's Monument Valley Trading Post. Every morning, Navajos would ride up together, often singing an old favorite about a girl who trained horses. The ringing falsetto of the verses would bounce off the canyon walls, followed by the rhythmic chanted chorus: *"Yoo shi yoo shi, yoo shi yoo shi, yo shin a ya, shin a aa ya, ya a wei ya hei."* [2] Inside the shop, the Navajos would buy and open a can of peaches, or perhaps a can of tomatoes with a bit of sugar scooped on top, just enough to bring out their sweetness. Seated in a circle on that low floor, they would pass around the container and a spoon, so that all could share. The addition of crackers turned this treat into a formal lunch. For the evenings, the Gouldings, like most traders, kept a guest *hooghan,* and provided a blue enamel coffee pot to put on the campfire. Most of those who stayed over were men, but women who came along were permitted to sleep in the laundry shed off the Gouldings' kitchen.

Between the bouts of socializing, afternoon was reserved for the stylized ritual of trading. A Navajo would stand and unfurl a handwoven rug or offer up a silver concho belt or bridle or blanket. Once a price was set, seller became buyer, taking out the value in potatoes or onions or velveteen blouses or brightly-striped vests. After each transaction would come the big question: *Dikwíí yidzííh?* How much is left? They picked out axes and shovels and metal parts to assemble into cookstoves. They loaded everything into burlap bags that they packed onto their horses, who waited for them in the Gouldings' corral. Last of all, if enough credit was left, they'd buy some candy or the fizzy soda, strawberry or orange, that the kids loved so much. Once done, the next Navajo would stand and Goulding or one of his relatives would ask: *Ha'at'iishą' ninizin k'od?* What do you want now? And so the pageant would proceed.[3]

Goulding's successful maneuvering to purchase his private island in the middle of the reservation had proved his eye for the main chance. When the Navajos and his business began to wither during the Great Depression, he displayed his shrewdness once again. In the autumn of 1938, Goulding heard from his brother-in-law, a stunt pilot in Los Angeles, that United Artists was scouting for a suitable Western landscape to shoot a cowboy movie. The Gouldings headed right for Hollywood in their old truck. Armed only with bravado and photographs, Harry strode into the studio in his grimy jeans and boots. Predictably, he couldn't get past the receptionist. He calmly mentioned out loud that he just might fetch his bedroll from the truck and settle into the anteroom to wait for an appointment. The man who was summoned to give Goulding the boot turned out to be the location manager for the great director John Ford. After he took one look at a photo of the Mittens with a Navajo on horseback in the foreground, the grizzled Indian trader found himself in a suite of offices with Ford, in front of a sandwich and a piece of pie. Soon enough, he also had a check for $5,000 and a charge to get a barracks erected at his trading post, rustic in flavor but luxurious enough to house a group of Ford's actors.[4]

Within a week, eighteen carpenters had done their job, the actor John Wayne was on hand, and Ford was making *Stage Coach,* the Western movie that propelled "Duke" to stardom and launched a lasting vision of America around the world. Until then, cowboy movies had mostly been inferior products, with lots of process shots and papier-mâché rocks. The glory of Ford's authentic location, though it belonged in reality to the Indians, seemed to seep into the character of the rugged white protagonist in the story of redemption that took place on the screen.

The Navajos gained employment, too, as extras. Traditionalists like Adakai were appalled. The movie men paid Navajos $3 a day in exchange for feigning death. They were courting evil spirits, summoning those who might impose the real thing. Still, there was no shortage of applicants. More to the point, in Harry's mind, the movies could ensure a steady stream of business for the Monument Valley Trading Post. For the crew, he charged $3 a night for a room or cabin, $1 apiece for the basement, which could fit up to ten people, 75 cents for breakfast and $1 for dinner. The production company furnished supplies for the Navajos, which Harry Goulding was happy to sell to them.[5]

As far as Ford was concerned, Monument Valley was paradise. He slept well. He ate well (Goulding's wife was a fantastic cook). He worked hard, felt healthy, and reveled in the clean, fresh air.

He wanted to come back and, eventually, he would. But World War II interrupted his plans. Uncle Sam wanted John Ford. The great producer was drafted to make movies for the government, memorializing the dramatic battles under way on other continents. Harry Goulding's money machine was temporarily closed.

The wily trader soon latched onto the possibility of yet another big score. Luke saw the evidence himself when he entered Goulding's one day and recognized, with a start, the stones littered across the counter. Some had a yellow cast; some contained yellow stripes. The gold from Adakai's mesa, he thought. The *leetso*.

Sooner or later, Goulding heard everything, and he'd gotten wind of the vanadium mining up in Utah and Colorado. Word got back to him that John Wetherill had found some of this carnotite stuff that contained it on the reservation proper. He eventually learned, too, that the Wetherills were helping Pep Redd in an effort to cash in on World War II.

Goulding thought that this was such a good idea that he just might appropriate it for himself. He wanted in, and he wanted in big. He aimed, in his words, to jump on the king.[6] VCA had been working only in the white world. But in December of 1941, just two months after its president and secretary sat down with Harold Ickes, VCA succeeded in leasing a carnotite mine in the Carrizos, near the New Mexico line. More recently, VCA had plucked the rights to a ridgetop across a broad valley from the Carrizos. Upon cinching this second Navajo deal, VCA pledged in a letter to the Interior Department that "we will extend our every effort to work this territory for the war effort first and then all concerned."[7]

This was the biggest company around, Goulding knew, just as he knew that VCA employees were bound to stop by the trading post at some point in their travels. Sure enough, a geologist came into the store and Goulding told him that he knew where some vanadium-bearing ore could be found, right there in Monument Valley. The geologist gave him the name of a contact: Denny Viles, he said, is the vice president and field manager, based at the company-run mill in Monticello, Utah.

"Well, if he comes down any time, I'd be glad to show him where it is," Goulding replied.[8]

He came on down.

Dennis W. Viles was strong, bluff, and hearty. He weighed a good 230 pounds, played a great game of golf, charmed the ladies, and was said to stop at nothing when it came to business.[9] Goulding, aware of Viles's hardball reputation, decided to play on it, to turn it to his advantage, reassuring him that "If you ever wake up in the night on account of you've done something kind of off-gate a little bit, you can think of what you've done for this bunch of poor old Indians and that'll just fix you up!"

He took Viles on a tour of the nearest *hooghan*s, showing him family after family subsisting on a half sack of flour, a little coffee, and maybe some jerky hoarded after slaughtering a goat. They need the jobs you would bring in, he told Viles. He didn't mention that he needed the jobs, too, that the Navajos would likely spend their wages on provisions at the Monument Valley Trading Post.

Viles kept pointing at different *hooghan*s. They made quite a pair, the stocky white man and the skinny one, ducking inside to find the same appalling poverty inside every single Navajo home. Goulding could see that Viles was suspicious, that he thought he was being played. Finally, though, Viles started to flush. "My God, Harry, I don't need to see anymore!" he cried out. So Goulding took him over to Wetherill's old deposit by the side of the road. It was carnotite all right.

Next, the trader embarked on a two-month search for the second Wetherill find. Having had no luck, he decided to set out bait: the stones on the counter. And sure enough, here came Luke Yazzie asking what, exactly, they were doing there.

Goulding told him they could be used in many ways, to make automobiles and airplanes. He said they were worth a lot of money, even more than the movies. "If you find these rocks," he told Luke, "bring them in."

Luke said nothing. But after he returned to Cane Valley, he rode his horse up to the place on the mesa where he had stashed the rocks. He looked them over. They seemed just like those on display at Goulding's. Automobiles and airplanes? Maybe the yellow dirt wasn't gold after all, but it might be precious nonetheless.

He was in his twenties, embarking on his second marriage. He had divorced an arranged bride and taken up with June Black, a pretty teenager he'd managed to run into "accidentally" time after time. He had children to support. He needed potatoes. He needed flour.

He took the rocks out of his hiding place and gathered more like them nearby.[10] He carried the haul back to his *hooghan*. He could hardly admit to himself that he was sorely tempted to disobey the word of Adakai. This was far too enormous to rush into. He wrapped the rocks in a cloth and hid them in a bush, and tried for months to put them out of his mind.

But when Luke felt the draw of the trading post again, those rocks were still there. He couldn't help inquiring further. "Which are the most valuable?" he asked Goulding. "Only a few have much value, but these few cost a great deal of money," the trader replied. He must have sensed that he was close to reeling in his prize.

Weeks passed. Luke approached his brother-in-law, Oscar Sloan, who had married Adakai's daughter Lillie and moved to the valley. Some of Sloan's new relatives in the quiet Red House clan pegged him as a bit of a smoothie. He'd been to BIA school and spoke English. To Luke, though, this education in the ways of the whites made Sloan a credible source of counsel. Lillie's husband advised Luke to grab this opportunity.[11]

Luke rode again from his green homestead through the vast, parched silence of Monument Valley, past the buttes and arches jutting into azure sky. The journey took half a day. This time, when he showed up in the trading post bullpen, he was carrying his bundle. He reached up to offer it to the proprietor.

Goulding peered closely at the contents. "That's it! These are the rocks. They're worth a lot of money!" Goulding exclaimed. He put them on his grocer's scale.

"Is there a road there?" Goulding asked in Navajo.

"Only a horse trail," Luke answered.

Already, the young man was growing uneasy. But Goulding gave his good friend a cold bottle of pop and a cigar. As John Ford had done for him, Harry invited Luke to share a fine repast upstairs at the oval dining table set with floral-pattern dishes, near the big radio and the piano and the huge stone fireplace. As he bade his guest farewell, Goulding told him: "Come back in seven days." The *bilagáana*—the white man—who was interested in these rocks would be waiting for him. Then he sent for Denny Viles.

Luke must have conquered his doubts again because he showed up at the trading post on schedule. Goulding ordered up some hay for his horse. Viles and another man were down from Utah, as promised. The guests all spent the night. After early coffee the next morning, the whole group set off in a car for a slow, jarring ride over old wagon trails. Finally, Luke had them stop in a canyon. They walked the rest of the way, a tiring hike up the mesa. Slowly they made their way across the holy place, the source of life for Cane Valley.

And then Luke led them to the squared-off cave and to a spot on the ridge where yellow stripes gleamed in the walls of rock. Viles' companion took out his Geiger counter, which instantly started to sputter. He and Viles brought out gunny sacks and filled them with samples. "This is really something!" Viles exclaimed. "It's going to be a big one!"

Luke was tired and hungry by this time, not to mention more than a little confused by their excitement. But Viles wouldn't be budged. He didn't want to leave.[12]

Oscar Sloan was on hand, too; he played the role of translator.[13] What Luke took from the conversation was this: He would get paid, without doing any work, just for showing VCA the special rocks. What Goulding heard was this: Viles promised to give Luke a job and keep him on for as long the company was working the mesa.[14] Between these two versions lay a canyon that would fill up with bitterness over many years.

Adakai was furious. Everyone in Cane Valley heard about it. He actually raised his voice. "What have you done?" he shouted at his favorite son. "I told you not to do that!"[15]

It was August of 1942.

Part II

THE SON

Fear and Frenzy

Chapter 4

The Power of Łeetso

month after Denny Viles discovered the secret of Cane Valley, a U.S. Army colonel named Leslie Groves got bad news. Far to the east, in Washington, D.C., he had distinguished himself with the Corps of Engineers as the overseer of construction for the Pentagon, the enormous headquarters for the Department of Defense, and he was delighted to be heading at last for an overseas command, right in the thick of the war. But the effort to develop an atomic bomb still was not proceeding as fast as the Army wanted, needed. No-nonsense, get-going Groves was ordered to give up his plans for combat and take charge of creating the ultimate weapon. He balked. He was certain that this crazy scheme could never succeed.

He had no choice in the matter, though, and he soon found himself promoted to brigadier general so he would have the necessary rank to push everything along at top speed. Because the Corps' main office for the program was located in New York, Groves called the whole enterprise the Manhattan Engineering District—the Manhattan Project, for short.

Since he had to make the Manhattan Project work, he flung himself into the mission. He began at the beginning, with the raw material for testing and making bombs. More uranium was coming from the Belgian Congo, but the risks of transport were a constant concern (indeed, over the course of the war, two of the forty shipments were lost in submarine attacks).[1] Groves acted immediately to take on the problem. Within a few weeks, he had established a domestic uranium purchasing program. As an experiment, the Corps ordered 80,000 pounds of uranium oxide from the waste of Union Carbide's vanadium mills, run by its subsidiary U.S. Vanadium in Colorado. Uranium, as hoped, was definitely present in the dump and the mill was able to separate it from rest of the leavings.

By the end of 1942, the Army's vanadium purchasers had signed contracts for uranium sludge—they referred to it as "B"—with both U.S. Vanadium and with VCA, which operated the Monticello, Utah, mill. VCA actually developed the process for recovering uranium from carnotite.[2] This pasty "vanadium waste" was resold to a single, shadowy customer, which of course was the hush-hush A-bomb program. It was shipped east to Pennsylvania for further processing.

For every six pounds of vanadium harvested (it *was* needed for armor plate), the government quietly got one pound of uranium for the special contract.[3] U.S. Vanadium and VCA were paid both for the uranium and vanadium content of the waste and for hauling it to Grand Junction, the Colorado town where the Manhattan Project had set up a special operations office.[4]

Though the tribal government didn't know it and was certainly not paid for it, Navajo ore was contributing uranium to a mighty effort that would change the world. VCA's eastern-reservation properties were part of the mix and in November of 1942, the company snagged the rights to the first Wetherill site by the side of the road south of Goulding's. The tribe had called this acreage the Combination Lode when putting it up for bid. Viles trumped two competitors with his offer of a signing bonus of precisely $739.83 in addition to the standard 10 percent royalty.[5] He promptly renamed VCA's new leasehold Monument No. 1.

He had a No. 2 in mind, of course, in nearby Cane Valley. He'd asked Luke Yazzie to help survey it and staked a claim. But potential pitfalls lay ahead: the tribal council still needed to determine whether or not to lease out the mesa, and if a lease was offered, anyone would be allowed to bid. Viles began to agonize over what size bonus to offer if a sale was scheduled.[6] He desperately wanted to win. But he was extremely cheap.

In the meantime, just as the government started siphoning the uranium out of the company's vanadium waste, Viles invited VCA's president out from New York to see Monument No. 1 in action. The two executives stayed, of course, at Goulding's guest quarters.[7]

The tribe demanded that Navajos be given preference for mining jobs and Viles complied. Luke was among the dozens who were hired at Monument No. 1, since it was ready to go and the negotiations over Cane Valley were just starting.[8] Adakai's son was issued a pick, a shovel, and a big jackhammer. Goulding was happy; every weekend VCA brought truckloads of Navajo customers from the mine to his trading post. As they purchased their supplies, Goulding would update them on the week's events from the war. Navajos were deeply involved in the big fight. Many were drafted, just as white men were. Some washed out of basic training because of the language gap, but a handful of the bilinguals would be plucked for a special mission. They sent messages to and from the big Pacific battlefronts in their native Navajo, a code that the Japanese could never crack.

The war also brought some of the People civilian jobs off the reservation. Just west of Flagstaff, Arizona, in the town of Bellemont, a munitions plant was hiring. One of Adakai's daughters—this one known simply as Adakai's Daughter—was soon employed there. She depended heavily on her own daughter, Juanita, Adakai's grandchild, who had once hoped for schooling but was consigned instead to herding sheep. Glimpsing life beyond the reservation's borders at last, Juanita was still pressed into service by her family. She was assigned to supervise the younger children during her mother's shift on the factory floor—at least until Adakai's Daughter arranged to marry her off. The groom was a Navajo co-worker who was once called Frank Big Thumb, but had since received the last name Jackson (though no one else in his family held the Jackson name). Frank Jackson was thirty years older than his adolescent bride.[9] Now Juanita Jackson had a new mission: this time she must care for her husband and produce heirs while he helped manufacture explosives for the troops.

On the *Dinétah* itself, the miners too supported the war effort with their labor, as Viles and Goulding never tired of reminding them. Adakai was not the only one who disapproved of ripping the innards out of Mother Earth. Whenever one of the laborers at Monument No. 1 expressed moral qualms about the digging, Viles took that man right over to the trading post for some jawboning from Harry.

Goulding had his spiel down pat. "The *ƚeetso* is the same color as the corn pollen," he'd say. "You could put 'em side by side and you couldn't tell 'em apart; they are the same yellow color exactly. We need that yellow dirt because it is strong like the pollen, and it makes bullets and helps in the war so much." [10]

After many late-night talks with the VCA men who lodged at the trading post, Goulding seemed to know that *ƚeetso* contained something even more powerful than vanadium. He wasn't the only one who guessed the secret. All over the Colorado Plateau, the miners and millers were talking about the Army men who pored over the vanadium waste piles. They all knew that the leftovers contained uranium, and it wasn't all that hard to figure out that the military had in mind a different use for it than coloring ceramics. "Kids read Buck Rogers and this type of thing," as one of the gossipers put it. [11]

So Goulding must not have thought much about the fact that he sometimes went overboard in his little chats with recalcitrant miners. He told them that their work would protect the sons of *Diné bikeyah,* that the bombs that went in the American airplanes would "do a lot more good than the enemy's bombs" because of the *ƚeetso.* [12] This argument seemed to do the trick every time.

The FBI, however, somehow learned of these discussions and deemed them disturbing. An agent telephoned Goulding and cryptically announced that he very much needed to see the trader, and soon. He gave Goulding a number and told him to call and reverse the charges any time he was going to be somewhere civilized, someplace with paved roads. So the next time that Goulding headed north of the reservation to Monticello for a load of flour to stock the trading post, he picked up the phone and let the feds know that he would be staying overnight with a good friend in that town. He took no chances. That good friend happened to be a lawyer.

The next morning, a couple of G-men grilled him at his friend the lawyer's house about where he got all this information he'd been giving the Navajos about uranium. Goulding couldn't help breaking into a wide smile when he finally heard what the big problem was. "We want answers, not grins," one of his interrogators snapped. So he explained that he had

just been trying to persuade Navajo workers to keep digging; he was helping the country's security, not undermining it.[13] The lawyer vouched for
him and the agents dropped the matter.

Viles apparently managed to refrain from revealing war secrets to his
laborers, but he frequently expressed how much he appreciated the Indians' sweat and toil. He had them working in quite primitive conditions
compared to those in the Colorado mines. One day, he told a group of
Navajo employees, "You folks are taking more vanadium out of this mine
per man in those wheelbarrows than the white people and Mexicans are
taking out where they have big equipment!"[14]

On May 15, 1943, Viles got a telegram from the War Department, re-
laying a message to VCA from the forces in North Africa. "Our fighting
men standing shoulder to shoulder with our gallant allies, the British and
the French, have driven the enemy out . . ." it read. "In this victory, the
munitions made by American Industry, labor and management played
a very important role. There is glory for us all in the achievement." The
sender signed only his last name: Eisenhower.

The trader had read that the Germans were promoting what he called
rotten, low-down, dirty propaganda about sour relations between Americans and First Americans. On his own initiative, he wrote a letter for the
Navajo miners to mail in response. Then he rode to the mine, stood by
the front of his truck, and grabbed twenty-six Navajo laborers to sign it.
One by one, they pressed the letter against the grimy fender, steadying
it with their dusty hands, and affixed their thumbprints (they couldn't
write, of course) next to the spots where Goulding told them he'd placed
their names. By the time they were finished, the paper was so crumpled
and dirty that it didn't seem fit to mail to a legendary wartime commander. Goulding hesitated, slept on it, but the next morning, he decided
to go ahead with his plan: "No, by gosh, I'm going to send it!"

This time, he was careful in his phrasing. The letter read: "We, the un-
dersigned, Navajo Indians of Monument Valley on the Northern Navajo
Reservation, have heard the telegram from our General. We thank you
for what you have said to us in your telegram. We will work harder to
get more vanadium from under the rocks on our reservation so the guns
and airplanes and munitions you need over there where you are fighting

will be strong. We are proud our reservation has vanadium to help win this war."

One of the names on the list was that of Adakai's nephew, Little John Holiday. And another one of the thumbprints belonged to John's cousin, Luke Yazzie.[15]

Eisenhower was delighted. He wrote directly to Goulding to thank "my good friends, the Navajos. . . . I wish I could shake hands with every one of them. . . . Their spirit is refreshing."[16]

Soon afterward, Luke got the chance to work even closer to home. The day of reckoning for the Cane Valley tract came on August 3, 1943. Strangely enough, only one bid was submitted. Not so strangely, the offer came from Denny Viles at VCA. Viles proposed what seemed like a generous bonus: $3,000, more than four times the amount he'd paid for Monument No. 1.[17] The Navajos accepted with pleasure.

Pep Redd was incensed. He insisted that he and Wetherill were never notified of the impending auction. The sale was advertised, but the timing was odd; bids were opened just thirteen days after public notice, an abnormally short period. Applicants generally had two to three weeks to hand in their proposals.[18] Redd told all who would listen that VCA had bribed some tribal official with $200 for favorable treatment, but he never offered evidence to back up the charge.[19]

Luke, too, felt cheated. As he had understood it, his name would come first on the paperwork and Goulding would be listed second as a witness. None of that happened, of course.

The words that delivered Adakai's mesa to the Vanadium Corporation of America were boilerplate legalisms rife with portent. *This indenture of lease, made and entered into in quintuplicate . . .* The VCA president signed evenly along the dotted line. The company secretary inscribed his name underneath with a grand flourish. Under the lease, VCA would be permitted to prospect and extract *carnotite and related minerals* for ten years and as long thereafter as it made economic sense to continue. The company was obligated to pay a royalty of 10 percent of the value of vanadium oxide *or the equivalent in other compounds.* Even the uranium, which the Navajos were unaware of, was locked up tight for the big corporation.

The Navajos did seek protections for their people and their land. VCA promised *to take appropriate steps for the preservation of the property and the health and safety of workmen*. The contract specified that VCA would *commit no waste on the said land and to suffer none to be committed* and ordered VCA to return the property *in as good condition as received*. Before surrendering the land, the company needed to make *a showing to the Secretary of the Interior that full provision has been made for the conservation and protection of the property.*[20]

Luke asked when he would receive his finder's fee, but felt, in his words, sort of ignored.[21] Instead of paying his uranium scout in cash, Viles unilaterally conferred a different honor. Like the federal Indian agents before him, Viles couldn't be bothered to learn a long Navajo name, so he replaced it with something that white men could pronounce. The mine itself was Monument No. 2, but he chose to name the rise where it was located "Yazzie Mesa," and on official maps it has remained so ever since.

Adakai was unimpressed. But Luke agreed to take a job there. He gave an explanation to his father that mirrored Harry Goulding's patter. "If *łeetso* can fight the enemy people and we say no, it will backfire on us," Luke told Adakai.[22] He maintained that selfishly withholding the ore from American soldiers would bring evil upon Cane Valley.

A few weeks after the big signing, the *bilagáanas* came to Yazzie Mesa to celebrate Monument No. 2. Viles brought along Page Edwards, a geologist who was the federal government's liaison at the Monticello mill where the uranium would be filtered from the vanadium stream. Edwards took photographs to mark the auspicious occasion. One of the pictures captured his curly-haired wife in billowing, high-waisted slacks and a blouse with rolled-up sleeves, and Denny Viles, in khakis and a pith helmet with a brim casting a shadow that obscured his face save for a big, broad smile. Between the two of them stood a somber Luke, his brow furrowed under a black cowboy hat, and old Adakai, dignity intact even in mismatched plaid shirt and breeches. He could hardly murder this group brought to Cane Valley by his own son, but he found a way to telegraph his contempt. He did not wear his heavy silver concho belt. And the patriarch's hair was held back by his bandana. These visitors did not merit his formal felt hat.[23]

As Viles added to his empire of Monument leases, the men of Union Mines were mapping the potential of the eastern reservation. They had answered the call of an ad placed by Union Carbide, the parent company of U.S. Vanadium, in trade journals. Wanted: mining engineers and geologists to work in the West. Young and restless, they signed up from lives that seemed too airless and sedate. One ran a factory floor in Kankakee. Another sold absorbent clay near the Georgia-Florida line. One was cloistered in a university lab, another behind a government desk. The most promising applicants were whisked away by train to New York for interviews. There, the chosen learned the true nature of Union Carbide's newest subsidiary.

The new hires packed up their cars and set off, with their wives if they had wives, suddenly flush with coupons for brand-new tires and for all the gasoline they might want, despite national shortages of both—the Japanese had seized the Dutch East Indies plantations that provided nearly all of America's rubber, and the government was hoarding fuel for the Army.[24] They drove through the Rocky Mountains, a big adventure in those pre-expressway days, and a slow one, too, with the Victory speed limit set at 35.

When at last they converged on their destination, they shocked the inhabitants of little Grand Junction, Colorado. The local gossips were inflamed. "What is your husband doing?" one neighbor asked one of the wives, who replied that she didn't have a clue. "Well, why don't you know?" the nosy woman persisted.[25] Most of the Union Mines wives stayed willfully uninformed, but nonetheless they pulled back after one too many inquiries and relied only on each other. They formed knitting circles, and gathered for cookies and coffee. Certainly their husbands were in no position to offer much in the way of companionship. They left for weeks at a time, returning sunburned and exhausted and close-mouthed, for the most part, about where they'd been and what they'd done.

All of the company's expenses were reimbursed by the federal government. Their cables were classified, but even so, they weren't allowed to use the U-word. They couldn't go to VCA's mines, because the company worried about possible industrial espionage. But they were still finding plenty of signs of S-37, SOM, and SOQ.

There was just one problem. The government had enough vanadium, the mineral that had provided uranium's cover story all along. In Washington, the vice chairman of the War Production Board wrote to the secretary of commerce to urge ending federal vanadium purchases. "It has developed that the Army is actively interested in this same vanadium program for reasons other than vanadium," he noted tactfully, but ". . . it cannot continue to be operated as such, by or under the direction of the War Production Board."[26]

In late 1943, officials in Washington sent a wire to their local man, Page Edwards, to close the sampling plant that VCA was operating for the government in Monticello.[27] Production at the Monuments soon ceased. All mining of carnotite ore was suspended in 1944—and would not resume for years.

But as far as the "reasons other than vanadium" were concerned, there was enough. In the end, 12.5 percent of the uranium used in the Manhattan Project came from the Colorado Plateau, including the Navajo vanadium mines.[28] That translated to some 2.7 million pounds of uranium oxide—yellowcake—purchased for more than $2 million, or 77 cents a pound.[29] Monument No. 1 was the source of more than ten thousand tons of ore. Monument No. 2, just getting off the ground, provided 243.72 tons.[30] VCA was still experimenting with its refining process and estimated it could only get at 35 percent of the uranium contents. If so, Monument No. 2 would have produced roughly 820 pounds of yellowcake for the Manhattan Project.[31] It was a small contribution but a contribution nonetheless. As was noted by the physicist Hans Bethe, who was part of Groves's team: "We wanted all we could get."[32]

By 1945, General Groves harbored no more doubts about the viability of building a uranium bomb, nor did the scores of researchers at the campus of a boys' school in northern New Mexico, which had become a secret city concentrating on the "gadget," as they were ordered to call their death-star invention. The science was airtight.

And it was evolving. The scientists of the Manhattan Project had managed to filter out a second element from their precious uranium supply that was even easier to split: plutonium. It seemed that a plutonium bomb would be even more deadly than a straight uranium bomb. But it was not as reliable, and it would need to be tested. At 5:29 on the morning of July 16, 1945, a plutonium bomb, code-named Trinity, was detonated in a remote slice of New Mexico desert. The bomb tower disintegrated and the soil was transformed into a sea of greenish glass. The fireball's smoking aftermath billowed into a stupendous mushroom shape. A new force had been set upon an unsuspecting planet. "I am become death, the destroyer of worlds," the chief scientist, J. Robert Oppenheimer, famously murmured. "Now we are all sons of bitches," concluded a physicist who stood next to him. Ever the engineer, Leslie Groves more prosaically compared the astounding explosion to what had been until that moment his most lasting achievement. "I no longer consider the Pentagon a safe shelter from such a blast," he wrote.[33]

The Army stood ready to employ either a uranium bomb or a plutonium bomb, or both.

Groves's Manhattan Engineering District had ordered a young lieutenant to Colorado to oversee the diversion of uranium from the local vanadium stream. Soon after Trinity, the officer received a telegram of thanks. "MED's mission has been accomplished" was the message. He was gratified, of course, but he hadn't been let in on the details, so he wasn't sure exactly what what had been accomplished.[34]

Understanding dawned about a month later, once he heard about the events of August 6 in the Japanese city of Hiroshima. An Army plane dropped a bomb containing a total of 140 pounds of enriched uranium in two different vessels. The uranium supplies were jammed together to reach critical mass. Neutrons collided, nuclei divided—unleashing the primal power of the universe for the second time on Earth. With a blinding flash, a potent shock, a multicolored boiling cloud so huge that it obscured the city, more than 100,000 people would perish. Three days later, a plutonium bomb replicated the Trinity success, this time over Nagasaki, killing another 100,000 Japanese.[35] The Atomic Age had arrived.

Chapter 5

Cold War

For a moment after the bombs obliterated Hiroshima and Nagasaki, the whole planet seemed to hold its breath. In 1946, after the Allied victory, the fledgling United Nations' very first resolution concerned ridding humanity of this terrible new threat. The UN created a commission to address this crisis, heralding the birth of a brand-new superbureaucracy.

The commission held talks that, predictably, failed before they even got off the ground. The Americans demanded that rules be set for enforcement of a ban before they would destroy the bombs they'd already made. The Russians insisted that the Americans get rid of their supply before figuring out how to keep anyone else from building more.

All too quickly, at the highest levels of the U.S. government, peace—or peace of mind, at least—had vanished. Intelligence showed that Russia was deploying conscripts by the thousands to old mines in the Soviet satellite states where uranium could be found. Just as feverishly, Communist construction workers were putting the finishing touches on enrichment plants. Aggressive action was called for. The American monopoly would not hold.[1]

On August 1, 1946, just days short of the first anniversary of the Hiroshima drop, President Truman created the Atomic Energy Commission (AEC), the successor, under civilian control, to the Manhattan Project.

The law he signed put the U.S. government in the happy position of reserving for itself the right to buy all the uranium on the market and also to set the price.[2] Almost immediately, though, it became clear that a shortage loomed, and that shortage could paralyze the $2 billion investment in America's bomb-production system. At the end of 1947, the AEC established a Raw Materials Division to flood the nuclear-war machine with as much uranium as possible, as fast as possible, and as economically as possible.

The job looked thankless. Uranium was more common on Earth than silver or gold, but it was rarely concentrated enough in one place to make mining practical. There were just three known sources of mineable uranium in the Western world, all of which had been pressed into service for the Manhattan Project, each with tragic flaws. The supply for the earliest experiments had come from a small Canadian mine at Port Radium where the ore had to pass over 1,200 miles of lake and river before reaching the nearest railhead. To make matters worse, the mine was less than thirty miles south of the Arctic Circle and the water route, involving seven portages past foaming rapids, was iced over completely for nine months of the year. Expansion was considered unlikely.[3]

Nearly 90 percent of the U.S. uranium stored from the Manhattan Project days came from Shinkolobwe Mine, the crucial Belgian Congo source. As at Port Radium, the ore had to make an arduous journey to get into American hands: 1,400 miles by river and rail before reaching the coast and then 7,000 miles more across the Atlantic. The losses to enemy submarines were not forgotten. And for all the trouble, the size of the deposit was in question; who knew how much was left?[4]

That left the vanadium-uranium beds of the Colorado Plateau—within the Navajo borders and without. The surroundings were remote and harsh, but the product was certainly not as vulnerable to enemy attack. Still, while the uranium at Port Radium and Shinkolobwe was found in dependable pitchblende ore, the carnotite of the American West seemed unpromising for the large amounts the Pentagon said it needed. The drilling and mapping of the wartime front company, Union Mines Development Corp., had revealed total reserves of about 1 million tons of ore, which would yield fewer than 2,500 tons of uranium oxide.

This was not much to feed the $2 billion beast. Were there other options in the world? The gold mines of South Africa seemed to be the best bet. About 20 million tons of the gold ore harvested each year contained about a quarter to a pound of uranium oxide per ton, averaging about half a pound. This was considered plentiful compared to the uranium in the carnotite stock. Then there were the small uranium deposits of Portugal. Perhaps uranium could be strained from sea water?

The Raw Materials Division was so desperate that it even considered spots where mere specks of uranium were present, such as phosphate rock in Florida and black shale in Tennessee. The drawback for both was the high price of getting at the stuff coveted by the AEC. Milling 10 million tons of phosphate would yield only a few hundred tons of uranium. Milling 10 to 15 tons of shale would result in just one pound of uranium—at that rate, it would cost somewhere between $40 to $60 per pound.[5]

There really didn't appear to be much choice. The AEC had to try them all.

Yet the situation was not nearly as hopeless as it seemed. As it turned out, the Union Mines reports on the Four Corners region made no mention of VCA's eastern Navajo leasehold, nor of Monument No. 1 nor Denny Viles's "big one," Monument No. 2 in Cane Valley. The reason: company rivalries.[6] VCA, after all, had shut out the Union Mines teams.

But VCA's troves were known to the government. One of the new AEC recruits was Jesse C. Johnson, who had worked in the wartime metals program, helping the government secure everything from tin to nickel. He was familiar with the sources of vanadium. Johnson recognized that there was definitely more uranium-vanadium ore out there than the reports had shown, and he realized too that this might mean even more lay yet undiscovered in the region. But there was no way the government would be able to explore so vast a territory—the Navajo reservation alone was roughly the size of Belgium—and there were no particular clues about where to start.

So he hit on the idea of getting others to do the job for them. If this was war, albeit a Cold War, then the AEC would raise an army. He spoke of volunteer prospectors as his infantry. He would encourage miners to seek their fortunes, and uranium, out West. To spark their interest, the United States of America would promise to buy any uranium in whatever form that they could find. Not only that, the government would guarantee a very nice price.

On April 11, 1948, the AEC sounded the call to arms, announcing that the commission would pay $20.40 per ton of uranium-bearing ore from the Colorado Plateau, beating by more than 50 percent the previous high price for any type of ore in the area.[7] That price would be good for three years. Anyone who found a new deposit would also earn a fine bonus, $10,000, on the first delivery of carnotite or similar rocks.

Of course, the commission was operating on hope at this point. Johnson was the liaison between the AEC's raw materials division and the military. Every time he met with the brass, the question came up: "How much uranium can you get?" Johnson was an ambitious man who liked to feel important. Despite his private fears, he told them not to worry. He ventured even further into perilous territory with numbers that were little more than dreams.[8] The Army officials, greatly relieved by Johnson's cheerful estimates, laid plans to expand the production lines for U-235 and nuclear bombs. He was going to have to deliver.

So just one month and one day later, the AEC sweetened its offer for "special rocks" from the Four Corners region, adding a six-cent-per-ton-per-mile allowance for hauling the ore to a mill and an extra 50 cents per pound of yellowcake from ores with 0.2 percent or more of uranium. These extras were intended to tempt the owners of closed mines to open up again.[9] Johnson was betting heavily on his infantry of prospectors, but he had decided to bring in the artillery to back them up. In other words, the AEC needed VCA. VCA's ten-year leases were still in effect. Jesse Johnson had worked with Page Edwards, the liaison to VCA at the Monticello mill, and Page Edwards had traveled to Monument No. 2 with Denny Viles. Through Edwards, Johnson knew that Monument No. 2, in particular, was a source of fine high-grade uranium.

To Navajo soldiers making their way back, the atom bomb was far from Topic A. They had stories to tell of exotic places far, far beyond the holy mountains. They took pride in the exploits of the Code Talkers. Embraced once more by the stark glory of *Diné bikeyah,* top priority went to regaining the internal balance that Navajos prized, the emotional symmetry disrupted by their military service. The returning veterans kept the medicine men busy. Over and over, in the great wide spaces late at night, fires blazed to warm the crowds camping for the ceremony known as the Enemy Way, cleansing the young men of their encounters with the dead of war. The ritual unfolded over three days and nights, with the medicine man building intricate colored sand paintings inside a special *hooghan* and chanting outside in the cold clear air. At first, everyone danced, with the women choosing partners, but as the tension built, two opposing camps enacted a mock battle, complete with an attack on horseback, rifle shots, and shouting. By sunrise of the fourth morning, "the one sung over" was free of evil. The songs declared: *Hózhǫ́ nahasdlį́į́'. Hózhǫ́ nahasdlį́į́'. Hózhǫ́ nahasdlį́į́'. Hózhǫ́ nahasdlį́į́'.* Over and over: "Conditions of harmony have been restored."[10]

Of course, exposure to the wider world had wrought changes that even the ceremony could not undo. The Marines, especially, evinced a less than reverent attitude; they tended to ad-lib the chants, throwing in a foreign phrase or two they had picked up overseas, and some of those phrases were a little risqué.[11] They were Code Talking in reverse.

The vanadium mines, open so briefly, were mere memories. The mills, far from the reservation, were all shuttered. With the war over, the market for vanadium ore plunged 72 percent between 1945 and 1946.[12] Instead of wheeling barrows filled with carnotite, there were sheep to herd, horses to break, crops to tend. Navajo men, veterans and nonveterans alike, were finding employment on the railroads that threaded the reservation's borders. These jobs took them far from home for long periods, but that was not unheard of anymore. Luke joined in; he even picked up a few words of English during his stints of train work. His family was still growing, the "finder's fee" he had expected from VCA had never come through, and the wages were sorely needed. The only other option was working for John Ford; the director had finally returned to film a trilogy about the American cavalry. After a long absence, the actors could at last ride again. If the AEC had its way, so would the miners.

Cane Valley's *leetso*—and any that could be gathered elsewhere—would be no good without processing mills to crush the rocks and make yellow-cake. Jesse Johnson also needed both of the old vanadium giants, Union Carbide's USV and VCA, for this crucial link in the supply chain. The method was almost the same as before, although now it was vanadium that would be the by-product. Jesse Johnson opened negotiations with Denny Viles[13] to buy uranium oxide from two treatment plants that the company would start operating in 1949. The government's goal was for VCA to spend $200,000 to refit an old vanadium mill in Durango and lease it from the government, its current owner. VCA would also build a brand-new mill in White Canyon, Utah. Neither was on the reservation, but if the talks went well, Navajo ore was to be shipped to Durango and a 10 percent royalty would go to the tribe.[14]

Johnson, nicknamed Jess, was not intimidated by Denny Viles's size. He too was a big man, tall and large-featured, with a prominent nose under brushy brows on a long face. But he knew who had the leverage in this relationship and employed the soft sell.[15] The AEC's man had mastered the art of compliments and expressions of courtly concern, and he also knew how to talk Denny Viles's language. He could match Viles's tales of business in South America and the Wild West with his own stories of work in frontier Alaska as a young mining engineer during World War I. This past included an exotic tinge of intrigue; the client he had listed during his visits to the field was his boss in the Navy's intelligence bureau. He had pledged allegiance as a civilian employee and agreed to report all activities of foreign vessels and locations of any German residents, as well as local public opinion and politics that "might have a bearing on the war."[16]

He offered terms to Viles and to Viles's counterpart at USV that would later be jokingly characterized as "a light form of bribery" by G. R. Kennedy, the owner of a smaller mining company working in the area.[17] The government would pay for exploratory drilling, in locales directed by USV and VCA. For Viles, Johnson threw in a prize that his company had sought for years: some old leases from the 1930s, in the Navajos' Carrizo

Mountains, that had ended up in the hands of the Manhattan Project's front company, Union Mines. A team of Union Mines geologists had reported back that this was definitive uranium land. VCA wanted the property, indeed had schemed in the past to get it through a double cross by one of the original partners, but the deal had fallen through.[18] Here it was, gift wrapped: completely surveyed and drilled, no risk at all involved. Jess Johnson had the lease transferred over.

VCA was thus able to move back into *Diné bikeyah* in a big way in late 1947 and early 1948. Over by the Arizona–New Mexico border, mining started up again in the Carrizos and on the nearby ridge. And, of course, where Arizona met Utah, Viles cranked up at Monument No. 2, still convinced that the mine on Yazzie Mesa was destined to become the richest of them all.

Back to work Luke went. Like his father before him, he left before dawn for the fifteen-minute trek up to the summit of the mesa. But Adakai had taken only what would grow again, paying with praise and blessings as he did so. Navajo land use was not always so benign—the land was overgrazed, timber overstripped—but Luke was skilled now in the ways of real violence. He drilled into the heart of the sandstone body, boring scores of shallow holes down in the tunnel and laboriously inserting blasting caps and wires. When he finished, it was time to detonate and run, run, run, as fast as the young Navajo boys had been taught to do first thing in the morning. He had abided by this custom throughout his childhood—Adakai made him do it—and could easily race away before the sparks turned to booms and the wall underground collapsed into chunks of *leetso* for the mills. The miners left columns of stone in place to support the tunnel's roof as they forced their way into the mesa's murky depths. The columns got longer and longer as they bored their way down.

At noontime, one of Luke's small sons would bring him a sack lunch, generally a piece of mutton rolled in frybread—mixed with flour, cooked in lard—and sometimes some canned goods. Whichever child had been elected for this honor would tarry to share the feast with his father. They would perch on the ore heap and eat and talk amid the fumes and the noise and the dirt until, in due course, Luke headed back underground to broach the mesa once more. At night, he would walk heavily home and lie down, exhausted in his dusty clothes while the toddlers swarmed all over their dad. They'd grab whatever was left of his lunch for a snack.[19]

For his toil, Luke received the same pay as everyone else, $130 a month. Since his efforts with Denny Viles had proved fruitless, Luke inquired of Harry Goulding whenever his errands brought him to the Monument Valley trading post. What about that extra payment he was owed? To hear him tell it, Goulding always reassured him, "Don't worry, your money is coming." Luke explained to his children that VCA was putting the bonus cash away for him and he would get at it eventually. They would be rich someday. He promised that they would.

The Navajo tribal council was unhappy. The mining company leases were legal, set up according to the regulations they had drafted, but Luke Yazzie's situation had revealed a glaring flaw. Delegates wanted to be helpful to the United States, and they were glad to accept royalties for the tribal coffers, but they felt strongly that their people should also be cashing in on the boom. Beginning in 1949, the council sought to recast the terms for prospecting and mining on Navajo land. A formal resolution noted that "the United States government, as well as many nations throughout the world, are vigorously seeking sources of uranium-bearing ores for development of atomic energy, whether for weapons of war or for peaceful and beneficial purposes . . ."

The documents already signed would remain in effect, so VCA's deals in the Carrizos, at Monument No. 1 and at Monument No. 2, were still in place. But for all the negotiations to come, the council set up a new procedure. The tribe would grant operating permits only to its own. The federal government would continue to be the only customer. The federal government would set the price. The federal government would establish ore-buying stations. The federal government would have the right to drill exploratory cores on the reservation. But it would be Navajos exclusively who would mine the ore.

The council's stance reverberated all the way from the Navajo capital at Window Rock to the American capital in Washington. The AEC's manager for the Colorado Plateau wrote a memo to the commission counsel at HQ, outlining what he saw as a big problem: "Several inquiries were received in this office from white men as to whether or not they could ship and sell such ore in their own names if they were to go in under an oral agreement with the permittee and develop these deposits . . . (but) we were advised that such ores would have to be mined, shipped and sold by the Indian."

The Navajos had every right to issue their decree. Under the 1868 treaty, the United States had agreed that no non-Navajo could "cross over, settle upon or reside in" the reservation without the tribe's permission. The only way around this would be for the government to hire its own miners and for the president himself to order them in. Those steps seemed a bit drastic. But, the local manager wrote, "it was apparent that this proviso was discouraging the development of uranium ore deposits . . ." Once lodes were located, Navajos had neither the experience nor the capital to speed massive amounts of ore out of the ground. Jesse Johnson's assurances to the military, and maybe the fate of the entire planet, were at stake. By this time, the Soviets had caught up, successfully testing their own A-bomb. President Truman made the stunning announcement in September of 1949. The threat was real; the race was on.

More countries were, like Russia, going Communist. Mao Zedong declared the People's Republic of China. Communists took control of large portions of Vietnam. An epic clash of ideologies was taking shape.

Let the white men in, the AEC entreated Navajo leaders at a meeting on August 1, 1950. The AEC's local manager offered a compromise: let the white men, in effect, sublet the uranium claims. This would allow individual Navajos, in addition to the tribe, to collect fees. But it would also offer access to mine operators with the know-how and equipment to do the job. The country could not wait.

The council agreed, setting up a cumbersome two-step. Only a Navajo could stake a claim, but a *Diné* claim holder could temporarily assign mining rights to outsiders. An assignment would be effective for only two years, though it could be extended for another two—a short leash compared to VCA's stranglehold on its direct leaseholds.

The change set off a frenzy. Individual Navajos rushed to enlist in Jess Johnson's "infantry." They knew their own grazing lands as intimately as

Adakai knew his, and now they could be rewarded for giving up their secrets. The tribe would make sure that, unlike poor Luke Yazzie, they would really get payment, not just promises. As people will, they responded to the lure of cash.

Prospectors lent out Geiger counters, urging families to take them on expeditions into the outback and they were happy to make a day of prospecting and picnics. Everyone knew about the hunt for yellow dirt. Everyone kept eyes peeled. And within a year, by 1950, came real results, the stuff of Jesse Johnson's dreams.

In the western Navajo lands, near the Grand Canyon, the Little Colorado River and the trading post at Cameron, Arizona, a Navajo prospector staked one mine after another, until he had more than ten. The Cameron finds were shallow paydirt, so close to the surface that miners would never have to dig a tunnel.

Far to the east and south, a Navajo woman sent her husband out to buy some baking powder in the white border town of Grants, New Mexico. Willing, but craving a drink first, he stopped in at the bootlegger—alcohol was illegal in Navajo country—and as he continued on his way, swigging wine, he got sleepy. He stopped for a nap on a flat rock at the foot of a mountain known as Haystack, and when he woke, reached for the jug again.[20] He found himself touching a shimmer of yellow in the rock. Wondering whether this was the *leetso* that everyone was talking about, dreaming of the bounty that lay in his grasp, he used another rock to break off a sample, proceeded to Grants, and took his chips to the mayor. The mayor sent it on to the AEC for testing. The rock was hot. Here again was uranium where none had been known before. It seemed to be everywhere. Deposits were showing up in a rough circle all around the edges of the *Dinétah*.

The boom was on, all over the Colorado Plateau, but the Navajos' world-class reserves were at the center of the action. VCA and U.S. Vanadium were no longer the only giants striding into the Indian lands. Over in the west, Rare Metals began blasting directly into the desert floor, while shepherds ambled past with their flocks. Far to the east, the oil company Kerr-McGee set up shop alongside VCA in the Carrizos. In the morning, miners walked up the pine-scented slopes, from their homes in the hamlets below—Teec Nos Pos and Lukachukai, Cove and Red Rock—and in the evenings, they headed back down from their jobs, just as the Cane Valley men did.

The Guardian, in the form of the Bureau of Indian Affairs, approved the leases on the Navajos' behalf, continuing to bow to the tribe's insistence on return of the land "in as good condition as received." Of course, the federal government was left to enforce these terms. Once the BIA signed off, whether damage was repaired or not, the land, and the legal responsibility for it, returned to the Navajo claim holder, who was more likely than not an ill-educated shepherd or farmer. In the end, the land reverted to the tribe.

The welter of leases and subleases under the new system often blurred lines of accountability. Small-scale adventurers began gravitating to Navajo territory to seek their own radioactive fortunes and some of those were fly-by-nighters who didn't know what they were doing. Sometimes the big guns and the new speculators worked the same claim in succession. For example, two Navajo friends named King Tutt and Paul Shorty staked a claim on a ridgetop where VCA was already ensconced, assuming that where there was a known deposit, more uranium must lurk nearby. They called their site King Tutt No. 1 and rented it to a parade of outsiders: First, Walter Duncan, Inc., which was owned by an Oklahoma oil tycoon. Then, Sylvania Mining, headed by the mayor of Thermopolis, Wyoming, and his vice president, a dashing pilot, auto racer, and noted ladies' man. Then the big time: their neighbor, VCA itself. And when VCA's two years were up, the Navajo partners picked an independent prospector named Charles Pickens to operate their mine. Paul Shorty, who could write his name in English but couldn't add or subtract, asked the wife of the Indian trader at Red Rock to maintain a checkbook for him. She tracked his bank account while he bought truck after truck, making sure that he didn't spend more than he had.[21] But it got harder and harder to keep similar watch over who had done what to the land.

Panic swept America. "Bert the Turtle," a cartoon character in civil defense helmet and bow tie, showed up on movie screens in classrooms everywhere, instructing young students to "duck and cover" if they saw a sudden white-hot flash. If they were lucky, an air-raid siren might wail a heads-up first—sometimes the authorities ran a test, sending chills through all within earshot—but truth be told, doom could strike at any second without warning. Quailing families built private fallout shelters and stocked them with canned goods.

Everyone knew how to prepare for nuclear war, or thought they did. But few outside the reservation borders were aware of the Navajos, barefaced and in moccasins, laboring to protect them from the Russians.

Chapter 6

The Obstacle

R adiation was still an emerging field of study, but everyone in the field knew of the horrific fate suffered by workers in the old metal mines of Eastern Europe, the same mines that the Soviets had begun to tap for their own nuclear arsenal. The case was a classic, first documented in medical literature in 1500. The Erz mountains were filled with minerals; the name, in fact, is the German word for "ore." The range marked the border between Saxony and Bohemia (and by post-war times, between East Germany and Czechoslovakia). Beginning in the Renaissance, miners tunneled through the mountains in search of silver, cobalt, nickel, bismuth, and arsenic, all of which they found in abundance. On both sides of the hills, the workers tended to die painfully in the prime of life, succumbing to damaged lungs and then a rapid spiral into severe illness. The miners themselves called the disease *Bergsucht,* "mountain sickness," and believed that it was caused by malicious dwarfs dwelling underground.[1] Not until 1879 did doctors discover that *Berg-sucht* was actually lung cancer. After Marie and Pierre Curie discovered radium in 1898, the two physicists turned to the Erz slag heaps, which, as they suspected, contained a steady supply of the newly identified element for their experiments. By the 1920s and '30s, radioactivity in the mines was fingered as the reason for the abundance of pulmonary tumors.[2]

The connection wasn't easy to make. The cancer generally developed about fifteen years after the first exposure and then it was often misdiagnosed as common tuberculosis. The prevalence among the miners of scarred lungs, or silicosis, also complicated the equation.[3] Yet it became clear that cancer of the respiratory system accounted for 50 to 70 percent of the deaths of veterans of the Erz mines.[4] In 1932, two Czech doctors published a landmark paper—in an American journal—that discussed a substance detected in the mines which they called "radium emanation." The authors linked the cancers to the cumulative effects of inhaling the "emanation" in small quantities over many years.[5]

By 1940, "radium emanation" was known as radon. Radium was one of the elements formed as uranium decayed. Radon was simply another step in this cycle, notable because it took the form of a gas. And what a gas: invisible but thick, about seven times as dense as air, the heaviest known to man. Half of any given quantity of radon transformed every four days back into solid form. The resulting microscopic particles were known as radon "daughters," and the daughters were all radioactive, too.

Radon diffused from the rocks in the mines. Drilling and blasting released still more of it. Colorless, odorless, inflammable, the gas offered nothing to alert the miners who inhaled it as the fumes spread through the mines' underground hallways. Radon daughters attached to the dust and water droplets that whirled through the air after dynamiting and these too traveled through the nose and mouth to lodge deep in the lungs, still tossing off particles and breaking down again, causing more exposure over time. The most dangerous of the particles, alpha radiation, would be easily blocked by skin, but once they were smuggled inside the body, alphas were free to join beta and gamma rays in damaging the cells, paving the way for mutations that spun wildly out of control. Mutated cells could grow unchecked into cancers.

One man on the Colorado Plateau knew enough about radiation to understand the implications for the local miners. It wasn't long before he started irritating Jesse Johnson, who brooked no obstacle to his plans for a mighty stream of Western uranium.

The obstacle's name was Ralph V. Batie. He'd been stationed in Grand Junction with the Manhattan Project from 1942 through 1945 while the uranium was salvaged from vanadium waste. After the war, he moved on to Oak Ridge, Tennessee, one of the "atomic towns" where the bomb-making process moved forward, and from there to Brookhaven National

Laboratory, a surplus Army base on Long Island that the AEC had converted into a center for peacetime nuclear research. When the mines and mills reopened in the West, Batie was recruited to return as the chief of health and safety for the AEC's Colorado Raw Materials Office. He took up his new position in 1948 and almost immediately started to worry about working conditions in the mines and mills, all cranking up, at Johnson's urging, for unprecedented production.

Batie was aware that the U.S. National Council on Radiation Protection had adopted a standard for radon in 1941 out of concern for workers who used radium to make luminous dials. The highest concentration of radon deemed safe by the council was 10 picocuries per liter of air. That amount was minuscule. (The curie was named for Pierre Curie after he died; it is a measure of the radiation produced by one gram of radium-226. A picocurie is one-trillionth of that amount. A picocurie has the same relationship to a curie that a penny has to $10 billion.)[6]

Given the Erz miners' history and the radiation council's limit, Batie wanted to find out how much radon gas was wafting through the uranium mines and mills in his region. He had worked with two young experts at Brookhaven who, like him, joined the AEC. Both of them had ended up in the New York health and safety office (the AEC's strong presence in New York was a legacy of the Manhattan Project). Batie traveled east for lessons from his friends on how to use radiation detectors. He also invited them to Colorado, hoping they would help him devise a safety program.[7]

His friends showed up in June of 1948. They never got to the Navajo mines. They toured four mills, including VCA's Durango plant. None existed yet in *Diné bikeyah*. For convenience's sake, the single mine they visited was also in Colorado. Only a couple of employees worked there, typical of the off-reservation sites. The visitors filled one-liter flasks with air and shipped the containers east for analysis. These were the first radon tests on the Colorado Plateau.

The results were disturbing. Even though the samples provided only a quick glimpse, not a full portrait over time, the numbers at Slick Rock, Colorado, looked a lot like the numbers reported in studies of the Erz mountains. Safeguards were definitely needed. The New York experts offered Batie a flurry of advice: All new hires needed a pre-employment physical. Mine and mill operators should think twice before choosing anyone who already had lung disease or renal problems—uranium had deadly qualities aside from radiation; its properties as a heavy metal were known to poison kidneys. At the mills, coveralls were essential and all employees needed to change them frequently; anyone directly handling yellowcake should wear thick leather gloves. The workers should shower at the end of each shift. The recommendations, the New Yorkers wrote in a memo, "are geared to good industrial practice and are being made without regard to either the legal or moral responsibilities of the AEC." These phrases were underlined in the copy that Jesse Johnson kept in his files: not so much because he felt strongly about "good industrial practice," but because he thought the phrasing gave him an out, at least when it came to the mines.[8]

The law that created the AEC held the commission responsible for uranium ore and its products "after its removal from its place of deposit in nature." The mills had to be licensed by the AEC and so did anyone who delivered the ore there. The lines of responsibility were clear in those cases. But mining did not require an AEC license.

The New Yorkers argued that the AEC might not *have* to oversee mining, but the commission still had the legal right to do so. It was simple: Just require the mills—which sold directly to the government—to process only ore from mines that met the radon limits. This would not be a first. The contracts with uranium mills already contained provisions that forced them to handle their ore purchases a certain way: they had to buy from independent producers, not just from their own operations. As for health protection, the AEC had just started requiring the makers of beryllium, another key ingredient in nuclear devices, to keep the metal down to certain levels both in the mills and in adjacent neighborhoods. The commission didn't have to flex its muscles like that, but it seemed like the right thing to do. After all, beryllium exposure could cause a chronic lung disease, and without the AEC, very little of it would be manufactured; the threat would not exist.

Why not follow the same course for uranium? It didn't occur to the safety experts that their approach might court controversy. Yet colleagues in the New York office gossiped that someone in Washington had gone ballistic. It was no surprise, then, when the order came down from head-quarters: AEC would keep its distance from the thorny issue of working conditions in the mines, leaving it to safety inspectors at the state level—safety inspectors who had no training in radiation. Safety inspectors with far less money for surveys than the AEC could command.

Ralph Batie, who had started all the uproar, refused to give up. With the AEC out of the mine-safety business, Batie went on to notify Colorado health authorities. If it was a state problem, well, then, he would do his best to make sure that the states took it up. The state medical men in turn alerted the U.S. Public Health Service (PHS).[9] General concerns about mining had prompted the PHS to start an "industrial hygiene" section back in 1914 when it was a radical notion that a working environment could affect health. The goal was to eliminate the prospect of workers paying for their jobs with their lives. But within the health service, this was a backwater, prone to sudden, sharp budget cutbacks. The PHS had studied the radium dial painters in 1928, but no one there had dealt with radiation for the past twenty years.[10]

It was amateur hour. Batie knew it, so he pushed ahead further. He invited Colorado's top two health safety experts to Grand Junction for training and a tour of uranium mines and mills. Jesse Johnson reacted with fury. He could not rescind the invitation without looking callous, but he could tighten a noose around his renegade employee. He imposed ground rules: Batie could show the state officials how to use the instruments. He could take the men out to the mines. He could even lend them the equipment to use later. But under no circumstances could he do any testing himself or even be present for any sampling.[11]

Batie obeyed the letter if not the spirit. He helped the state experts get Q-clearances from the FBI, which allowed them access to classified information, so they could go to the mines on their own.[12] But he hosted a meeting afterward with both the state and the PHS to check the results. By this time, March of 1949, nearly a year had passed since he first sought help from his own agency. The state's numbers were similar to the first samples taken by Batie's shunted-aside New York friends. Even scant as it was, the data clanged a resounding alarm.[13] The director of the Colorado Health Department scheduled a conference in Denver that

May to look into the radiation problem. At the same time, in response to five thousand inquiries from would-be ground troops in Jesse Johnson's prospector "army," the AEC and the U.S. Geological Survey published a pocket-sized handbook on how to hunt for uranium. They sold it for 30 cents, hoping to fan even more interest.[14]

Meanwhile, miners and millers—in Colorado, in Mormon Utah, and on the Navajo reservation—were still breathing radon, still unwittingly ushering alpha, beta, and gamma daughters to dance through their respiratory systems. One of the state officials, frustrated and frightened, leaked the results of the preliminary testing to the *Denver Post*. On July 7, 1949, two articles appeared, one stationed prominently at the top of the front page and a second, shorter one on page 2 with added details. Both stories focused on a VCA mill where a chemist had been observed stirring uranium with his bare hands and workmen were seen eating lunch in radioactive sections of the plant. Radioactive particles inside the body could cause lung cancer and leukemia, the *Post* reported, and might contribute to stillbirths, deformities, and sterility.

The shorter article noted that "Ralph V. Batie . . . confirmed the findings of the state officials. 'Definite radiation hazards exist in all the plants now operating,' he declared."[15]

That did it. Denny Viles was outraged. So was Jesse Johnson, who phoned angrily from Washington. He dispatched a deputy to Grand Junction for an emergency meeting. Ralph Batie was in deep, deep trouble.

"Keep your mouth shut," the aide ordered Batie before the group sat down.[16] The five men in the room were all federal or state employees except for Denny Viles.[17] The agenda had a single item: chewing out Ralph Batie. The AEC and VCA presented a united front. Stay away from the mines and mills. Keep out.[18] As instructed, Batie absorbed the verbal blows in silence. Yet he still planned another trip to the uranium mines for the fall.

Within weeks, Johnson himself was headed west with Batie on his mind. This persistent fellow was really turning into a headache—a one-man bottleneck. Johnson's life was complicated enough without this prophet of doom. He had guaranteed the Army a flow of uranium, and amazingly enough, the ore just might be there in the ground. But the uranium-bearing rocks outside the reservation also contained significant amounts of lime and the lime was gumming up the works at the processing plants, counteracting the acid used to separate uranium out of the ore. Until Johnson could find some method that could work with lime, he was even more dependent on production from Monument No. 2. Among its other virtues, Monument No. 2 ore happened to be very low in lime. Viles, of course, controlled this precious store. Not only that, Johnson needed a new mill to get all that ore converted into yellowcake. He had been pushing Viles to move faster on his White Canyon mill, which would process uranium ore with high amounts of copper.[19] Jesse Johnson desperately needed to keep Denny Viles happy. And Denny Viles was sick and tired of Ralph Batie.

Johnson bought a spiral notebook from a stationery store in Grand Junction to jot down his musings during the trip. On August 25, 1949, he drove straight away to Durango and Denny Viles. After an overnight stay ("Royal Motel—very good," he wrote), Johnson inspected VCA's mill. Viles showed him samples of carnotite containing 1 percent uranium, an exciting amount.[20] Johnson numbered the reminders in his notebook from his meeting with Viles. Number 10 was "Safety limit. No mining. No October trip." Batie's trip, that is.

Johnson's schedule was jammed. He grabbed the 10:40 a.m. train to Salt Lake City to meet with some businessmen about building a station where ore samples could be pulverized and tested for uranium content so accurate prices could be set at the mills. He flew back to Grand Junction ("Monarch Airlines 3:15–45 minutes late") in time to dine with a mill manager who had some thoughts about treating that vexatious high-lime ore.

But Batie's name kept recurring in the pages of his notebook. Johnson listed topics for a meeting on August 29 with the top brass at the Grand Junction office. A fireproof warehouse. Secure lines for phone calls. Leasing six Buicks; they were cheaper than Fords. And "Cancel Batie Oct. trip. Define Batie's work within realistic limits." He added firmly: "No radioactive hazards but silicosis"—a lung disease linked to many forms of mining. Johnson simply would not allow uranium to pose a distinct peril of its own; he would not let cancer be an issue.

He put together a group of the most important issues to raise on his return to Washington. "Discuss with Safety—Batie's proposed trip in Oct." By now, Johnson had a solution. He had come up with better uses for the time of his front-line safety man. Instead of checking radiation and radon levels in the workplace, Batie should escort visitors around the Grand Junction office. He should also drive between the mines and mills to check the mileage, so haulers could be called out if they padded their costs when seeking reimbursement for expenses.[21]

Ralph Batie got the point. His travel allowance was suddenly depleted. Jesse Johnson had grounded him.[22] There was no one to appeal to; at the end of the month, Johnson was promoted to deputy manager of the Raw Materials Division, making him the heir apparent for the top job.

Still, Batie's outreach had been effective in keeping the safety question alive. On August 25, the same day that Jesse Johnson hit the road for Durango to talk with Viles, Colorado state officials were meeting to discuss radiation with the Public Health Service. On August 30, only a day after Johnson told the Grand Junction managers to rein in Ralph Batie, a coalition from Colorado—including the state health department, the bureau of mines, and the Colorado Industrial Commission—formally requested the surgeon general—head of the PHS—to examine the risk to workers. Just as the AEC officials were joined by Vanadium Corporation of America for Batie's dressing-down, the state of Colorado had an industry partner. VCA's great rival, Union Carbide's U.S. Vanadium, echoed the call for a scientific review.[23]

U.S. Vanadium executives may have had a motive less pure than the good of the miners. A federal health survey would tack away from Colorado toward Indian land, where its competitor held sway. On the reservation, no one could argue that all agencies of the federal government must yield to the states. The tribe was a sovereign nation under the Treaty of 1868, which limited state power in the *Dinétah*, and the United States government had promised to care for the Navajos as their guardian. Even if the AEC didn't feel like taking on the task, other agencies could—and should—step in. In November of 1949, a PHS "sanitary engineer" took a brief run from his base in Salt Lake City to three mines on the Navajo reservation, all of them operated by VCA. He visited the King Tutt mines near Oaksprings, Arizona, in the east and, across the broad Red Valley, the operations in the Carrizo Mountains. And of course he made his way to Cane Valley to visit Monument No. 2, where Luke Yazzie and about fifty of his neighbors—a much larger force than at any of the Colorado mines—were drilling and blasting and hauling and hammering, following the rich veins of ore deep into the mesa.

The readings he took at the Tutt and Carrizo mines were troubling, but the results in Cane Valley were shocking. Radiation there was ten times higher than the level suggested as a maximum by Ralph Batie's colleagues from New York.[24] Two months later, in January of 1950, an engineer from the U.S. Bureau of Mines came by to take radon samples at Monument No. 2. His findings were similarly off the charts. The gas was present in varying amounts from 4 to 750 times the standard that had been proposed.[25] The workers were told nothing.

In the spring of 1950, the Public Health Service launched a bigger, two-pronged study: a continuing survey of human health combined with monitoring the conditions in the mines. To gain access, though, the PHS researchers had to accept the companies' terms and that meant staying low-key to the point of deception.

Denny Viles offered them a model. He was well aware of the cancer concerns after the Batie dust-up, but he made no mention of those in his dealings with the Office of Indian Affairs on the subject of the study. He wrote on April 11, 1950, to the Navajo superintendent to confirm a seemingly generous offer. VCA would transport its Navajo mine workers "free of charge" up to the Monticello mill for Public Health Service physicals. "Further, we will allow to those Navajos in our employ one day's pay for the time required," Viles added.[26] No one seemed too worried or hurried. It took three months for the government to pass the good news along to the chairman of the tribal council. "I feel sure you will recognize the value of such a study of the health of the Navajo," wrote the local medical officer. The federal doctors would take blood and urine samples and also, he noted matter-of-factly, chest X-rays. The uranium miners, he added, "will be told if there is anything wrong with them."[27] Yet another half-truth. This one would prove fatal.

The very next day, the PHS checked radon and radiation at Monument No. 2. One reading, taken at the center of a tunnel just after a round of drilling, showed the gas in concentrations more than nine times the standard. A second reading collected about twenty feet from a mine opening at the foot of an incline within the tunnel revealed radon at twenty-three times the standard.[28] Samples at mines all over the Colorado Plateau were coming back in the same dangerous range. For Monument No. 2, in particular, this was the third set of numbers—more, now, than just a snapshot of the mining conditions. The PHS officials agreed among themselves to keep this explosive information quiet, at least until they could figure out what they were going to do about it.

Jesse Johnson was promoted to the top spot at Raw Materials on December 25, 1949, a lovely Christmas gift. After the holidays, Ralph Batie was told that the new director wanted him fired for stirring up trouble. He had certainly lit a fire under the PHS. A chemist there wrote in February that his latest radon results were "appalling" and "beyond all expectations." "It is my opinion that a control program must be instituted as soon as possible in order to prevent injury to the workers," he added.[29] But Batie knew he had to step away if he wanted to save his job. He asked for a transfer to the AEC station in Idaho. Unsurprisingly, this request was promptly granted.

Pugnacious even in surrender, he couldn't help firing one last shot. Just before moving to Idaho Falls, in the spring of 1950, Batie checked on Monument No. 2. A Navajo crew was drilling an open pit without first wetting down the ore to minimize dust. VCA had water trucks available onsite, but the superintendent apparently felt it was too much trouble to drive the five miles to the closest source, the Frog Ponds, as the twin watering holes were known locally. So many tiny bits of rock and radiation choked the air that Batie could barely see the bottom of the pit.[30] Because Cane Valley straddled the Arizona-Utah line, he called inspectors from both states, suggesting that they shut down the job until water was supplied. He left without knowing whether anyone followed up.[31] His position at Grand Junction remained vacant.

With Batie gone and the weather warming, Monument No. 2 received another visit, this one from his nemesis. Jesse Johnson brought along his wife, and Denny Viles escorted the power couple to Cane Valley. Jesse chose a business outfit of pants and a white Oxford shirt, a straw hat and a tie, while his wife Alice donned denims and a casual blouse. She loosely knotted a sweater around her shoulders to protect herself from any cold breezes in case the temperature dropped while they were out. The Navajos they'd come to see wore bright orange hard hats, their skulls well protected from falling rock. But their mouths and noses were wide open to that insidious dust, that invisible gas. After repeated memos from Batie and those he had inspired, Jesse Johnson must have understood the danger they were in, but it is unlikely that he had much to say on the subject. The Johnsons posed for photographs near one of the support columns at a tunnel entrance, a pillar of rock shot through with yellow flashes—*leetso*, object of the government's desire.[32] Afterward, Viles struck a cordial tone, writing to "Dear Jesse" to express more concern for the director's wife than he had for his employees: "I hope Mrs. Johnson suffered no ill effects from the two rough desert trips and I look forward to seeing you on my next trip east."[33]

Such pleasant interludes were rare for Johnson. More than 80 percent of the country's uranium stores were still coming from overseas, and members of a joint House-Senate committee on atomic energy were increasingly frantic that the supply line might fray, robbing America of its capacity to arm more bombs in an emergency. And emergencies, big ones, appeared imminent: A wall of Communist forces poured into South Korea in 1950. The panicky congressional committee was driving everyone at the AEC, from the commissioners on down, to find more domestic uranium and get it into the system as fast as possible.[34] The whole world hung in the balance.

As always, Johnson soothed. "Tell me how much you want, let me pay an attractive price, and give me 18 months or two years," he said.[35] Both the committee staff and his superiors at the AEC greatly appreciated his calming words. Privately, though, Johnson was less sanguine. Soon after his first anniversary as raw materials director, he wrote to an aide, "We are still under terrific pressure and I see no end so we shall have to accept it as a regular part of our job." [36]

One of the fretting PHS scientists, Duncan Holaday, got a taste of the commission's atmosphere when he stepped into an occupied taxi in Grand Junction. He was leaving town after a meeting and realized with a start that he was sharing a cab to the airport with Sumner T. Pike, acting chairman of the AEC. After introductions, Pike made clear that he knew all about the radon studies, and he was worried, but not about safety. The huge, and hugely expensive, bomb-making factories were finally taking shape. Plutonium was going to be manufactured on the Savannah River, in South Carolina—an addition to the original plutonium refinery in Hanford, Washington—and uranium would be enriched in Portsmouth, Ohio, as well as at the Manhattan Project's Oak Ridge, Tennessee, site. "We don't have the uranium in sight to get those plants operating," Pike said. "We have just taken a horseback gamble that by the time they are completed, the uranium will be available. We have got to have the production from those mines."

His cabmate retorted, "This is perfectly possible for you to do, but this can be done without any undue health hazard. It requires control measures to be instituted." Pike did not reply. [37]

In January of 1951, AEC and PHS medical officials met in Washington and agreed that they didn't know enough about radon to settle on a safe concentration. Duncan Holaday, who attended, agonized in a letter to a colleague, ". . . this situation cannot be allowed to continue until we have enough information." [38] Straining for compromise, he suggested a caravan of health officials through the towns where the mining executives were stationed. They could meet with each one separately to discuss control measures. Hitting the circuit would take far more time than simply gathering all of the companies together, but it had the advantage of being less likely to attract attention. Holaday had concluded that he must show far more deference to the mining companies than Batie had in order to get anything done and, his conversation with Pike notwithstanding, he had already displayed a flair for diplomacy. He'd sent a strongly worded letter the previous fall to Denny Viles, but he had topped the page with this heading in all capital letters: CONFIDENTIAL.[39] His AEC counterparts warned that the one-on-one meetings must be just as discreet. After Viles's volcanic reaction to the spread in the *Denver Post*, "the AEC considers it essential that there be no newspaper publicity on this matter," Holaday wrote.[40]

Unaware of the furor in remote health agencies, eleven Navajo leaders gathered at the handsome eight-sided sandstone building in Window Rock that housed their council chambers. The octagon, with its east-facing entrance, resembled an overgrown *hooghan*. The Works Progress Administration had built it for the tribe during the Depression, and murals, a WPA trademark, adorned the circular walls of the great meeting room. This small group of delegates, an advisory committee to the full eighty-eight-member council, had been summoned from across the reservation by their white superintendent. Allan G. Harper was the local face of the Guardian, the Office of Indian Affairs, on behalf of the secretary of the interior, on behalf of the president of the United States. He had scheduled a two-day hearing. The subject was uranium mining and Harper (who as usual did most of the talking) opened with a declaration of discontent. "The situation is not satisfactory," he said, but he wasn't referring to the working conditions that were so disturbing to so many federal safety experts.[41] Harper meant the amount of ore moved out of the ground. He echoed Sumner Pike: It was not nearly enough.

Under the rough-hewn beams supporting the high ceilings, Harper appealed to the tribe's patriotism, reading aloud from a letter sent by Jesse Johnson's deputy, who had journeyed from Washington to sit in the audience. "We would like to stress the urgency of development of the uranium resources of the Navajo Reservation . . ."

" 'Stress the urgency,' " Harper repeated, "which is a clue to the urgency of our meeting today."[42] He wanted to cut red tape. He wanted to gear up. He wanted the Navajos to allow a processing mill—maybe even more than one—on tribal land. He had an interpreter on hand for those who spoke no English and had invited a number of mining men to testify. The first to speak was Denny Viles.

Viles suggested that any white man who came to mine on the *Dinétah* in the future should take a Navajo partner—not just a landlord. The partners, or as Viles called them, "the Navajo boy and the outsider," should divide proceeds equally.[43] This was a very generous proposition, particularly from the man whom Luke Yazzie had accused of stiffing him. A 50-50 split would certainly motivate Navajos to come forward with information on the whereabouts of *łeetso*, a prime goal of any change in the rules. But Denny Viles, of course, had his own interests at heart. He had already locked in treasure on his own terms, with no individual Navajos involved at all. His contracts with the tribe for a 10 percent royalty were good for as long as the ore held out. Adopting his idea would just leave less money for his competitors. Predictably, the other mining executives showed little enthusiasm for Viles's suggestion as they took their turns before Harper and the delegates on the council panel.

Even for the Navajos who understood English, the business and bureaucratic jargon was a bit much. By the afternoon of the first day, a council delegate named Joe Duncan spoke up: "There are quite a few Navajos interested in that uranium and they are here to find out what the outcome of this meeting is going to be. And now we are just sitting here and getting confused."[44]

A little later, Sam Ahkeah, the tribal chairman, cut to the heart of the matter. "There have been quite a few recommendations made what to do and how to operate this, but there is one thing that we have not heard yet and that is for the benefit of the Navajos just how much money has been derived out of that uranium that has already been dug. How much have the Navajos received from that that has already been mined? What are we getting out of this uranium? We are in the dark there."[45]

Incredibly, the man who held the top position in the Navajo government had no idea how much money uranium was bringing to his people. An attorney for the AEC who was in the audience suggested asking Viles. That may have been a sensible response, given how ill-informed the Guardian of the Navajos appeared. Harper jumped in to deflect the question. "We can answer that a couple of ways," he said. "One way would be to give it in dollars." Instead of being so straightforward, he mentioned that the income of Navajos in one particular district of the reservation was derived as much from mining as from livestock.[46]

The Navajos were clearly having trouble prying even basic information from the white men in their chambers. Nonetheless, they kept trying. News had filtered in from Colorado about the *Denver Post* article and the state health director's conference. On the second day of the hearing, the tribe's vice chairman, Zhealy Tso, asked about the reports.

"People have said that this uranium is a very dangerous substance to handle with your hands and it will impair your health. Is that true?"

"I would say definitely the other way," replied the other mine operator to whom the question was addressed. "I have several boys who have been with me fourteen years and they are the healthiest men we have working for us."[47]

"May I interpose here to say that a study of this problem has been in progress by the United States Public Health Service," Harper added, "and that we hope to have a very definite report from doctors who have been examining a great many Navajos working in this field. We hope to have a report from very competent people on the question."

After these replies, which were misleading at best, the two white men quickly changed the subject.

Chapter 7

A Hundred Tons a Day

D enny Viles didn't care much for the cancer warnings delivered by the Public Health Service, but he heard the AEC message loud and clear: produce, produce, produce. He knew exactly where in his empire he needed to focus his efforts to wring more uranium from the ground. In the spring of 1950, the big man drove up to a company mine north of Durango and asked a thirty-year-old up-and-comer named Bob Anderson if he'd like to take a trip. Anderson, an Idaho native from a gold- and silver-mining family, naturally said yes to the boss. He'd been the first foreman in VCA history to keep a crew working up in the mountain deep-snow country all winter long. He assumed that Viles was planning to reward him with a pleasant excursion.

"I'm going to New York Monday and I'll be back Thursday," Viles said. "Be down there early Friday." Eager Anderson was at the Durango mill a day ahead of time, asking all his colleagues, "Where's he going to take me?" No one knew. He phoned Viles that night to ask what he'd need to bring along in the morning. "Oh, just your hat and light," Viles said. "When do we leave?" Anderson asked him. "I'll meet you at the scale house at six o'clock," Viles replied.

The next day, they departed right on time, descending from the high green Rockies until they crossed the reservation border to the brown Indian lands. By noon they had covered 170 miles and arrived at Monument No. 2. Anderson was too preoccupied at first with internal concerns to focus on the strange, spectacular desert landscape; hunger was beginning to scrape at him and the realization was dawning that he faced a six-hour drive back from this godforsaken place before he would eat his next meal. He vowed to himself that, in the future, he would always pack a lunch whenever he traveled with Denny Viles. The boss introduced Anderson to VCA's on-site superintendent, Carl Bell, and the three men donned hard hats with miner's lamps fastened in front. They toured the whole place, walking through two big gulches on the property, one known as the South Rim and the other as the North Rim, and all through the rest of VCA's forty-acre leasehold. Anderson managed to forget his gnawing stomach long enough to focus on the busy Indians and the bright yellow, red, and black rock they were retrieving from the tunnels. It was the most colorful work site he had ever seen.

At the end of the hike, Viles asked, "What do you think of it, Bob?"

"It's a beautiful mine," the young man replied.

Viles didn't care about that. "Do you think you can make a hundred tons a day out of there?"

"I don't have any idea, but if it produces ore like it is today, I don't see any reason why we couldn't make a hundred ton a day out of it."

Viles turned to Bell, the superintendent. "Well, Bob will be in contact with you," he announced. "He's in charge here now. He'll be coming down right away." [1]

Anderson would never be certain whether his battlefield promotion was a spur-of-the-moment decision or a premeditated act. In any case, he was soon ensconced at an office in Durango with authority over a number of VCA mines, including all of those on the reservation. Shortly afterward, Denny Viles's new regional director took the bumpy dirt road back to Monument No. 2. Carl Bell was taking a vacation, and Anderson would run the place while he was gone.

This was a whole new world, and Anderson felt lost there. Most of the Navajos looked alike to him. He could pick out only two very old men from the crowd. The mesa itself was also impossible to read. Viles was not one for exploratory drilling; he didn't care to spend the money. So Anderson had no solid information about likely hot spots and wasn't quite sure what to do with his crowd of identical laborers. He started two or three of them digging in one arbitrary place, then another two or three in another, and so on, until he had spread them all across the VCA claim. When he brought the time book around and asked, "What's your name?" most of the men appeared not to understand. One of them handed him a grocery bill.

He figured that under these circumstances, someone was bound to sneak off and still try to collect a day's pay, and by sheer luck it turned out to be one of those distinctive old men. By 9:00 a.m., Anderson noticed that he was missing, and when he asked around, nobody seemed to know where the truant was. On Day Two, Anderson spotted the man arriving and asked, "What did you do yesterday?" With gestures the old Navajo made his excuses; it seemed that he'd had a headache. Anderson berated him: "I'm going to dock you for the full day and if you ever do that again, I'm going to fire you. If you get sick or anything else, you have to tell somebody that you're going to go, because we thought maybe you might be hurt."

Anderson started to walk away, but the Navajo miner came up close and shook a finger at him. "Dona Shawna," he said; at least that's the way Anderson heard it. The new boss asked a different worker what the man was saying. The other miner obligingly translated: "He's calling you a mean, bad man."

This was far from the last challenge to his authority. On an exceedingly hot day soon afterward, he repeatedly caught one miner resting and trying to cool himself in the shadow cast by a boulder. Fed up by mid-afternoon, Anderson ordered the laggard to join some of his colleagues in dumping waste ore from a mining rail car over the side of a cliff. Later, Anderson saw one of the mining cars start rolling down the canyon. His lazy friend came running; so he could in fact move fast! He managed to explain, without the benefit of English, that he hadn't done it on purpose; it had not been revenge.

The Navajos continued testing their new overseer. Anderson assigned a driller to make a pattern of six-foot holes in a wall of rock so that enough dynamite could be packed inside to blast the ore to bits. He thought the job would take a day and a half. But that evening, there was already a hole everyplace he'd wanted a hole. The interim superintendent was no pushover; he picked up a six-foot steel rod and jabbed it inside to gauge the length. The resulting shock almost tore his arm off. The openings were all too short, each just about two feet long.

"You're laid off," Anderson spat at the Navajo. Soon, the miner had five co-workers who spoke varying degrees of English descending on the "mean, bad man." They explained that the poor guy owed the trader and that he had a large family. But Anderson remained unmoved, noting that for all the torrent of words, they never once said that he promised to go back to work and finish the job right. When Carl Bell, the local foreman, returned from his travels, Anderson told him what had happened. "If you want to rehire him, why go ahead, I don't care. I just couldn't let him get away with it." Bell grinned. "Aw, he's getting pretty fat. We'll let him stay off for a month or two and thin down a little bit." [2]

Anderson made one more change during Bell's absence and this one would prove much more momentous, although it didn't seem so at the time. In one tunnel, a tramway for the mining cars that hauled the ore out to the surface ran right past an area that was dotted with uranium, but had never been worked. He decided to set off a few rounds of TNT to see what was behind the wall of rock. By the time his stint was nearly up, he had thirty people working on a streak of ore just an inch wide. Before he headed back to Durango, he and Bell shared a laugh about that, too.

But the crew kept at it, and on his next trip, Anderson saw that the little stripe was growing wider. On the trip after that, the men were blasting from a seam a full thirty-five feet across and it ran clear through the property, six hundred feet from the South Rim close to the North.

They had stumbled on the hidden heart of Yazzie Mesa. Entombed for all these decades under the herbs and berries used by Adakai in his powders and potions, under the brush nibbled by the sheep, under the water collected by Luke and his cousin, a gigantic mass had been constantly transforming like the evil shape-shifters of Navajo lore. The miners had been working mere capillaries; these were major arteries. Now VCA was intent on freeing the long, thick channels of *leetso* with the help of the men of Cane Valley. This lode of uranium could save the country. And it could make a fortune.

The Navajos dug four more tunnels into the ore body and Monument No. 2 shifted into overdrive. The miners found astounding riches. Anderson noticed part of a petrified tree jutting out by the tramway. The fossil was black. "Why don't you get in there and dig that out?" he asked one of his men. Once excavated, the tree turned out to be one hundred feet long and five feet wide. The wood once present had been replaced over eons by a few hundred tons of rock that ran 12 percent uranium and 12 percent vanadium.[3] Anderson instructed the workers to put a bucketful on each truckload leaving Monument No. 2, blending the high-grade ore in with lower-grade ore to bring the average up. He could make subpar shipments meet AEC standards that way and send even more product out. Most of the ore was still coming from underground shafts, but in one area the crews started strip-mining, too, simply blowing the top off oncesanctified ground.

It was the spring of 1950. These discoveries probably led to the safety shortcuts and the resulting dense clouds of dust that Ralph Batie witnessed in the new pit about that time, and probably also explained why Jesse Johnson undertook the difficult journey to the site a few months later. But all in all, the Atomic Energy Commission was not very welcome at Monument No. 2. The usually irrepressible Viles wanted to keep all outsiders at bay. He even demurred when the insatiable AEC offered to provide free drilling—free!—to help define the contours of the mother lode. Anderson finally wrangled permission from Viles for fourteen federal core holes on the north end of the property. Thirteen came up blank. Only one contained minerals in the soil, and not much at that. Viles must have been relieved, but Anderson couldn't resist showing off to one of the government geologists. He escorted the scientist to the one mineralized hole and proceeded to point out a few things and hazard a prediction or two.

About a year later, Anderson's geologist friend brought more than a dozen colleagues with him to make an inspection. A lone Navajo, with one wheelbarrow and one shovel, had spent three or four days working the slope where the holes had been drilled. He had stacked up six feet of ore, with three big specimens on display next to the pile. One chunk was red, one yellow, and one black. Each was solid uranium. If any of the government drillers had worked just a foot or so over, they'd have found hot high grade all around.[4]

The stuff was running from 5 percent to 15 percent uranium and the company didn't want to risk losing even a pound or two of ore that rich. VCA put brooms in Navajo hands, and ordered the workers to sweep up the bright yellow dust on the ground; it was that valuable.[5] More valuable than the labor force, apparently. You could get thousands of Indians cheap, after all.[6] The supervisors paid no attention to whether or not the Navajos wet down the drilling sites to keep their respiratory systems clear, but they made certain that the ore in the trucks was watered to help keep every tiny pebble in place during the ride to the processing plant. For that, they fenced off the Frog Ponds in the valley, two hand-dug lakelets fueled by the springs that had brought Adakai there. The VCA men told the kids they couldn't swim there because the mine needed more water. Adakai's Daughter raised objections; the Frog Ponds watered Cane Valley's crops and stock. VCA had built an airstrip at the mine by then and Adakai's Daughter was flown to Window Rock in a tiny plane to negotiate. But the company and the tribe had already come to terms and she had no leverage.[7] Monument No. 2 was also one of the few uranium operations where the crews bothered to place tarpaulins over the loads. VCA wanted to block the escape of errant rocks as the rigs jiggled over the rough reservation roads—not for safety's sake, but because the chunks were worth so much.

Those who were in on the doings at Monument No. 2 were convinced that it was richer even than Charlie Steen's Mi Vida mine, a colossal find in 1952 that brought a flood of national publicity to the off-reservation uranium boom. Steen was a white man, a Texan, with an irresistible story: a penniless petroleum geologist, barely able to feed his family, he had persisted in looking for uranium in an area near Moab, Utah, that had been written off by the government explorers. On the day that his borrowed drill bit broke, he finally decided to give up. The samples he had managed to collect before the breakdown appeared as unpromising as all those he had found before. But on a whim, he placed the rocks next to a Geiger counter. They registered stupendously high radioactivity. And so Charlie Steen became the "Uranium King" in newspapers all over the country. He bought a plane and held huge parties at the local airport, with steaks and booze for all. He bestowed Lincoln Continentals on all four of his kids, even the ones who didn't have a driver's license.[8] His good fortune inspired an episode of the *Lucy-Desi Comedy Hour* that features Lucy and Ricky Ricardo prospecting for uranium near Las Vegas with Fred MacMurray.[9]

Monument No. 2 kept a much lower public profile. But in the self-contained world of *Diné bikeyah,* everybody knew that something really huge was going on at the mesa east of Monument Valley. Suddenly, one hundred Navajos were working two shifts a day, six days a week. Luke was among them, of course, and so were his cousins and nephews and friends. The Cane Valley Navajos made it clear that they wouldn't stand for strangers in their midst; they hazed new hires from distant parts of the reservation until they quit, some in tears.[10] Still, the job was so big that VCA had to bring in reinforcements from neighboring Dennehotso and Mexican Water on the other side of Comb Ridge—the locals grudgingly agreed that these Navajos were "close enough" (Adakai's wives had grown up in a small valley between the two hamlets). The Backbone made the commute so arduous—they traveled by foot or on horseback—that these employees brought their families along; a makeshift city of white canvas tents and lean-tos sprouted on the slopes. They christened the community with the company's name: "I live over at VCA," they'd tell Navajos in other sections of the reservation, and everyone knew exactly where they meant, even though Denny Viles also controlled mines that were churning out ore over at King Tutt Mesa and in the Lukachukai Mountains. This was the big one, the big, big one. Too busy to farm or hunt, too far from their traditional grazing lands to tend and butcher their flocks, the newcomers took to buying canned food. Because the company had constructed dirt roads for hauling Monument No. 2 ore to the north, the mine workers used their earnings to buy trucks of their own. No more Long Walks. They could motor in style the fifteen miles to the trading posts at Goulding's or in Mexican Hat. But there still were no decent roads to their old homes.

A downtown of sorts sprang up right by the mine. Adakai's enterprising son-in-law, Oscar Sloan, started a small café. Oscar's wife—Luke's sister—cooked mutton stew and frybread for a sweaty, hungry crowd that combined lunch with fevered gambling on various card games until the break was over.[11] The state also opened a school in a corrugated-metal shed on a flank of the mesa. It was a long walk from Cane Valley uphill through sand and rubble, but the thirty or forty children who attended were fascinated by the place. The teacher was white. She distributed paper and crayons to her small students; they were not familiar with these objects. One of Adakai's great-granddaughters—Juanita Jackson's oldest daughter, Eunice—noticed an orange on the teacher's desk, so she drew a circle and colored it with the crayon that matched the white lady's round ball. She had never seen such a thing in her life.[12]

Even when they weren't in class, Adakai's youngest grandchildren and his burgeoning brood of great-grandchildren swarmed through the mining site. They loved to watch the grownups run out of the tunnels; they loved to hear the dynamite explode. On Saturdays, the one day of the week when everything was quiet, the children of Cane Valley would find their way to the powder. They knew how to spark it and make a light, the way the miners did. They'd grab some and take to the dark tunnels for the day. The water dripping down the walls was very cold and nice to drink; the yellow dirt was soft enough to mold into little animals or pretend cigarettes. Sometimes the mining supervisors or watchmen would try to chase them back out through the narrow corridors, but the kids knew where to run and hide away.[13] The drills and jackhammers had opened the mesa for play in a way that the young Luke Yazzie could never have imagined.

Luke, by this time, was well known to Bob Anderson, who was coming to respect the Navajos in his employ. They weren't lazy, he realized. Quite the opposite. They simply paced themselves differently than Anglos, Anderson thought. A typical Anglo miner worked fast through the morning and was tuckered out by late afternoon, reduced to cruising around the site and chatting with his friends. A Navajo was slower but steady, just as good at 4:30 p.m. as he was at 8:00 a.m. You probably get the same amount of work out of both, Anderson concluded.[14] He believed that the Navajos were perfectly suited to the hand sorting practiced at Monument No. 2. They were patient and had very sharp eyes.[15]

Anderson's early frustrations had subsided, but they didn't entirely go away. The mesa took on the trappings of a rowdy frontier outpost, largely due to the presence of the bootleggers who routinely showed up on pay-days. Anderson was aware of this, but did little to clamp down despite the whiskey-fueled trouble that generally followed. One time, the on-scene superintendent ordered a worker under the influence to go home and sober up. Instead, the angry Navajo placed a charge right on top of the motor of a three-quarter-yard power shovel. He did a very nice job of blowing up the machine. VCA's insurance paid nearly $15,000 and the offender ended up in jail.[16] Another time, a different drunkard broke into the superintendent's house and found the boss's gun. He carried it toward a truck parked nearby, where the weapon's rightful owner was monitoring a group of workers loading ore. The man with the gun fired unsteadily, but he managed to hit a Navajo in the front seat. The victim died.[17]

The other big problem for the white mine managers was the marked tendency of Navajos to disappear. Some saw no need to keep working once they had enough money to get out of debt and qualify for credit at the trading post. Others left whenever they were called to a ceremony. The summons could come without warning and the events could take anywhere from three days to more than a week.[18] A ceremony was simply more important than any job.

Luke Yazzie was typical. He got fired about once a year for absentee-ism or drunkenness.[19] But VCA always hired him back. This was not an exceptional favor, though Goulding had asked Viles to keep Luke em-ployed for life. The company did as much for anyone who only slipped up occasionally.

Luke kept pushing for special status, for acknowledgment that he was, as he liked to say, "the founder."[20] He felt strongly that he was helping the United States defend itself and he was helping the tribe win royalties and he deserved the reward that he believed he had been promised. When-ever Bob Anderson or Denny Viles paid a visit, Luke would approach to seek improvements for his home in Cane Valley and a good water well for his family. Though he asked "in a kind way," as he described it to others, the executives replied with vague assurances that somehow never panned out. Sometimes they told him to ask Harry Goulding, but Goulding had taken to avoiding him.[21] Harry frequently came to the mine, but on these occasions he always managed to elude Luke and his nagging. And whenever Luke walked in the front door of the trading post these days, Harry seemed to have some pressing need in the back room and he would not emerge until Luke had gone away.[22] Luke took his business more and more often to the trading post at Mexican Hat, which passed through several different owners. Mexican Hat was just about the same distance, and anyway, Harry didn't sell liquor. At Mexican Hat, he could get a can of beer.

Luke suspected that Harry and VCA had struck some kind of deal and had left him out. Though Harry would publicly deny all his life that he had ever asked Viles for any payment for Monument No. 2, and this appears to be technically accurate, Luke's instincts were right on the mark.

Soon after VCA signed its Monument contract with the tribe, Goulding received a check in the mail. It was from the company, made out in the amount of $480, and right there on the check it said that Harry was a prospector. To hear Goulding tell it, the money was totally unexpected. He told Viles, "I can't get out and go to prospectin' for you, I got this tradin' post." Viles replied, "We don't want you to. You do as you please, or else you and I are going to have trouble!" The big man told the skinny trader, "You don't have to do anything. I just wanted you to get a little check out of it, and the company did. So that's all there is to it. You're not obligated in any way."[23]

In the 1940s, that amount "wasn't little bitty!" as Goulding would finally confide years later.[24] He was well aware, though, that VCA was reaping many millions and the payment was a token. He cashed the check. Another one appeared, and then another. They kept on coming like clockwork for years.[25] Every winter, Goulding and his wife would leave the trading post in the hands of an employee or relative and travel to Phoenix for a vacation. Viles would meet them there and host the Gouldings in a high-rise that Harry described as "a swanky son-of-a-gun."[26] The rough-hewn Gouldings were ill at ease in these surroundings, but Viles insisted. Eventually—it's not clear how long this took—Goulding told him, "I think you've worn that pencil down to where you're gonna have to pinch it." He grew uncomfortable with his "prospector" status, too. John Ford's cavalry films brought in both movie crews and tourists. In 1953, Harry tore down the two rock cabins where he had housed guests and built a motel. Three years later, he expanded the place, doubling the number of rooms. The uranium miners were flush with cash that they spent right away. The trading post was prospering. "I don't think that you need to carry those checks on forever," he finally said to Denny Viles.[27] There is no evidence that he ever asked Viles to pay even a penny to Luke.

VCA also tried to reward Goulding by helping him get a uranium contract of his own on Yazzie Mesa. The company had found five acres containing ore just outside the Monument No. 2 leasehold. The council had changed the rules and a Navajo had to stake the claim. So VCA took care of the engineering and surveyed the area and Anderson, in his words, "got an Indian," and the Navajo, whose name was Walter Scott, partnered with Goulding.[28] Scott got the nod because he worked for the company and spoke good English.

In true VCA fashion, this maneuver was not just a favor but also made good business sense. Viles and Anderson recognized that the tribal council wasn't likely to grant an additional lease on the mesa to VCA. Monument No. 2 brought $200,000 a year to tribal coffers, a full third of the uranium royalties paid by operators of Navajo mines.[29] Even so, the delegates were starting to realize that the Navajo government had been shafted. Viles's initial bonus payment of $3,000 had been small change, as it turned out; the tribe could have raked in millions had the council known how vast the deposit was. The royalty, the standard fixed rate of 10 percent, was an even better bargain. Even Anderson admitted that the tribe had been lowballed; if the Navajos could renegotiate the terms, they could easily command 40 percent of the take.[30] But of course, VCA was locked in. The contract stayed in effect even after its ten-year term expired for as long as the company kept producing ore—and Monument No. 2 wasn't running out of ore any time soon.

So the council felt that the company already had quite enough, and there was no way VCA was going to get hold of that five additional acres. But Scott was VCA's Indian and Goulding was VCA's white man. Scott would help Goulding lease the acres in exchange for royalty payments; Goulding would take the bulk of the profits from the mine; and they would guarantee that ore from the five-acre plot would be milled at VCA's plant in Durango. If VCA had let Luke Yazzie in on the arrangement, it might have helped to make up for the terms of the original lease. But once more, Luke was kept out of the loop.

That was just as well, because, crafty as VCA might be, the company didn't always get its way and this was one of those times. Even though its hand was invisible during the lease applications, the tribal delegates weren't sure they wanted Goulding, either. A Navajo entrepreneur named Cato Sells surfaced with a competing bid for the land and won. He later staked another claim on the other side of Monument No. 2, making a VCA sandwich, and became one of the few Navajos to gain substantial wealth from the reservation's uranium rush.

VCA would perform other kindnesses for Goulding, the most notable being a road that the company bulldozed from the mine to the trading post. The company was always happy to provide Harry with the use of any equipment that it had on hand. "It was such a wonderful association!" Goulding would reminisce later.[31]

Viles and Anderson were pleased, too. By 1953, Anderson's daily quota for Monument No. 2 had tripled, from one hundred tons of ore to three hundred. He always met the goal.

That June, Jesse Johnson wrote "Dear Denny" a note about VCA's production: "We are deeply grateful to you."[32]

Bob Anderson, constantly urging more uranium faster from his troops on the ground, didn't trouble himself about the radon gas that he'd been told was seeping through the stone halls underneath. He knew the situation was dangerous. Duncan Holaday of the PHS had made this clear to Viles. He knew that something could be done about it too. Holaday had explained to Viles that VCA could install fans to blow fresh air into the tunnels to dilute the gas inside, that they could close off old workings to quarantine the radon drifting off the exposed ore, that they should seal pillars containing high-grade ore.[33] Holaday raised the radon issue with other VCA executives as well.[34] Anderson's superiors all brushed off the earnest young chemist's warnings and so Anderson did, too. He knew that Monument No. 2 had one of the poorest ventilation records but the mine had "pretty much a slave labor type of thing over there," Anderson thought, and why bother messing with a good thing?[35] Though Duncan Holaday had pointedly noted that cancer was certain to hit the miners, he'd also said that it could take ten years or more for the disease to show up. That wasn't a very compelling argument to Denny Viles, who didn't even want to waste time and money on exploratory drilling. Viles was in this to get as much as he could while he could. He was not one to worry about the long run.

In May of 1952, the PHS and the Colorado Health Department tried to send up a flare. Holaday, along with two other health experts, published what they called "An Interim Report of a Health Study of the Uranium Mines and Mills." They noted the epic levels of radon in the Colorado Plateau uranium operations, higher than in the killer mines of Bohemia. They summed up the medical findings of the physical exams. No clear-cut patterns had emerged, they acknowledged, but they explained that this was no surprise, because the latency period for cancer had not yet elapsed.[36] And then they made their recommendations: Improving ventilation to keep the radon at less than 100 microcuries per liter; wetting down the rocks while drilling, in order to keep down the dust; giving respirators to the workers; mandating daily showers, frequent changes of clothing, and preemployment physicals. These were nearly identical to the proposals of Ralph Batie's colleagues from New York four years before. And they met the same fate. They were ignored.

Jesse Johnson wrote a seven-page memo about the report to the commissioners of the AEC. "There is no doubt but that we are faced with a problem which, if not handled properly, could adversely affect our uranium supply," he warned them. The problems could be corrected in the United States, he said, but "communist propagandists may utilize any sensational statements . . . to hamper or restrict uranium production in foreign fields, particularly at Shinkolobwe."[37] His assertion was laughable; the Belgians in fact were already far more conscientious on this score than the Americans. They built a lab in the middle of the Congo to measure radon. They ventilated their mines and they removed broken ore as fast as possible, to minimize buildup of the deadly gas.[38]

Even worse, in Washington, the Public Health Service issued a soothing press release. The surgeon general was quoted as saying, "Many of these measures have already been instituted by the industry." That statement was completely false.[39]

Holaday was unaware of the bulletin. Upon seeing it for the first time more than thirty years later, he would react angrily: "It makes me blush for the PHS." He denounced his own agency's official announcement of his report as "a collection of half-truths, weasel words and evading responsibilities."[40]

The "Interim Report" was distributed to all of the mining companies, although not to the miners, of course. Holaday determined that installing a ventilation system would cost between 50 cents and a dollar per ton of ore. The government was paying $20–$30 a ton and production costs averaged anywhere between $11 and $19 a ton—about $15 a ton in the Monument Valley area.[41] But if blowing air into the mine ate away too much at profits, Holaday suggested to the AEC's Grand Junction manager, the government could pay a ventilation allowance to companies following the recommendations in the report. Such a bonus would drive up the cost of the finished yellowcake by a mere 50 cents a pound, he calculated. The idea didn't fly.[42]

By this time, the Public Health Service was out of the air sampling business, but the U.S. Bureau of Mines was testing for radon during inspections. More than a year after the report came out, in July of 1953, a Bureau of Mines engineer visited Monument No. 2. He took ten air samples. All of them were orders of magnitude above the radon standard recommended in the Interim Report. One was 90 times higher. One was 120 times higher.

VCA was into higher-grade ore, and more of it. The samples were more toxic than ever.[43]

Even without a glimpse of the spin practiced at PHS headquarters, Holaday knew that his big report had landed with no discernible thud. He and his colleagues recognized that part of the problem was that their work was far from definitive. There was so much turnover in the mines that the doctors had examined different men in 1953 than in 1952, in 1952 than in 1951, in 1951 than in 1950. The total number of exams had been relatively small, no more than a few hundred each year. And the group as a whole had only very brief mining experience. Scary results would clearly be needed to shock the AEC and the industry into taking any meaningful action. The public health experts decided that they needed to think big, to find as large a pool of uranium miners as possible to follow for a long period, perhaps fifteen years or more. They needed a good baseline picture of the miners' health. They needed to know how to contact the same men again and again, even after the miners left their jobs.[44]

They could not continue depending on the mining companies to bring workers from the field to the mills. To be sure they didn't miss anyone, they needed to venture out to the mines—out to the tunnels and pits, the tiny one- or two-person "dog holes" and the most massive big-time operations, no matter how remote. But they didn't have the vehicles. They didn't have enough staff. They didn't even know where all the mines were.

So they were forced to seek help. They needed the AEC. Surprisingly, the AEC did not reject them out of hand. Jesse Johnson, the raw materials director who had practically clapped his hands over his ears whenever the subject of lung cancer came up, was still in his post in Washington. But the commission had very practical reasons to keep tabs on the miners. They were excellent guinea pigs.

The military wanted to know about the effects of moderate doses of radiation. "Advantage should be taken of any opportunities for the study of the biological effects of radiation, particularly in man," a Pentagon research committee had recently concluded.[45]

One of the AEC's medical consultants was particularly enthusiastic. William F. Bale was trying to figure out the risk run by the elite researchers in the national labs, who were being covered by special hazard insurance that the government had purchased. Bale, a radiation expert at the University of Rochester, was no stranger to studies with human subjects. He had already been deeply involved in experiments on terminally ill hospital patients who were injected with uranium and plutonium and other radioactive substances. These patients had not been fully informed of what was going into their bodies or of the possible consequences.[46]

Other AEC doctors had been more squeamish. Subjecting people to internal doses of radiation "would have a little of the Buchenwald touch," one wrote.[47] The physician was interested in the response of healthy males in the twenty- to forty-year-old age group, but noted that the AEC would face substantial criticism if it conducted such research, even on volunteers.

But here came the Public Health Service with a perfect group of subjects. In this case, the experiment would consist of simply allowing natural events in the mines, and in the miners' lungs, to unfold without explaining the hazards involved. In a note to his files, Bale paid what he considered to be a high compliment to Holaday and his supremely tactful PHS colleagues: "They seem to have conducted their work so far without unduly alarming miners as to hidden hazards that may exist, or in any way impeding mining operations."[48]

For the sake of soldiers and scientists, then, the AEC was in.[49]

It was settled. The summer of 1954 would provide a grand adventure for two research teams assembled by the PHS. Like the mappers of Union Mines before them, they would venture out from Grand Junction. Each group of six physicians and technicians would travel in a convoy consisting of three trailers to live in, another to serve as a doctor's office and lab, a mobile X-ray truck, a 250-gallon water trailer, a generator, and a Jeep station wagon. The vehicles came from the AEC.[50]

Despite the newfound air of cooperation, there was plenty of mutual mistrust to go around. The AEC offered, for example, to store all of the miners' fourteen-inch by seventeen-inch chest X-ray films at its Grand Junction office. The public health team was loath to give the commission so much control over the evidence, "especially if our own technicians could not get in to use the photo equipment."[51] Instead, the PHS decided to expose two films for each man, reading the first one "wet" in the field for a preliminary diagnosis, then discarding it, and taking the second to Washington for safekeeping.

For the AEC's part, the sore point, as always, was publicity. A commission public-relations man in Grand Junction insisted that his agency remain invisible to the press. All announcements about the upcoming X-ray tour were to come from the PHS, and the AEC's role was not to be mentioned under any circumstances.[52] The AEC didn't want the companies to know that it was back in the health investigations business, however peripherally. This caution seemed excessive to the point of silliness; the miners would surely see the "Atomic Energy Commission" label stenciled onto the doors of the convoy's Jeeps.

The medical teams set off in June and were immediately overwhelmed by the primitive conditions. They improvised, sterilizing needles with a pressure cooker and, when they ran out of rubbing alcohol, with liquor—they bought so much at one local shop that they were embarrassed. The roads, with boulders and shrubs sticking up here and there, were brutal. The engine block on an X-ray truck cracked, the tailpipe and muffler were knocked off a Jeep, vehicles got stuck in sand and had to be pulled out, tires blew constantly. Tempers flared in the cramped quarters. Two of the medical men started throwing punches at each other. People forgot to deliver notes and credit cards when they got back to civilization, and these omissions caused no end of trouble for the next group entering the field.[53]

The public health men showed a particular interest in Monument No. 2, which had the largest number of workers at any one mine. "Viles is the man," one of them noted. "Hold for Duncan." Only Holaday, with his track record of keeping things close to the vest, could smooth the way with VCA for the medical convoy to come through.

A contact man drove a Jeep to Yazzie Mesa ahead of Team Two and arranged a schedule for 102 miners. As usual, the journey was arduous. An engine valve broke in the high desert, causing a three-day delay.

After the doctors arrived, each miner stepped into the X-ray trailer at the appointed time. It was the first stop on a medical assembly line. First, his case number was assigned and pictures were taken of the inside of his chest. Then on to the examining trailer, which tilted whenever someone entered or left, never failing to irritate the technicians engaged in lab work. Urinate in a cup, get jabbed for a vial full of blood, submit to a long list of questions: Work history. Medical history. A person who will always know where to reach you. The idea was to be able to follow these men over cancer's long latency period. But a cultural chasm yawned. Many of the Navajos could not spell their names and did not know their Social Security numbers. They tended to list their birthdates as the first or fifteenth of the month or as "Christmas." They would not reveal—and often claimed not to know—their wives' names. They also generally denied all symptoms and past illnesses. The Navajos, of course, spoke little or no English, and it was impossible to tell how skilled the interpreter was.[54]

The medical team headed off on a 130-mile trip to the next stop, a BIA school in Cove near the Lukachukai mines. Along the way, the bouncy ride over dirt and gravel roads broke loose the bolts holding the motor in place on one of the trailers. The motor crashed into the radiator, causing enough damage to necessitate yet another detour to yet another distant garage.[55]

At summer's end, the two teams had examined 1,319 uranium miners, only 181 of whom had been seen in previous years. Only 246 of the 1,319 were from Indian country. And none of them had been warned by their doctors of the suffering and death that might lie ahead.

Duncan Holaday felt like a vulture.[56] He was not the only one. "How far can I go in making public our real concern for U mining hazards?" a colleague jotted in a note to himself.[57]

The answer: not very far at all. Holaday had granted an interview to the medical editor of the *Salt Lake Tribune* in July. He had not sought the limelight—the reporter had been tipped off about the study by someone at the Los Alamos Lab—and staying true to character, he'd been vague about the reasons for the tour, never once uttering the word "cancer." Even so—perhaps because of his growing frustration—Holaday had allowed himself to speak of "hazard" and "shortened life span."

The AEC's director at Grand Junction was mortified when he read the story. He feared that Holaday's choice of language would disturb the industry.[58] And the industry was not to be disturbed.

Chapter 8

Endings

Adakai had lived to be an old man in a loud, chaotic world that bore little resemblance to the harmony he worked so hard to instill in Cane Valley. He tried to set an example. Bitterness was not the Navajo Way, and he bore no grudge against Luke. After the initial bout of yelling, the patriarch and his son returned to herding sheep, gathering up the cows, and playing cards together.[1] Luke was nearly as skillful as the Gambler; his winnings were enough to buy a truck.[2]

Yet Adakai could not avoid the knowledge that six days a week, under the direction of the white man, Luke was just one of many from his family biting the mesa with steel teeth. A whole new generation was failing to heed his teachings. No longer did his grandchildren obey, even when they disagreed with his directives, the way little Juanita—Juanita Jackson now—had reluctantly gone along when she was forbidden to leave for school. Juanita's husband, Frank, had become a uranium miner. Luke's sons worked at the mine, and so did the sons of Adakai's daughters. Despite their grandfather's teachings, they rammed their way where they had no right to be and they set off fire and smoke inside. They broke the stillness with the clangs and rumbles of large machines and they fouled the pure air with a sharp acidic tang.

Somewhere along the way, either too busy or too tired, they stopped marking the seasons with offerings and sings.

Adakai did not give in easily. One day, whispers traveled through Cane Valley that Paul Jones, the new tribal chairman succeeding Sam Ahkeah, had just arrived on the scene, having driven north from Window Rock to see *Hostiin Adíka'i*. All of the neighbors ran to the patriarch's *hooghan* to watch their highest elected leader alight from his car. Adakai, they assumed, was asking the council chairman to stop this abomination, the invasion that had transformed his home. Jones heard him out, but though he too had grown up in a sheep camp, he had gone on to graduate from high school. He was a speaker of English, a modern man, and he was determined to lift the tribe economically.[3]

Their encounter evoked the sweep of change across Navajo country. Both of these elderly men were held in high esteem. Both were deeply concerned about their people. But otherwise, they could not have been more different, as was immediately apparent from the way they dressed. Jones wore suits and spectacles, and his coiffed hair was snowy white. Adakai was probably twenty years older, but every strand that he tied back in the traditional bun remained as black as the obsidian used to make arrowheads.[4]

The battle was over. Jones wanted the royalties and the jobs and would not yield to Adakai. The conversation changed nothing.

Soon afterward, Adakai fell into decline. From his sickbed, he could hear the jackhammers tearing at the mine and the site's incessant blasts.[5]

In those days, the family always kept a wagon and two horses at the ready in case someone needed urgent help from the white man's doctors. Adakai's mysterious ailment was deemed important enough to hitch up the team. The odds were not good for the Gambler. The patient didn't always reach his or her destination; the wagon had carried Juanita, for instance, in distress during her first labor, only as far as the top of Comb Ridge before breaking down. Desperate, she had to squat outdoors to give birth to a daughter, Eunice, on the Backbone of the World.[6] Adakai fared better on his ride. The wagon made it up the steep climb and all the way down again, and through the difficult journey overland to the nearest "Indian hospital." But the white physicians could not save him. Just six miles from Window Rock, closer to Paul Jones than to his home, he perished. Some of his relations thought that he died of heartbreak. His youngest wife, Anna Sling, and their daughter Lillie—the wife of Oscar Sloan—traveled south to make arrangements for a burial there. *Hostiin*

Adíka'í's remains did not return to his beloved and despoiled valley.[7] With his voice stilled, it seemed as if the mining of uranium from Cane Valley would continue forever.

All afternoon on workdays, the Navajos at Monument No. 2 prepared the sinuous channels of uranium for the big explosions that signaled the end of the shift. VCA's supervisors liked to let the blasts rip just as it was time to go because the worst of the grit and dust would have settled by morning, and the men could start right in collecting the chunks that had been hurled from the mesa walls.

So at quitting time, Yazzie Mesa's factory whistle was a series of loud ka-booms. As the men working in Cane Valley descended to their homes, a giant ball of golden dust—loosed from the detonations—chased them down the hill. Sometimes the cloud moved faster than they did, overtaking them and dividing them from the world. To the families watching as they approached inside the gloom, they seemed a dim caravan of yellow ghosts.

In the evenings, the uranium fog settled on the *hooghan*s in the valley.

The federal mining inspectors noticed. They complained about the proximity of the houses to the blasting, just as they had complained about the interior radon levels. Both complaints had the same effect: none. The regional chief of the Bureau of Mines went so far as to send a letter to Denny Viles about his attitude.[8] But no one imposed a fine. No one shut down a mine. Like the Public Health Service, the Bureau of Mines had no enforcement authority; the agency could only observe and comment. The Atomic Energy Commission had made a conscious decision to back away, and the state mining inspectors had little access to the tribe's dominion.

The tribe itself knew little or nothing about radiation, and had little or no inclination to learn. The mining simply meant too much to the Navajos' bottom line—they received $600,000 to $650,000 a year in uranium royalties, providing about a quarter of their annual budget of $2.5 million.[9]

Uranium was hardly making them rich. They actually were receiving more money from oil leases. Their expenses were high. Sovereignty meant taking on responsibility, and in 1955, the royalties covered the cost of just two *Diné* programs: $500,000 for law and order (eighty-one tribal police officers and seven tribal courts stretched way too thin) and $100,000 for a scholarship fund (Paul Jones assigned more value to a white-style education than Adakai did).[10]

It is possible that the Navajos should have been receiving more, even under the less-than-lucrative terms of the leases that the Indian Office had approved on the tribe's behalf. At VCA's Cottonwood mine, north of the reservation, workers were murmuring about an odd development. Company personnel sometimes slipped them $50 or $100 when they were hauling ore to the Durango mill. Their instructions were to give the money to the assayer, who was expected, by prearrangement, to double the amount of ore recorded from that load. The drivers suspected that the company was cooking the books. The mill, of course, had to report its totals to the government, but if ore came from Cottonwood rather than Monument No. 2, there would be no Navajo royalty due.[11]

Tribal officials must have gotten wind of the rumors. The Navajos established a mining department. They decided to station two men at the VCA mill to monitor the sampling.[12]

The village of "VCA" began to take on an air of permanence. Viles offered to build a wooden house for any family moving to Yazzie Mesa with a miner. Most preferred, though, to replace their original tents and shacks with round mud *hooghan*s that they built themselves, like the ones in the valley, and Viles respected their customs. Still, signs of change crept up the hillsides. Down below, Luke's wife June washed his uranium-crusted work clothes by boiling water on the fire, adding powdered soap and scrubbing the steaming laundry with a washboard. But up on the heights, perhaps inspired by the heavy equipment all around them, a few of the new residents used their earnings to install gleaming new washing machines in their summer shade enclosures. They had no electricity, of course, so they powered their purchases with gasoline engines.[13]

Viles also lived at a worksite. In his case, this was a promontory known as Vancoram Hill, on the south side of Durango, by the mill. He had moved in 1948 from the Monticello mill to the new one in this Colorado town of twelve thousand. Soon afterward, he was promoted from VCA's head of Western Division mining to the company's vice president of mining operations all over the world (to replace him in the old job, he hired Page Edwards, the Metals Reserve man who had accompanied Viles to Yazzie Mesa just after the lease was signed).

Yet rather than relocate to New York, Viles stayed put, and he and his wife took their place as leading citizens. During Durango's annual Spanish Trails Fiesta, when the men donned Western wear and the ladies put on Spanish or "squaw" dresses, the hot ticket in town was an invite to the party at the Vileses' home on high. Their two-hundred-plus guests dined on turkey with all the trimmings, and the view out the big living room window was stunning whether the foothills were wreathed in mist or overlaid with shining beams of sun.

Durango was a joiners' paradise, with some sixty active clubs for the women alone. Claire Viles was president of the Garden Club; she lectured on African violets and, for one reception at the Elks lodge, flew an exotic arrangement of birds of paradise, red ginger, and anthurium all the way from Hawaii. Denny was president of the Chamber of Commerce, a director of the First National Bank, and a bigwig in the local Republican party.[14]

The Vileses vacationed in London, Paris, and Monte Carlo. They hosted a constant flow of guests from such farflung points as Johannesburg and Antigua. His style of hospitality was to show off the rugged scenery of the region, and he had completely lost his reticence about Monument No. 2. With the addition of the airstrip, the mine became the highlight of his tours. A charter plane could get there from Durango in half an hour.

The president of VCA came west for a typical frenetic Viles weekend: A Friday trip to a beautiful hiking spot with a cocktail party upon return. A flight on Saturday to breakfast at Goulding's new motel, followed by a visit to the mine and its riches. Back to Durango in time for an afternoon rodeo. Sunday lunch in a quaint Victorian mining town nearby.

Viles gave his boss a look at the newest addition to Yazzie Mesa. Right next to the mine, he had constructed a mill—a pre-mill, actually, which he called an "up-grader." The idea was to avoid wasting any of the rock from the mesa's fertile ground. The company had focused on two ore beds, one on top of the other, each containing an almost unimaginable abundance of uranium. But the layer that separated them also included uranium, though in lesser amounts. The upgrader ran the lower-grade rock through a grinder, harvested uranium from the resulting grit, and wet it down to make a concentrated slime. This process could take rock that was anywhere from four-hundredths of one percent to nine-hundredths of one percent uranium and churn out a product that was twenty-five hundredths to thirty hundredths of one percent uranium.[15] It wasn't anywhere near the 5 percent and more that emerged from the prime deposits, but it was good enough to ship off to Durango for further refining into yellowcake. VCA stored the leftovers in two big piles that grew and grew.

Viles's upgrader meant even more jobs for Navajos. Ben Stanley, yet another of Adakai's grandsons, was in his middle teens when he graduated from playing in the tunnels to hiring on as a hauler between the mine and upgrader. It took an eighteen-wheel, twenty-ton truck to take the loads up to the mill in Durango. But less than a mile separated the Yazzie Mesa operations, so young Ben used a simpler mode of transportation. He rode a donkey, traveling the same way that Adakai's mother had favored back before the first prospector appeared. All day long, Ben hoisted ore at the mine onto his mount, unloaded it at the upgrader, and went back for more. When the mine added an overnight shift to boost the totals even more, the blasts began going off in the morning, too. Ben guided his donkey through swirling flakes of green and yellow.[16]

Mighty Monument No. 2 helped power the United States to a landmark moment. For years, Jesse Johnson's taskmasters had spurred him on. "Several times during the year I have felt that we almost pushed you too hard," AEC chairman Gordon Dean wrote to Johnson in one Christmas note, and then ladled on the praise for bearing up and bringing the uranium in. "My hope for the Commission is that you will keep pushing," wrote Air Force Brigadier Gen. James MacCormack, who represented military interests at the AEC.[17] And Johnson did keep pushing, paying out millions in bonuses, building roads through mountain and plain, drilling exploratory core holes through red cliffs and lonesome buttes. He sent out pilots in low-flying planes to aim radiation scanners at the ground, and on the fifteenth of every month he posted maps of their findings at twenty locations around the country. This tipsheet for prospectors stirred up so much excitement that it was said if one of the scout planes circled back over an area to take a second look, the ground below would be covered with claim stakes within a couple of hours.

In 1956, Johnson announced with pride that yearly domestic uranium ore production had risen from 70,000 tons in 1948 to nearly 3 million tons. He had fulfilled his mission-impossible. He had made America the free world's leading provider of uranium.[18]

No one trumpeted a second milestone delivered by the mine that same year. The Public Health Service confirmed the death of a forty-eight-year-old man on February 14, 1956. He had been employed at Monument No. 2 and was one of the legions examined by the medical teams traveling the Colorado Plateau two years before. Ironically, the deceased was not a Navajo. It was Carl Bell, the foreman who had laughed with Bob Anderson about the foibles of their troops, the supervisor who'd been willing to keep the crews digging until they found the mother lode. No autopsy was performed, but lung cancer showed up on X-rays and in cells from Bell's bronchial tissue. The diagnosis was irrefutable.[19]

And then all of a sudden, Johnson applied the brakes. This had nothing at all to do with the death of Carl Bell and everything to do with the fact that Johnson had performed too well. Not knowing for sure that his uranium problem could be solved in the American West, Johnson had also traveled the world to help other countries exploit their reserves. In the early days, before the big surge of mining on Navajo land, he'd signed contracts to buy uranium from South Africa, Australia, Portugal, and of course from the old stand-bys, Canada and the Belgian Congo. He had to honor these. In also promising to buy all of the uranium discovered in the United States, he overshot the mark. He saw what was coming for months, dreaded what he'd have to do. On October 28, 1957, he did it.

"We have arrived at the point where it is no longer in the interest of the federal government to expand the production of uranium concentrates," he announced. No new claims need apply. Johnson's "infantry" of prospectors was ordered to stand down. After all the flogging to find more, more, more uranium, the industry was shocked. "If you can find it, you can't sell it!" an incredulous Charlie Steen remarked. Anger rained down from the miners upon the man who'd made them. An acquaintance tried to buck him up: "Jesse, you got too much uranium, but if you hadn't found more than you needed, you wouldn't have had enough." [20]

There was no denying, though, that Johnson's words signaled the beginning of the boom's end. The active mines kept on churning, but their owners knew that once they were played out, the game was up. The timing was terrible for Paul Jones's push for good jobs in Navajo country. In addition to VCA's upgrader, three full-fledged uranium mills had just opened on the reservation, much to the tribe's delight. VCA still sent Monument No. 2 ore to Durango, but Kerr-McGee, Rare Metals, and Texas-Zinc Minerals Corp. had hired hundreds of Navajos to grind carnotite from other reservation uranium mining districts. Now their days of employment were numbered, too. They might have years left, but surely not decades.

The Atomic Energy Commission abandoned downtown D.C. in 1958. The White House, the U.S. Capitol, the Washington Monument, and the Lincoln Memorial would all be decimated in the event of an atomic attack on the nation's capital, but the AEC planned to survive nicely, thank you, well outside the zone of destruction that could be expected from a 20-megaton bomb. After much consideration, the commissioners bought a farm twenty miles northwest of the city near the tiny burg of Germantown, Maryland. Even though the location was thought to be safe, the AEC situated its building along a north-south axis, the better to absorb a blast. Reinforced concrete backstopped the brick façade. Construction cost more than $13 million, 30 percent over budget.[21] In this giant fallout shelter, the increasingly restive Duncan Holaday crossed paths with Jesse Johnson for the first and only time.

Holaday, still deeply involved in the Public Health Service field studies, visited the new headquarters in 1959 for discussions with the commission's health and safety officials. Unexpectedly, one of Johnson's subordinates showed up and led a nonplused Holaday off to meet the man who had whipped up the uranium frenzy in the first place. Suddenly, he found himself in the Raw Materials Division, face-to-face with the personification of the AEC's sensitivities about radiation in the mines.

Johnson was not at all hostile. He was familiar with the study's latest results and seemed sobered by them. The medical teams out in the field were by this time following some 3,200 uranium miners and the trends were frightening. A total of ninety-one people had died since the study began. Three years after VCA's Carl Bell passed away, the list of lung cancer deaths had grown to at least six, with a possibility of nine because of three suspicious X-rays. Sticking just to the confirmed cases meant the total was between two and a half to three times the number expected.[22] There were at least ten other cancers, including two of the pancreas, one of the liver, and one of the colon. Eighteen fatalities were attributed to heart attack or "sudden death."

Most important, about fifty miners in the study group had been mining uranium since 1942. Sixteen of these longtime veterans had died— four, a stunning 25 percent, from cancer of the lung. The most recent medical tour had included some new tests. Technicians had collected the saliva and mucus that miners produced when asked to cough to see if they could find atypical cells that might be related to a malignancy. Hair roots were examined under a microscope for damage, which could indicate radiation exposure. Uranium miners were showing more abnormalities than coal miners or nonminers. Nonmalignant lung disease was also on the rise: silicosis, fibrosis, tuberculosis. The researchers had not reached statistical significance. The time for articles in all the best scientific journals had not arrived. But taken together, the evidence suggested that the worst was yet to come.

Perhaps because the pressure to produce had cooled at last or perhaps because President Dwight D. Eisenhower had just established a Federal Radiation Council to advise on general matters of health and exposure, Johnson suddenly acknowledged the problem.

"Just what shape are those mines in now?" Johnson asked Holaday.

Holaday told him.

"Well, they don't sound so good," Johnson said. "Those things ought to be gotten under control."

One thing hadn't changed. Johnson, speaking in the passive voice, refused to take responsibility for the mines. The agency had already, if belatedly, started cracking down on radiation in the mills. As the AEC granted licenses for these facilities, it was unquestionably in charge of mill working conditions. Soon after Johnson cast a chill on the overheated mining industry, the agency conducted a series of mill inspections and found that most mills failed to check contamination levels or keep records of exposure. Follow-ups the next year showed little change. By the time Holaday came to Germantown, the commission was issuing stern directives, mill by mill: begin sampling air and liquid in your plants without further delay.

Holaday, inspired, seized the moment: "Well, Mr. Johnson, you know, your own mines, these mines, some of them are not in such good shape either."[23]

Your own mines? Johnson was dumbfounded. His aide informed him that the during the great prospecting rush, the commission had indeed staked some uranium claims that were on public lands at Forest Service and Bureau of Land Management sites rather than on the reservation. The commission was currently leasing fifteen properties directly to mining contractors.

AEC mines. With high radon. And, evidently, a lung cancer epidemic on the way.

"Get busy," Johnson told his staffer, "and see what you can do on those things. They have got to get controlled."

Earlier in the year, Johnson had watched a Bureau of Mines engineer lambaste a group of uranium company officials for the consistently high radon levels and pitiful efforts at control. The engineer said he had recently been to a mine where the radon was at seventy-nine times the concentration considered safe, and it wasn't hard to figure out why. The ventilation system was nothing more than a five-horsepower fan forcing air through a four-inch drill hole. "You people have bigger fans than that at home," the engineer scolded.[24]

Johnson could not bring himself to be so straightforward. He delivered a mealy-mouthed speech on the hazards of radiation to the American Mining Congress that fall. He rambled and hedged, glossing over harsh judgments with qualifiers—high radon levels "may present a definite health hazard"—and in the end tried to sound an optimistic chord: "I have no doubt that the uranium industry will successfully solve its radiation problems." He would say later that this hadn't been his proudest moment.[25]

He did take one small action. He turned to the outspoken engineers at the Bureau of Mines, for help within his own domain. He asked the bureau to conduct radiation surveys at all of the AEC leaseholds and threatened to close those that couldn't meet safety standards. Within a year, ventilation and dust control at the AEC properties were much improved. He touted this success to Congress as proof that radon could be minimized "without unduly prohibitive costs."[26] Jesse Johnson had come a long way. It just wasn't soon enough, or far enough, to avert disaster.

For all of his early crusading, Holaday was as masterful a rationalizer as Johnson. Johnson worried that forcing the radiation issue with the companies would cost him the uranium he had promised the Pentagon and Congress. Holaday's priority was the miners study. He spoke boldly enough in private, but he and his fellow researchers knew that if they said anything to the miners themselves, the PHS would lose access and all the precious data it was accumulating. He wasn't comfortable, far from it. Several times, he considered writing an anonymous letter to the hard-hitting syndicated newspaper columnist Drew Pearson.[27] But he decided that publicity would backfire and kill the study. He played by the rules.

To a colleague looking in from the outside, though, the terms of the medical study were impossible to defend. James G. Terrill, Jr., worked in a new section of the Public Health Service, the Division of Radiological Health. This division had been formed as the public grew ever more aware of possible hazards from radiation, whether from atomic weapons testing or from the fledgling field of peaceful nuclear power. Terrill familiarized himself with the long-term medical exams of the uranium miners. The more he learned about his agency's negligence, the more horrified he grew.

"My opinion is that we may yet be the center of a national scandal . . ." he wrote to a colleague. "When large numbers of uranium miners die of lung cancer, PHS will be asked what it did about the problem, and the answer will have to be, not much, we did too little too late." [28]

He was shocked that neither the AEC nor the PHS had felt any obligation to step in to protect the miners. "The only conclusion an objective observer can reach is that someone has abdicated his responsibility. . . . We can plead lack of money or lack of authority but the fact remains that aggressive leadership could have accomplished more than has been done."

Yet even as the doctors recorded more deaths, mine inspections on the Navajo reservation grew more lax. The tribal mining engineer was overwhelmed. The mining department employed two men who were supposed to check each operation twice a year. But there was so much activity over so wide an area that they found it impossible to keep pace. [29]

The Bureau of Mines was similarly understaffed. And while the state mining inspector in Arizona was an aggressive sort who actually closed down one or two mines for high radon levels, he had trouble gaining access to Indian territory. So, starting in 1957, the Bureau of Indian Affairs asked the U.S. Geological Survey for help. Geologists who knew next to nothing about radiation or uranium mines were sent into the field with minimal training on unfamiliar equipment. The tests had to be done at a certain time, in certain temperatures. Often as not, they fumbled so much that they simply gave up. [30]

By this time, many of the smaller mines, emptied of their highest-grade ore, were shutting down. Mysteriously, the tribal mining engineers insisted that all excavated ore too low-grade for the market be stockpiled at the mines, so the waste remained when the operators left. Though the mine portals were left unguarded and unsealed, the inspectors signed off on them, and the land was returned to the Navajos.

By 1960, the number of lung cancer deaths in the study group had reached ten—five times the number expected. The number of heart disease deaths was eleven times higher than predicted. Three times as many miners revealed abnormal cells in their cough tests as had in 1957.[31]

The wheel turned in 1962, after the Soviets blinked in a stare-down over missiles they had installed in Cuba, the closest Communist country to the Americans. The United States had an arsenal of launch-ready nuclear weapons that far outnumbered the Soviets' store.[32] But coming so close to the brink made President John F. Kennedy recognize that even one or two Soviet bombs reaching a U.S. target would be too many. The superpowers that had nearly kindled World War III began instead to tiptoe away from their Cold War. It wasn't over: the Berlin Wall, Vietnam, tussles over influence in Africa, Latin America, and the Middle East all lay ahead. But from the terror of those two weeks in October came a series of agreements to limit the number of nuclear weapons on Earth.

What did the United States get for its headlong rush to collect uranium? From the early 1940s through the first half of 1964, the government acquired 270,000 tons of uranium oxide, the yellowcake that came out of the mills, ready for conversion to the easy-split state required for atomic bombs. The bulk of that, 250,000 tons, was purchased between 1950 and 1960. Only a small portion was used.[33] Since the overall number of weapons was not likely to grow, the highly enriched uranium already in place could simply be recycled in newer models; it didn't get stale. The government was left with the world's largest store of raw and highly enriched *łeetso*.[34]

Jesse Johnson retired in 1963, taking up a life of travel, relaxation, and consulting gigs. Denny Viles retired, too, leaving a host of problems in the lap of Page Edwards. Lung cancer was much on Edwards's mind. He worried about the conditions at the mill in Durango.[35] VCA shut it down, but then replaced its capacity by buying Kerr-McGee's newer mill in Shiprock, New Mexico, the reservation's largest town.

The Public Health Service had halted its large-scale examination tours in 1960 and declared definitively that uranium miners faced an elevated risk of pulmonary cancer. In the medical journals, a steady stream of articles began appearing, based on the study's results. Grounds for denial were harder and harder to come by.

Edwards jotted notes to himself throughout 1963 and 1964: "OK to physical and X ray employees who have not had physical, thereafter have X-ray annually"..."Mon 2 Examinations STOP"..."Mon 2 re-examine TB possibility"..."Radon mtg in Dgo morning of 9-2-64. Called Dr. Holliday [sic] and he said meeting not open to operators ... Information from meeting will be sent to operators 9-4-64."[36] In 1965, he got tested himself. His cough specimen showed normal cells.[37]

As the disturbing scientific evidence mounted, Monument No. 2 wound down. After more than a decade of fevered excavation, Yazzie Mesa had given up the best of its ore. Edwards decided to wring what he could from the upgrader's gritty tailings piles, just as he'd done for the government in the old Manhattan Project days. He thought he could harvest more than half a million pounds of uranium over the course of three or four years.[38] He built large tanks to treat the leftovers with sulfuric acid, which freed the uranium from the sands. Once the solution had enough uranium in it, ammonia was added. The chemical reaction left a sediment that was filtered and partly dried, then sent off to the mill. Later, Edwards tried the same basic recipe using waste from the mine itself. The workers crushed the rocks into one-inch bits and piled it atop sheets of polyethylene. They poured the acid on the top of the heap, let it percolate downward, and caught the solution at the bottom. They'd send it through the pile again and again until they had enough uranium in the liquid. Add ammonia, filter, dry, and ship.[39]

Still, layoffs could not be avoided. By 1966, only twenty-two Indians and three white supervisors were still working at the once-bustling mine on the mesa.[40] One of them, of course, was Luke Yazzie.

The following year, on the clear and cool morning of March 9, the lead story in the *Washington Post* concerned the city's air being ranked fourth dirtiest in the nation. But a smaller headline below the fold drew the attention of the secretary of labor when he picked up his paper that day: "Hidden casualties of Atom Age emerge; uranium mine occupational hazard." Reporter John Reistrup had interviewed a twenty-year veteran of the uranium mines, a fifty-six-year-old white man who was dying of lung cancer and had filed for workman's compensation in Colorado. Union Carbide Nuclear, which had employed him, was fighting the $12,000 claim. The *Post* reporter contacted two Public Health Service researchers about their published studies and the federal gridlock that had kept forceful action at bay. One of the men he reached was Duncan Holaday, who felt free at last to talk in public without parsing his words. All the miners who would be examined had been examined. No longer need he fear an end to X-rays and cough tests and peering at hairs. With nothing to lose, Holaday unloaded a plainspoken warning, an informed prediction based on many years of experience: "There'll be more. We haven't seen them all."

The labor secretary, whose name was Willard Wirtz, was taken aback. He knew nothing about any of this and he thought that he should. President Lyndon Johnson, who had named him to his post, regularly mentioned occupational safety as a priority in speeches. When the reporter telephoned him later that day, Wirtz took the call. Asked whether his department had authority over the uranium mines, he found himself at a loss for the answer. By the close of business, both men knew that the Public Contracts Law of 1936 required that companies which supply products to the federal government must guarantee a safe and healthful workplace. The Department of Labor had had the power all along.[41]

On June 10, 1967, Wirtz issued a regulation declaring that no uranium miner could be exposed to radon at levels that would induce a higher risk of cancer than that faced by the general population. He accomplished in three months what the combination of at least three other federal agencies and four state governments had failed to do for two decades. But the AEC was already letting most of its mill contracts lapse. Safety standards came just in time for the industry's collapse.

———————

Within two months of Wirtz's pronouncement, the Vanadium Corporation of America was no more. With the market shaky for its mainstays, vanadium and uranium, VCA merged with Foote Mineral Co., the world's leading purveyor of lithium salts.

By then, Luke Yazzie had worked at his namesake mesa for so long that he qualified for three weeks' paid vacation.[42] But he wouldn't need to rest from his mining work much longer. The new owner retained Page Edwards and Bob Anderson as executives and Job One was shutting down the fading mine. The old VCA hands halted the dynamiting and collecting of ore. They milked a few last loads of uranium out of the waste with their acid-and-ammonia method. They brought in visitors to check out the trucks and loaders, selling off as many as they could. Just to be certain that they hadn't missed any of those extra-good spots, they instructed a skeleton crew of Navajos to spend a month drilling holes around the mesa. Satisfied that no big fossilized trees or thick veins of ore remained, they told the Navajos one day that they were done, done for good. The white bosses gave a few of the miners a ride home in their trucks. The company men kept on going out of the valley, to new careers in Colorado with Foote.[43]

By 1969, all of the old VCA leases in Navajo country were ripe for termination. It was clear that ore had not been produced in paying quantities for some time. According to the contracts, the cessation of mining was grounds for the land to be returned *in as good condition as received.* Howard B. Nickelson, who oversaw the closings on the government's behalf, was one of the ill-trained men from the Geological Survey. His sympathies lay squarely with the companies: They had helped to keep the United States a superpower, feeding the nuclear weapons that kept the Communists from overrunning the world. They were capitalists, fully participating in the system of the free world. They had to make a profit, didn't they? If they had to close every single hole, how could they do that?[44]

The genial Bob Anderson returned to his old turf to accompany Nickelson on his rounds, first through the east reservation leases and then to Monument No. 2. When they reached Yazzie Mesa, the abandonment was not complete. Anderson pledged that the area would be fully cleaned up and the Guardian's representative took him at his word. "No final inspection is planned and it is recommended that the leases can be cancelled," Nickelson wrote in his report.[45]

Monument Valley supplied nearly 1.4 million tons of uranium ore to the American people; most of that came from Monument No. 2.[46] As a marker of sorts, the miners had left one stone pillar in place, blasting around it over the years as they followed the uranium down from the surface. With the mining over, the memorial stood thirty-five feet tall on a silenced summit, a measure of just how deeply the mesa had been maimed.

TOXIC
LEGACY

Part III

THE GRANDCHILDREN

Aftermath

Chapter 9

Fallout

As the jobs at the mine disappeared, so did the families who had moved into VCA's "village" on Yazzie Mesa. A few joined Adakai's descendants, settling into Cane Valley, but the rest melted away to their own home places on the other side of Comb Ridge or dispersed to some of the uranium mines that were still limping along outside the reservation. The departing villagers left behind a raft of rusting cans; the charred centers of their campfire rings were all that remained of the cedars that had once flourished on the hill. The outsiders had chopped down all the trees.

Adakai's granddaughter, Juanita Jackson, bucked the tide. She had gone away from the valley when the newcomers were moving in, and she returned when the others were moving out. Her husband, Frank, spurred her comings and goings. After Adakai's Daughter arranged their marriage, he had, as custom dictated, followed his in-laws and his wife back to Cane Valley. But despite the steady wages available at the mine, Frank yearned for his own family in Shonto, a high plateau to the west.

Familial tug-of-war ensued. The Jacksons relocated to Shonto, staying long enough for Juanita to give birth to their fifth child in July of 1960, a girl they named Lorissa. While the baby was still in her cradleboard, they returned again to Cane Valley.

Then back to Shonto. Adakai's Daughter had fallen ill and was admitted to a hospital close to Shonto, so the Jacksons pulled up stakes again to be near her. During one of Juanita's visits, her mother confided that the

white doctors thought she might have something called cancer.[1] Whatever she had, it soon killed her. A few years later, Frank started coughing
and gasping for breath, diagnosed as tuberculosis. Whatever he had, it
soon killed him.

After his death in 1964, the young widow and her brood, number-
ing seven by then, set off for Cane Valley once more. They had no great
distance to travel, but it took nearly two years to get there. Juanita's truck
overheated in Kayenta, a ramshackle town that had grown up around
John Wetherill's old trading post. To make matters worse, one of the toddlers cried out that he was thirsty. In a quintessentially Navajo twist, a
woman in a nearby *hooghan* heard his bawling, fetched water, discovered that her Salt clan was also the clan of Juanita's great-grandfather—
Adakai's father, Man With the Red Hair—and made the offer that such a
kinship tie called for: "It's getting late. Spend the night."

In the Navajo Way, those who give help get help. Juanita took on chores
for weeks, and soon, without anyone having to discuss it, she set up a tent
outside the home of the Salt Clan Lady. Then she collected two-by-fours,
little by little, until she had enough to jerry-rig a tiny house.[2]

Of course, Adakai's people wanted her back. Her maternal aunt visited
Kayenta with a message: We are building you a nice home in Cane Valley.
She brought a letter from the tribe and a paper for Juanita to sign.[3]

The Navajo government was announcing what everyone on the reservation would soon be calling "the ten-day program." The tribe was
divided into 110 local governments called chapters, and some of the
chapters were about to reap a windfall. Federal money would flow to improve housing and provide employment at the same time. The government paid for temporary construction teams; each chapter that qualified
for the grants hired locals to build a new foundation for any resident who
would contribute the materials.

A brainstorm struck Juanita's cousin, Ben Stanley. He ran his truck up
to the Monument No. 2 tailings, where he still spent so much of his working day, and helped himself. The sandy leftovers were perfect for making
cement.[4] The men mixed the sticky paste by hand in a wheelbarrow and
took it out in buckets. With the foundations poured and set, more than
two dozen neighbors worked together to finish the job.

Four stout, strong houses soon lined up, miles apart, in the shade of the cottonwood trees. One was for Ben, one for his brother, one for his aunt and uncle, and the last was bait laid to lure Juanita away from the Salt Clan Lady. She succumbed, leaving Kayenta and installing herself and the children in the nice new place, with its provenance etched in the front stoop: 1965. MV 2.[5] Hers was in the nicest location in the valley. On a slight rise with a sweeping view of Comb Ridge, it hugged a wall of rocks in the back that protected it from the wind.

In the waning years of Monument No. 2 and increasingly after it closed, other neighbors, including Luke, took up Ben's idea. The herbs and berries of old were now scarce by the mining complex, but the mesa was once more a source of sustenance, it seemed. Chunks of ore, nicely squared-off by the blasting, littered the ground over by the old tunnels. The people of Cane Valley used the rocks to fashion bread ovens, patios, and cisterns. They used the waste sands to make not just foundations but also stucco walls.

There was plenty to go around. Despite the recycling efforts of VCA's Edwards and Anderson, which had eaten away at the tailings, the piles left behind with the inspector's blessing were more mountains than mounds. One covered ten acres, the other twenty. Just five hundred feet separated the two.[6]

Ten years before VCA gave the mesa back to the tribe, four Atomic Energy Commission scientists had warned that such detritus had high radon and radiation levels and should be closed off from the public. "The likelihood, for example, of children playing on these heaps should be considered," they wrote in a journal article in 1959.[7]

The descendants of Adakai, having somehow missed that issue of the *AMA Archives of Industrial Health,* were happy to have the artificial hills in their midst. As predicted, the youngest valley residents dug caves into the tailings in the summer and sledded down the slopes during winter snows.[8]

Luke Yazzie found yet another use for the waste. For the first time in more than twenty years, he could devote full attention to his sheep. Now that the top of the mesa was shaved off, the tailings were the tallest point around. He rode each day to the top of a pile, where he could keep an eye on his grazing flock for miles. He sat directly on the sand underneath his horse. The animal served as his workday "summer shade," where he kept office hours.[9]

Good riddance to the mine, he thought. Good riddance to VCA. He had been badly cheated, but now at least he and his cousin-neighbors had their valley back.

He had time now to teach his boys, and Juanita's boys, too, how to break the wild mustangs that roamed the canyons. The admiring youngsters seized on the similarity between his name and the title of a recent Paul Newman movie, dubbing him "Cool Hand Luke." There were no theaters nearby in which to see the film, so they may not have been aware of Newman's role: that of a prisoner who refused to cave in to authority and ultimately paid the price. The nickname fit better than the kids, or Luke himself, could know.

Luke also reclaimed the gulch that divided the South Rim from the North Rim at Monument No. 2. He planted an orchard of trees bearing green apricots, and he planted the Navajo staples: corn and melons and squash. The farm had a natural irrigation system; it caught water on both sides from the raised parts of the mesa. Every rain passed through the rubble littering the old mine site before it ran downhill to soak deep into the ground. The sun-dried soil took on a yellow tinge.

Ben told his uncle he thought the farm's yellow dirt must be uranium. "I don't think so," Luke replied, and he shared his bounteous harvests with all the families in the valley. They were grateful; with the mining jobs and wages gone, they needed the food.[10]

Uranium houses went up in the other mining areas of the *Dinétah*, too. Over in the east, Paul Shorty used his new trucks to haul ore down from the mine that he and King Tutt had staked out. He gave the rocks to friends, who put them to good use in dozens of buildings at a nearby spot known as Oaksprings.[11] To the south, at Haystack in New Mexico, at least two houses had uranium walls and a third was surrounded by a nice strong uranium fence. The story was the same in Cove, Tuba City, Teec Nos Pos, Tah-chee. Everywhere, resourceful people made do with the offerings of the land.

On the other side of Goulding's, in Utah west of Monument Valley, Mary and Billy Boy Holiday bought a *hooghan* from a medicine man. They paid a fair price: $50, a sheep, and a canvas tent. For the most part, the Holidays were happy with the purchase. Because the house stood next to the trading post road, the kids could walk to catch the school bus instead of riding horses for hours before they even got on board. The single drawback was the bare dirt underfoot. When the ten-day program came to their chapter at Oljato in 1971, the Holidays jumped at the chance to get a real floor. The same thought occurred to their ten-day contractor that had occurred to so many others in the uranium belt. He suggested using sand and crushed rock that had washed down from an abandoned mine in the mesa behind the *hooghan.* It wouldn't cost a cent and it would make fine cement. As promised, the six-inch slab was so level and smooth that the Holidays could lay their sheepskins directly on the floor and enjoy a good night's sleep.[12]

While federal money was helping to install uranium in reservation houses, the government was preparing to take uranium *out* of non-Indian homes. The Navajos had no idea that by this time, 1971, doctors and state authorities were in an uproar two hundred miles to the north, in the lily-white town of Grand Junction.

Within a mile of the AEC's Western nerve center, the Climax Uranium Co. transformed ore into yellowcake in a converted beet-sugar mill on the north bank of the Colorado River. To reduce the size of the waste pile, the mill had opened its gates once a month since 1952 to anyone who wanted to cart away some sand. At first, contractors used it in roadways; they had asked for and received the AEC's blessing to do so. After all, drivers seldom had prolonged contact with the pavement. But then gardeners came, too. The fine powder was acidic so they sprinkled it on the soil to nourish their roses and tomatoes. And after that the situation got out of hand.

In 1966, the Colorado public health department accidentally discovered that tailings had been used in houses, churches, and schools, generally as bedding on which floors and foundations were placed. The state health officials, alarmed, made sure this stopped. To have the people of Grand Junction irradiated in their own homes, even at low levels, was unacceptable at best, perilous at worst. From under the houses, radon was exhaled in the same way that it was in the mines; the walls acted as an incubator for radon gas just as the mine tunnels had.

The state asked the Public Health Service for money to investigate the situation in Grand Junction, but in 1968, an AEC reviewer weighed in, recommending against the grant. Any high radon levels found in Grand Junction homes were probably the result of natural radioactivity, not the tailings, the AEC argued. Having put the kibosh on the funding, the AEC tried to slam the door on any further requests by conducting its own surveys in portions of Tennessee and Florida that were high in natural radiation. But the Grand Junction houses contained radon at levels one hundred times higher than the highest amount found in the AEC control group. Anxious to keep this news from getting out, the commission suppressed its own report, stamping it "For Internal Use Only."[13]

It looked like a replay of the mining experience was in the cards. But this time, the state went to Congress. Grand Junction's representative in the House was a Democrat named Wayne N. Aspinall who was well-positioned to help. He chaired the House interior committee; more precisely, he ruled it. And he also headed the raw materials subcommittee, a unit of the special Senate-House atomic energy committee. That got the AEC's attention. Glenn Seaborg, the Nobel laureate who had discovered plutonium and was at this time serving as the AEC chairman, noted in his office diary that the United States had "a moral obligation" to remove Grand Junction's contaminated material.[14] When the victims had a patron with clout, the connection between the government's hunger for uranium and the hazards of exposure were easily laid bare.

In the Home of the People, Juanita Jackson was laughing at her children's puns and weaving rugs in her valley home, and Mary and Billy Boy Holiday were enjoying the fine new floor in their cozy *hooghan*. In Grand Junction, surveyors drove the streets and alleyways in a lead-shielded scanner van to ferret out "hot" houses. Ads ran in the local paper and a toll-free hotline was established. The government yanked out tainted material, replacing foundations and floors. Where the crews found contaminated rooms that didn't meet building codes, they even threw in a bonus and upgraded electrical systems. In many cases, the value of the repairs exceeded the value of the house. Authorities also wanted to be sure that no one would ever unwittingly build a new house in a polluted spot. The tailings-fertilized yards were dug up and purified with new soil. If a tree came out, a sapling went in. If a lawn was ripped up, sod was put down.[15]

All told, four thousand private and commercial properties in and around Grand Junction eventually had tailings removed, at a cost of $250 million. The debris was stored at the millsite, by this time posted and fenced, and later buried at a federal disposal cell specifically designed to hold radioactive waste. No medical examinations were conducted before, during, or after the removal project, but the Colorado health director had made an impassioned plea: Don't wait for a long, drawn-out study before purifying these homes. Don't wait until outbreaks of cancer and genetic defects tell the tale.[16] Congress agreed, implying that the residents of Grand Junction deserved better treatment than the uranium miners had received at the hands of their government.

On the western Navajo range, between Monument Valley and Flagstaff, new lakes appeared in the arid scrublands as if by magic. These were the old uranium pit mines, some of them a mile wide and 130 feet deep, transformed into oases fringed with green. Water pooled here from above and sometimes from below. The rain water collected; water rose from the aquifer that had been pierced by mining.

Lois Neztsosie was one of the women who trudged all day, herding, through the vast silent desert around Cameron. For long years, her animals had gleaned sips here and there from puddles forming in depressions in the sandstone. With the arrival of the lakes, Lois could lead her one hundred sheep to drink their fill at the same time. She quenched her own thirst as well, parting the surface film with her hands and then leaning down to swallow. She took care to get her water from the side opposite the animals, for hygiene's sake. She was pregnant, then a new mother, then quickly pregnant again, and she wanted to stay healthy.

At dusk, if she was too far from home, Lois camped out, rolling under a bush for shelter. When she was away overnight, she got in the habit of filling and refilling a small container with a drinking supply as she moved from one lake to the next.

Despite the newly abundant water, her flock failed to thrive. The birth rate dropped, and the few new lambs that did appear had a hard time walking. Some were born without eyes. Lois' husband, David, wondered whether the sheepdogs were mating with their charges. He also suspected witchcraft. Trained as a medicine man, he tried to fight the spell by burning cedar and herbs and gathering the sheep around the fire to inhale the healing smoke.

The livestock were not his only worry. A mysterious sickness affected the couple's two youngest daughters. Laura, born in 1970, had a weak right eye and was prone to stumbling. Arlinda, who came along the following year, developed ulcers in her corneas by age five. A few years later, she was walking on the sides of her feet.

At the Indian Health Service hospital, doctors were mystified. Experts concluded that both girls suffered from a rare genetic disorder. There was another possibility, but no one considered it until many years later. No one connected the children and the sheep.[17]

Back in Cane Valley, Juanita Jackson worked hard to get by. Adakai's granddaughter sat for hours at her loom, then sold her weavings to trading posts. She fashioned jewelry of turquoise and silver, which she hawked to tourists at a Utah state park near Mexican Hat. She made pottery in the traditional manner, wrapping her creations and placing them in the ashes of a wood fire to bake.[18] She got some help when a new man from Shonto showed up, instructed by his mother to shoulder some of the endless chores. As intended from the start, they married. Two more children arrived in the compact house that Ben Stanley had helped to build for her.

Her new husband, John Black, set Juanita on the road again. They picked crops, moving from farm to farm around Phoenix. These were unfamiliar fruits and vegetables to Navajo farmers: tomatoes and lettuce and onions. But the money was good and they could come back to Cane Valley when the harvest was done.

The older children were big enough to help. The youngest children needed to be with their mother. As for little Lorissa . . . well, for her, Juanita had big plans. Lorissa had attended kindergarten and first grade during the family's sojourn in Kayenta. On the other side of Comb Ridge from Cane Valley, over at Dennehotso, the BIA ran a boarding school. Juanita's plans to go to class had been foiled long ago. But Lorissa would do it. Lorissa would get an education.

Just one problem presented itself. Lorissa hated the school. The atmosphere was harsh; the children were required to speak English and forced to mop floors. She longed for Cane Valley. She had worked hard at home, too, of course. Her mother assigned Lorissa to cook for the six boys. Sometimes she sent Lorissa to make tortilla bread for Anna Sling, Adakai's younger wife—not so young anymore. But in Cane Valley, Lorissa could bask in the warmth of a huge extended family. She could ride horses and sometimes her brothers would let her join in their shoot-'em-up games. Even if her mother and siblings had to leave for a while to pick crops, she would much prefer to stay with her uncles, her aunts, and her many "grandmas" than at the institutional school. Her mother was making her give them up.

One day, when she was enrolled in the school's fifth grade, she sought out a cousin who'd also been dispatched to Dennehotso from Cane Valley, and together the girls hatched an escape plan. They sneaked away on a sunny Saturday, piling on many layers of clothing because the early spring weather was still so unpredictable. After crossing an arroyo, they started up Comb Ridge, the Backbone. Hours later, upon reaching the top, they lost the trail, but they started down the other side anyway, figuring they'd just keep going in the right direction. At first, the descent was easy.

Suddenly, though, the cliff dropped away, straight down. The cousin went ahead, grabbing at plants all the way. Lorissa sat by her ten-year-old self on a ledge, trying to decide whether to go back the way she'd come. She was scared.

But after what seemed like endless agonizing, she decided she wouldn't retreat. She wanted home that much. She pushed off and slid fast, and it wasn't as bad as she thought it would be.

Day was nearly done by the time the girls reached Cane Valley. They walked together along the bottom of the rise, looking back at the undulating wall that they had conquered: red heights fading into a pale tan down below; rough block patterns that resembled carvings in the rock. Their sense of triumph ebbed as they realized they were going to get in trouble. They hid behind a sheep corral for a while, racking their brains for a way to explain their presence. Failing to come up with anything beyond the simple truth—"I was homesick"—the girls emerged just as Tony Yazzie, one of the "grandfathers," came out of his house. (He married one of Adakai's daughters.)

He was shocked when he spotted the runaways. The "grandfather" took Lorissa's cousin to her father to be dealt with. Juanita was off on her migrant farm route, so the "grandfather" acted in her stead, driving Lorissa back to school the next day.[19] For her difficult climb, she had earned just one night's freedom.

The following year, Lorissa was sent so far away that she couldn't possibly hike back. This happened because Ben Stanley's wife, Mary, had had a dream. When she woke, Mary told her husband, "There's someone that's coming to see me." Early in the morning, he would come.

In Navajo tradition, the sand paintings prepared by the medicine man reflect the world as it is, and changes to the painting change the world. A story can become real while you're telling it. So the Stanleys weren't surprised at all when strangers showed up in the valley two weeks later, not long after daybreak. A white man and his wife. It was him. The man that Mary had thought into being.

He was a missionary, a Baptist from Montana. He wanted to hold a revival at the Stanleys' place, to preach for everyone in the valley, and Ben and Mary let him because of the dream. The missionary came back again and held another revival, and came back again and brought more ministers from all over the country. One of them, from South Carolina, really liked the Cane Valley children. "Can we have two of those?" he asked. Ben and Mary gave him a pair of their children; they could go to school and be well fed and learn the white man's ways with a gentle family that would treat them more kindly than the BIA.[20]

Christianity took hold in the valley. Juanita's second marriage was over and she was no longer making the migrant-picking rounds, so she sent her children to Bible school at Ben and Mary's for a week or two each summer. After each session, the girls stayed and stitched clothing for their families. Luke Yazzie's son, Luke Jr., began thinking about becoming a preacher himself. The "grandfather" who returned Lorissa to Dennehotso built a white wooden church. He used uranium tailings, of course, and rock from the mine, for the foundation.[21]

The Christians found a family off the reservation for Lorissa as well. Juanita was determined that her daughter, like it or not, learn to read and write and do sums and go on to get a good education. Lorissa soon left in a car with strangers, driving to Santa Rosa, California. She had no idea what to expect. Her host family held her back a grade to join their daughter's class. Lorissa resented that. Just as Bob Anderson hadn't been able to tell one Navajo from another, Lorissa thought that all the white people looked alike. And the vineyards looked so different than the desert grazing lands.

When she got home for vacation, Lorissa couldn't make her tongue form Navajo sounds at first. But once she said one word, it all came back to her. Juanita taught her how to weave and she produced a skinny, short cloth adorned with stripes. The sides were uneven. She was jubilant, back in the *Dinétah*.[22]

Then fall rolled around again and she was off to a different Baptist family, this time in Vancouver, Washington. For a class project on wool, she set up a loom and showed off her new weaving skills to the other students, doing the best she could with store-bought yarn. She got an A. She earned other A's too, but this one was the only one that mattered to her.

The pattern was set. In the summers, Lorissa was one of The People. Her back ached at the loom, but Juanita told her, "Always finish what you start," and she finally sold a rug to the trader at Mexican Hat for the goodly sum of $35. She and her siblings and cousins lived outdoors. They loved to load a truck bed with barrels and drive to a well at the base of Comb Ridge. Whoever wasn't pumping ran under the gushing water for a shower. The teenagers were scolded for getting soap and shampoo in the family drinking supply.

But during the school year, Lorissa would always be sent packing, an educational nomad on the Christian road, to people who looked and acted nothing at all like her or anyone else in Cane Valley. Vancouver again, then Blanding, Utah, then Coos Bay, Oregon, for the last two grades of high school. At the rehearsal for graduation, the white kids started talking about possible careers. Lorissa's seething about being forced so far from home spilled into contempt for all things school-related. "I'll tell you one thing I'll never do," she declared to her classmates. "I'll never be a *teacher.*"

She had never stopped hating, absolutely loathing, the nine months she had to spend as an expatriate each year. But later on she often reflected that the repeated bouts of exile may well have saved her life.

Chapter 10

Avalanche of Suspicion

T he Grand Junction scandal led Congress to consider the source: the tailings pile itself, and the radioactive mountains at twenty-one more inactive mills around the country. Though the tailings, by definition, had been stripped of most of their uranium, there was plenty of radiation from a host of different elements. All of the products of uranium's decay mingled in the waste, and they too were breaking down and throwing off dangerous particles. The problem would not dissipate any time soon: thorium-230 has a half-life of 75,400 years; it transformed into radium-226, with a half-life of 1,600 years. Radon, polonium, bismuth, radioactive lead: all were present in the piles. The heavy metals in the tailings posed their own dangers, separate and apart from radiation.

The alpha, beta, and gamma particles flew off on dust in the wind. Rain dripped through the heaps, and, with nothing to catch the resulting mixture underneath, kept right on going into the water table underground. What was the impact of all this contamination? How much damage did it do?

Not surprisingly, these questions had already been raised and had languished without resolution. The AEC researchers writing in 1959 about the piles had called for more study. In 1966, the same year that the Colorado Health Department learned of Grand Junction's tailings-construction boom, federal researchers looked into the possible contamination of the Colorado River by mill wastes in the watershed. The report, from the Department of Health, Education and Welfare, concluded that there was no immediate danger, but urged controlling the spread of the tailings because no one knew what their cumulative effects might be down the line. The document even mentioned two of the Navajo mills—the Rare Metals facility at Tuba City and VCA's upgrader in Cane Valley. HEW noted that the tailings could affect Indian families in the area and could spread through some of the dry washes in the valley.[1] The prescription: abandoned piles should be covered with dirt, or with an oil-film cover, or seeded with vegetation, to seal off the dangerous material for ten or twenty years. Someone needed to be held accountable for the long term— who exactly this would be was apparently above the authors' pay grade.

This report was published three years before Howard Nickelson let VCA turn Monument No. 2 back to the Navajos with the tailings piles still open and in place.

Yet, how could Nickelson have proposed effective measures, if he'd wanted to? Rare Metals, to its credit (and by order of the state), applied chemicals to form a crust over the pile when it closed the Tuba City mill in 1967. But the crust was no match for the hot blasts of desert wind. The topping cracked and wore away, and by 1971, Arizona authorities were telling Representative Aspinall that the effort had failed and tailings dust was escaping again.[2] Rare Metals, of course, like VCA, had already been allowed to leave the reservation and any liability behind.

By this time, however, a new federal player had entered the picture. The U.S. Environmental Protection Agency had been born in 1970, the same year the first Earth Day was celebrated. When the EPA was three years old, the Navajo tribal chairman at the time, Peter MacDonald, turned to the young agency's administrator for advice. MacDonald believed strongly in tribal self-determination and he was not at all opposed to mining uranium, as long as the Navajos got their fair share of the profits. Indeed, he was negotiating with Exxon to harvest *leetso* with the tribe as a full partner in a joint production venture, not merely as a lessor of land.[3] But the reservation contained four abandoned mills by this time: Cane Valley.

Tuba City. Mexican Hat. Shiprock. Now that Congress was publicly investigating dangers posed by tailings piles, MacDonald wanted to know what the tribe could do to protect The People.

It took two years, but in 1975, the EPA dispatched nine radiation experts from their base in Las Vegas to *Diné bikeyah*. By this time, the tribe's plea for help dovetailed with signals from Congress. Lawmakers were considering a federal program to contain the tailings and wanted to get a feel for the scope of the problem.

The Indian Health Service tipped off the team leader, Joe Hans, that the tribal government—the same tribal government that was so worried about mill site radiation—was training Navajos in the construction trades again, this time at the tailings pile in Shiprock. The students, unprotected by masks or respirators, were practicing their moves on bulldozers and excavators, shifting tailings from one spot to another. Hans put a stop to this. He also noticed that the Shiprock mill was topped with not one, but two, layers of roofing. When the inner layer was ripped out, sheets of yellowcake powder rained down.[4]

At his next stop, Monument No. 2, Hans broke the bureaucrat's cardinal rule: don't stray beyond your mission. From the upgrader site on the mesa, he noticed the hand-built houses in the valley below and made the connection to the houses at Grand Junction. Had Cane Valley's residents served themselves from the open piles he was examining? It would have surely been the practical thing to do.

He returned a few months later with his colleagues. They brought hand-held radiation scanners, air samplers, portable generators, and other fancy machines and headed straight to the houses. To his dismay, seventeen of thirty-seven tested homes contained radioactive material. At one of them, occupied by Ben Stanley's sister, Bessie Cly, the meter's *beeeeep* sounded so long and so loud that the EPA technician began muttering that there must be something wrong with the equipment. He left and got another instrument from his truck. But when he tested the house again, he got the same ear-splitting noise.[5]

Hans thought the residents of Cane Valley faced hazards far worse than those in Grand Junction. The Navajos were not just living with sands piled under or against the house, which was quite bad enough. Adakai's children and grandchildren had incorporated tailings directly into the homes themselves, in the exterior stucco, on inside walls as "plaster," in mortar for stone footings. One person had installed a uranium-ore fireplace. The risks of gamma radiation and radon were unacceptable, Hans thought. He would never live in such conditions himself and he didn't think that anyone else should have to.

He wrote to EPA headquarters in Washington, recommending that the agency clean up the most contaminated homes, on the Grand Junction model, or relocate the occupants.

His higher-ups said no. He tried the Indian Health Service. No, again. Finally, he got the message. No one had the money to decontaminate these sites, and no one was willing to go to bat to get it.[6]

So once more, Hans returned to Cane Valley, this time with a Navajo translator. He aimed to deliver a warning, at least. He set up a projector and a screen, and proceeded to show Adakai's puzzled descendants a film about radiation. He quietly suggested that it might be wise to move.

What was this *bilagáana* talking about? This was land. This was Mother Earth. This was their mesa! How could it be dangerous for the *Diné*?

Much as Luke Yazzie had come away from his conversations with the VCA thinking he had a deal, several families in the valley left the presentation under the impression that Hans made them a promise. They thought the white man was telling them that the government would build replacements for their dangerous houses. Whether Hans blurted out a pledge that he certainly pursued but could not keep, or whether, as he would maintain later, something got lost in the translation, nothing happened. Most of the Navajos who had gathered for the odd movie premiere in their valley eventually decided that the long silence afterward must mean the problem wasn't *that* bad.[7] Besides, everyone seemed fine.

Only Bessie Cly and her husband, Larry, were unnerved enough to take action. They had seen how shocked and upset the tester had become at their home. It took them a couple of years to save up the money to build a new house, but they finally did it. They dug a foundation and raised four new walls right next to the old place, and moved their family a few dozen yards away. Eventually, they demolished the radioactive house by attaching chains to a truck and pulling it down. They left the debris on the ground.[8]

Hans wrote a report for the EPA, naming names and listing numbers. For some reason, the Clys' place didn't make it in. But the memory of their house stayed with him. It was one of the "hottest" in the valley.[9]

In 1977, President Jimmy Carter named James Schlesinger the first U.S. secretary of energy. The fledgling Cabinet-level department inherited the nuclear weapons program and, with it, the problem of what to do with the abandoned mills. Joe Hans grabbed the opportunity to press his case anew, urging DOE to clean up at least the nine most dangerous houses in Cane Valley.

For two more years, the people had been living in these death traps, bombarded by particles, drawing radon daughters into their lungs with every breath. Hans was frightened for them, as frightened as Duncan Holaday had been for the miners. He wrote to the DOE contractor that was charged with assessing how much work needed to be done at the old mills and estimating the costs.[10]

Please, he asked, add these contaminated houses to your checklist. Take care of Oscar Sloan's place, he implored, and of Jesse Black's. Remove the radioactive material from the homes of Cecil Blackmountain—one of the mine's last workers—and Ned Yazzie, who had been partially paralyzed when the brakes failed on a VCA truck and he plunged off the mesa. Fix the structures in the compound built by Tony Yazzie—the "grandfather" who took Lorissa back to school and put up the church. Do something for Adakai's grandson Ben Stanley and for Ben's mother, Anna Cly—one of Adakai's three Annas. The other names that Hans put forward were those of Luke Yazzie and Juanita Jackson Black.[11]

None of them knew that he'd done this, of course.

Cancer had once been so rare among the Navajos that researchers marveled. A Phoenix doctor writing in a 1956 medical journal article noted the *Diné*'s apparent resistance to this deadly class of diseases. And at first, it seemed to the PHS researchers who kept track of such things that white uranium miners were coming down with cancer, while their Navajo counterparts were not.

But 1972 was a bad year for the men of the broad and dramatic Red Valley in the northeastern part of the reservation. Overlooked by the Carrizo and Lukachukai mountains, which were riddled with old uranium tunnels, Red Valley was named for the bright scarlet hue of the cliffs ringing the plain. In scattered clusters of homes, once-active men lay wheezing and exhausted, plagued by sharp pains piercing the insides of their chests. Lee N. John died on January 19, survived by his widow Mae and eight children.[12] Clifford Yazzie, husband of Fannie and father of fourteen, died in April.[13] Billy Johnson, married to Louise and the father of four, died on May 21. Todacheenie Benally, leaving wife Rose and thirteen children, died on May 28.[14]

Fannie Yazzie had sold off sheep and pawned jewelry so she could take her Clifford to the VA Hospital in Albuquerque. There, she met nine other Navajo women with nine other husbands who were dying of cancer. The patients had something in common besides their sickness; they were former miners all.[15]

Perhaps more Navajos came down with cancer later than the white men because they did have special genetic defenses. Perhaps it was because they rarely smoked—cigarette use was frowned on as sacrilegious, because herbs were occasionally puffed at ceremonies. Perhaps it was because the study group was skewed toward whites, who worked at the more accessible mines. Perhaps Navajos were more often misdiagnosed at first. The latency period was longer, for whatever reason, but in the fifteen years after uranium's heyday, well within the range of the Eastern European miners' experience, something happened, and kept happening. The cancer death rate among Navajos doubled from the early 1970s to the late 1990s, a period when the overall U.S. cancer death rate registered a slight decline.[16]

There was no more talk of cancer immunity among the Navajos.

The symptoms became familiar. First, a lump on the neck. Then, shortness of breath. Then, spitting up blood.

Red Valley's delegate to the tribal council was an engineer who had worked for the Navajo minerals department. His name was Harry Tome. Tome remembered hearing complaints about health back when he was visiting the mines on official business back in the 1960s, but the thought had never occurred to him that handling uranium might be dangerous. By this time, whenever he attended prayer meetings at the pan-Indian Native American Church, his fellow worshippers were more likely than not trading talk about the deteriorating state of their lungs. Nine times out of ten, the ill were former uranium miners. Tome watched the death toll mount among his constituents with growing dismay. He visited some doctors, who explained radiation to him as "a dangerous smoke you breathe in." He understood the concept—he was an educated man—but he knew that most of the elders wouldn't.[17]

He attended a Red Valley chapter meeting and tried to tell the people what he'd learned. He urged them to pass a resolution asking the tribal council for help, and after some prodding, they did, but the council felt the fault lay with the federal government, and the federal government should pay. That was the beginning of a long road. Tome got in touch with a reporter for the *Albuquerque Tribune,* and connected the writer to distraught widows and anguished, ailing miners. He lobbied Congress, persuading both New Mexico senators and a congressman to try for a law that would pay compensation to the dying and their families for the sacrifice they'd made for their country. But the bills did not pass.

By 1978, in a community with several hundred families, twenty-five Red Valley mining veterans had fallen to lung cancer. Harry Tome had spent five years flying back and forth to Washington to no avail. He asked Representative Harold Runnels of New Mexico, one of his frustrated champions on the Hill, whom to contact about filing a lawsuit. Runnels suggested Stewart L. Udall, a former Arizona congressman and interior secretary under Kennedy and Johnson who had left the government and joined a law practice in D.C.

Udall, a scion of a pioneering Mormon family prominent in Arizona politics, knew about uranium and he knew about Indians. He had grown up in the small town of St. John's, not far from the reservation. After serving as an Air Force gunner on B-24 missions over Western Europe, he played guard for the University of Arizona basketball team. He was

elected to Congress in 1954, where he won a seat on the Interior committee, which included jurisdiction over tribal relations.

While in Congress, at Paul Jones's urgent request, he had fought to
keep the Rare Metals mill open when it looked for a time in the late 1950s
like the AEC might let its contract lapse. He had helped the Hopis undo
a prospecting agreement that a village council had unwittingly signed, all
the while wishing that the tribe would reverse its stubborn stand against
uranium mining, which he saw as a great economic boon.

At the announcement of his nomination to the Cabinet, he had irked
Kennedy by joking that just as the president-elect was qualified to be his
own secretary of state, Udall could well appoint himself Indian commissioner. ("I don't want the job," JFK curtly interjected.[18]) The brash young
Westerner had gone on to make a name for himself as an environmentalist, but he had not delved deeply into the radon problem in the mines.
Once the new safety standard was in place, though, he had readily agreed
to cooperate with Willard Wirtz. He made sure that his department's Bureau of Mines lent its expertise on radiation to Labor's enforcement of
the new safety standard.

Tome was not optimistic that this big shot would help him, but he
moved west on Pennsylvania Avenue to Udall's building, drew a deep
breath, and headed for the seventh floor. Udall, for his part, was surprised
to hear about the Navajo in his waiting room. Curious, he invited Tome
into his office, sat and listened, later traveled out to Red Valley, and then
decided to take on the case.[19]

It was actually tougher to sell some of the potential plaintiffs. The locals were wary of getting all tied up in the white man's courts. And some
of them didn't believe that uranium could cause all this suffering so long
after the mines had closed. When Mae John signed on and became a
leader in the fight, she acquired the ridicule of her neighbors and a new
nickname, "Check," for her presumed motivation.[20]

Tome wore a second hat in the tribal government. Besides his council
position, he served on the Navajo Environmental Protection Commission, which was by this time four years old. In this capacity, he soon heard
again from the Red Valley chapter, now fully aroused, this time about the
state of the abandoned mines. The timbers at the open portals were rot-

ten and collapsing. The children played in those tunnels. Some families used them as corrals, fencing their livestock inside when the cold and snow arrived. What if they caved in? And with the old miners dying, the question naturally arose: how much radiation were the Navajos and their animals being exposed to?[21]

The combination of Udall's planned lawsuit and the old open mines made an enticing story for CBS News. In late May 1979, the environment commission assigned a staffer to take a crew from the television network out to Oaksprings, near the King Tutt and VCA mines in the eastern Carrizos. They visited some of the old tunnels with a Geiger counter and then stopped in to see some former miners. In one home, the tribal staffer offhandedly stuck his detector against a wall. The instrument screamed. Embarrassed, he quickly placed it on mute and watched the needle dance.[22]

Evidently, the Navajos' "Grand Junction" problem was not confined to Cane Valley.

The beleaguered director of the tribal commission already knew all about Joe Hans's discovery at the foot of Monument No. 2. Harold Tso had sent tribal staffers to the Las Vegas EPA for training and in turn had provided Hans with the translator for his Movie Night. He was pushing hard on the issue of the tailings piles—in 1978, Congress authorized a cleanup—and he was hoping that Hans would succeed in his attempts to get the Energy Department to include the "hot" houses when the time came.[23]

But Oaksprings was nowhere near a mill, and Congress had only told Energy to decontaminate the mills—without a word about the mines. By the spring of 1980, Tso's staff had discovered sixteen more Oaksprings houses built with Paul Shorty's gift rocks. At least three of them registered readings higher than the King Tutt mine, the source of the ore.[24]

Tso cobbled together enough federal money to replace a handful of houses and then faced an agonizing decision: what to do about the people who lived in the others. He was a Navajo, Fort Defiance–born, and he knew how hard they had labored to build the uranium houses with their own hands. He knew how poor they were and how hard it would be to start again from scratch. But he was also a radiochemist who'd done graduate work at Colorado State University, and he was a former field lab supervisor for Project Gasbuggy—the AEC's ill-fated attempt to explode an underground nuclear device to stimulate natural gas flows (it worked, but the gas was unusable because it was radioactive). He knew what radiation could do.

In the end, Tso decided he just couldn't let anybody stay. The tribe evicted the remaining families in the spring of 1981 and placed padlocks on their doors. They were left to find shelter wherever they could. Needless to say, they were furious—not at Paul Shorty, not at the mining companies, not at the government, but at *him*. Who was Harold Tso to upend their lives, to turn them out of their own homes? Who was he to say that the blessings performed before they moved in would not protect them?

One of the dispossessed, Clifford Frank, vowed to go take his cabin back. But in truth, there was little he could do. He lay in bed many miles away, at the Indian Health Service hospital in Shiprock—a nonsmoking husband and father in his fifties who had worked at one mine and come home at the end of his shift to sleep in another. Years later, he was slowly surrendering to the cancer that was eating away at his lungs.[25]

Of the roughly 3,500 uranium miners in the PHS study group, 144 cancer deaths were counted by 1974. Statistically, researchers would have expected about thirty. The PHS estimate in 1978 was about 200 cancer deaths, with about 160 of them classified as "excess." Two more PHS scientists went public, venting this time to the *New York Times*. "What we refused to do thirty years ago, we are paying for today," one of them said. "What we refuse to do today, we will pay for in thirty years."[26]

Forty-five medical researchers gathered in Albuquerque on February 27, 1981, to discuss a series of puzzling signs that something was amiss in the Four Corners area of the American Southwest. The medical school at the University of New Mexico had convened an "unsponsored meeting"—academic argot for a conference with no subsidies to help defray the costs—but scientists were interested enough to travel from as far as Texas and Washington, D.C.

The presentations put forward one oddity after another. Sex ratios were off. Miscarriages were up. In the uranium corridors of New Mexico and Utah, the number of birth defects had significantly increased, but not in other parts of the same states. The mining areas of Utah had even higher rates than those near the nuclear test sites where the finished product had exploded in ferocious displays. Among Navajo teens, reproductive, breast, and bone cancers were as much as seventeen times higher than expected. The statistics on brain tumors were murkier, but still worrisome.

The scientists' chief suspect was the old uranium mines. As the day wore on, Marvin Legator, who had traveled from the University of Texas Medical Branch in Galveston, grew increasingly distressed. "I came to this meeting cold, not even having heard anything about it, and I have to go away thinking, hey, we really have something here," he told the others. "It looks to me like it is a really big problem. We don't know the dimensions of it, but I come away from this meeting saying there is something here that we should really look into on kind of a priority basis."[27]

Representatives from the EPA, the Indian Health Service, the Labor Department, and the Centers for Disease Control were on hand (the Nuclear Regulatory Commission, successor to the now defunct AEC, had been invited but no one from the NRC attended).

"I heard the comment that the agencies were intrigued," said Frank Dukepoo of Northern Arizona University. "I hope they are a little bit more than intrigued. I hope they are moved by what happened here, what they see."

Dukepoo couldn't stop himself. As the only geneticist in America of Indian ancestry—his background was Hopi and Laguna—he felt duty-bound to prick the cerebral detachment that ballooned through the room. "What will the agencies do?" he burst out. "Will they fight over their jurisdictions? Who has priority in this area, that area? What message do we take to the Indians who, after all, are the research subjects in this grand study we are about to embark on. History will record what we do. What will we do? Will we use our education, our expertise, and knowledge for the position and prestige that we may become another Indian expert?

"You talk about chromosomal abnormalities, sperm analyses, and the like, as priorities. And I can appreciate that, being a geneticist. On the other hand, I think one of our main priorities would be to inform the tribes of the issue at hand."[28]

Herbert Abrams, of the Arizona Center for Occupational Safety and Health, felt compelled to step in. He agreed: "There is a problem in the sense that there is excessive radiation in the area. We don't need to know any more about the harmfulness of radiation. We have no evidence that it does anybody any good. We have a lot of evidence it does harm . . . Think of each of us living in a house where there's excessive radiation coming out of the walls. We sleep there, we spend most of the hours of our life in that house. It's not doing us any good . . . It may be doing harm, even if we can't prove it today.

"Something ought to be done," he concluded.[29]

Richard M. Auld arrived on the reservation in 1982, fresh from his residency in internal medicine at University of California–San Diego. He was posted to the Indian Health Service clinic in Shiprock at the edge of the northeast uranium belt. He had heard nothing from his colleagues about the recent "birth effects" conference.

Over the next two years, he treated six cases of stomach cancer. Two of the patients were women, eighteen and twenty years old. Rick Auld thought this highly unusual, not least because the incidence of this particular type of cancer among Navajos had historically been 10 percent of the U.S. average.[30] He returned to the San Diego area, this time on a two-year fellowship in gastroenterology at the Scripps Clinic and Research Foundation in La Jolla, to search for an explanation. He teamed up with William S. Haubrich, a prominent gastrointestinal specialist.

Their review of IHS medical charts showed that stomach cancer on the reservation had increased sharply in 1975—indeed, 82 percent of the cases had occurred since then.[31] This suggested, given cancer's latency period, that something had changed during the 1950s or '60s. The increase kept up through the mid-1980s.

Patients typically died within five months of their diagnosis. The doctors' research ruled out hereditary factors, medications, alcohol, and smoking as possible causes. In a conversation with a doctor at the New Mexico Tumor Registry, Auld mused aloud: "I should probably try to look at a toxin." The reply came instantly: "You should look at uranium."[32]

Auld plotted the locations of stomach cancer cases on a map. They clustered strikingly around the sites of uranium mines and mills. He and Haubrich discovered that incidence of gastric cancer was fifteen times the national average in some areas near uranium deposits and mills.

And the disease was not limited to former miners. In two western parts of the reservation filled with old pit mines, stomach cancers were developing in women ages twenty to forty at two hundred times the U.S. average.

As Auld pored over medical charts in California, a National Park Service ranger named Steve Cinnamon was jockeying for a promotion near the Navajo community of Cameron, in Arizona. To get one, he needed to demonstrate his ability to sample and test water. Though he wasn't aware of it, he was based near a section of the reservation where stomach cancer was on the rise. He approached an acquaintance, Donald Payne, who was an environmental health officer for the Indian Health Service, to ask for help with his technique.[33]

Payne agreed, so the two men set out to practice by sampling forty-eight wells and livestock watering holes in the area. What they found appalled them. The EPA had not determined the maximum safe level for uranium in drinking water (in 2000, this would be set at 30 picocuries per liter), but it was clear that Cameron's water supply contained huge amounts—as much as 139 picocuries per liter in wells and up to 4,024 picocuries per liter in the lakes that had formed in abandoned pits. The water in many of the pits also had high concentrations of the uranium by-product radium-226.[34]

Despite Payne's job with the IHS, he had never seen the pits before. He was amazed by the sheer size of the things. In a report to the tribal government, he wrote that "the Indian Health Service, as the primary public health providers for the Navajo people" should "make every effort" to warn residents not to drink from the shallow wells or let their livestock drink from the pits. The tribe, Payne wrote, "must mount a concerted program to restrict access of livestock to the heavily contaminated pits and impoundments."[35]

Steve Cinnamon and Don Payne were sampling in the very plain where Lois Neztsosie had heralded the coming of the "lakes." Unknown to them, uranium was also weighing on the mind of a neurologist down in Albuquerque who was examining dozens of children who seemed to have the same syndrome that afflicted the two youngest Neztsosie girls. It had a name by now: Navajo neuropathy.

Navajo neuropathy patients had liver damage, dimmed vision, and most dramatically, fingers and toes that gradually fused and stiffened into hooks. They tended to die young. The average age of death was ten.[36]

In the spring of 1978, the neurologist Russell Snyder had a chat with Helen Nez, the mother of a two-year-old in serious decline, a little girl named Euphemia. He asked the mother where she lived and she told him: near a uranium mine, an abandoned pit, not in Cameron, but in the center of the reservation by a hill called Tah-chee. Snyder warned her, belatedly, that uranium was dangerous.[37]

Two years later, the IHS sent Laura and Arlinda Neztsosie for an examination by Russell Snyder. Laura was ten; Linnie, nine. In a letter to their reservation doctor, Snyder considered whether "heavy metal intoxication" was the cause of their problems. But he concluded that "by far the most likely possibility is a hereditary" disorder.[38]

By the mid-1980s, the toes and fingers of both girls had frozen into Navajo neuropathy's hallmark claws. The older Neztsosie children chopped wood for the fire and cleaned the house when they were home from boarding school, but the two youngest felt left out. They couldn't help at all. They couldn't even walk. They could only crawl around on the sandy floor.

Indian trader Harry Goulding shows a Navajo uranium prospector how to use a Geiger counter. *Photo courtesy of Popular Mechanics.*

Cold War legacy

The Navajo reservation contains some of the world's richest uranium deposits. From 1944 to 1986, nearly 4 million tons of uranium ore were mined to supply material for nuclear weapons and fuel for reactors. Today, more than 1,000 abandoned mines dot the 27,000-square-mile reservation. Shown are mine locations identified to date by the Environmental Protection Agency:

● Abandoned uranium mine   ☐ Reservation boundary   ▨ EPA study areas

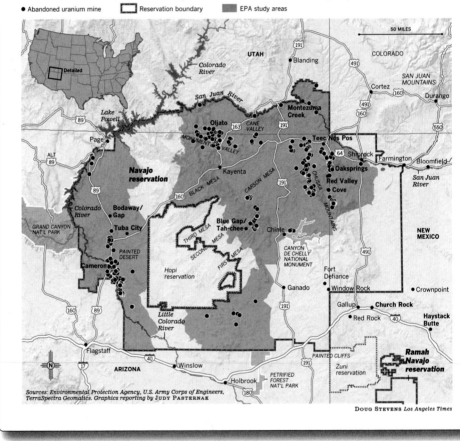

Sources: *Environmental Protection Agency, U.S. Army Corps of Engineers, TerraSpectra Geomatics.* Graphics reporting by JUDY PASTERNAK

DOUG STEVENS *Los Angeles Times*

Abandoned uranium mines identified by the EPA as of 2006 in the land between the Navajos' four sacred peaks. *Map by Doug Stevens/Los Angeles Times.*

From left, Mary Elizabeth Edwards,
Luke Yazzie, Adakai, and Denny Viles,
at Monument No. 2 in August 1943.
Photo by Page Edwards/Courtesy of the
Palace of the Governors (MNM/DCA),
Negative No. #HP_2006_19_a.

Denny Viles with Navajo miners at Monument No. 2.
Photo courtesy of Fort Lewis College, Center of Southwest Studies.

Massive buttes and rock spires in the Navajo desert—sacred landmarks to their neighbors, icons of the American West to filmgoers around the world. *Photo by Gail Fisher/Los Angeles Times.*

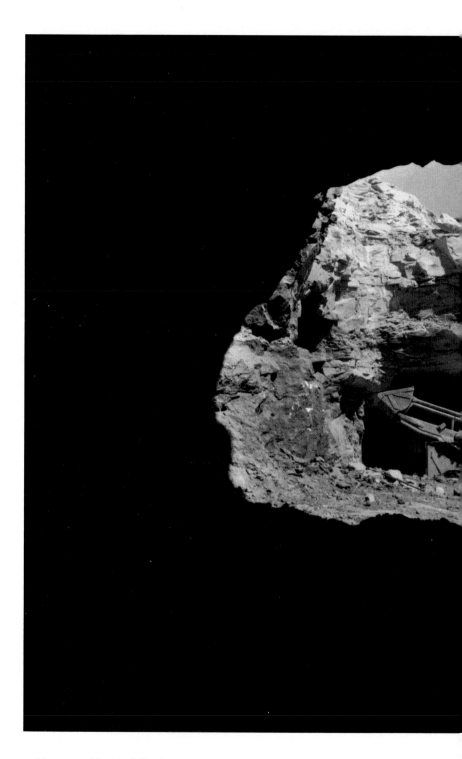

Monument No. 2 in full swing. *Photo courtesy of Fort Lewis College, Center of Southwest Studies.*

Atomic Energy Commission car stuck in the sand during the difficult travels of medical teams examining Navajo miners in the 1950s. *Photo courtesy of the U.S. National Library of Medicine.*

A Public Health Service team setting off to conduct physical exams of workers at the uranium mines. *Photo courtesy of the U.S. National Library of Medicine.*

Juanita Jackson, granddaughter of Adakai.
Photo by Lorissa Jackson.

The cozy house that Juanita Jackson's family built, using plenty of uranium, to lure her back to live in Cane Valley.
Photo by Judy Pasternak.

One pillar of ore that the miners left in place as they blasted down from the surface, a measure of the maiming of the mesa that still stands there today. *Photo by Gail Fisher/Los Angeles Times.*

Luke Yazzie, about fifty years after he disobeyed his father and set off the uranium mining boom in Cane Valley. *Photo by Murrae Haynes/Courtesy of the Palace of Governors (MNM/DCA), Negative No. HP_2006_19_b.*

Laura Neztsosie examines her checkbook, finding a way to hold the pages open despite her fused and stiffened fingers, a hallmark of Navajo neuropathy.
Photo by Gail Fisher/Los Angeles Times.

When the Vanadium Corp. of America abandoned the Cane Valley mine, the mining men abandoned their cars. *Photo by Gail Fisher/Los Angeles Times.*

The "Hear Our Voices" crew at work.
Photo courtesy of Monument Valley High School.

Digging a grave in 2005 for a former uranium miner with lung disease who had put his thumbprint on a government compensation acceptance letter just the week before. *Photo by Gail Fisher/Los Angeles Times.*

Lois Neztsosie quenching her thirst at a natural spring in the twenty-first century, just as she did from the pit mine "lakes" in the 1960s. *Photo by Gail Fisher/Los Angeles Times.*

Laura Neztsosie being pushed in her deceased sister's wheelchair by a relative. *Photo by Gail Fisher/Los Angeles Times.*

Mary Holiday shoveling the dirt where her contaminated *hooghan* once stood. *Photo by Gail Fisher/Los Angeles Times.*

Elsie Begay near an earthen *hooghan* she occupied after moving out of the original dwelling in her aunt Mary Holiday's compound. *Photo by Gail Fisher/Los Angeles Times.*

Lorissa Jackson by the side of the road to Cane Valley, with the back door to Monument Valley in the background. *Photo by Judy Pasternak.*

The EPA wrecking crew taking down the Cane Valley home of
Anna Adakai Cly in 2008. *Photo by Judy Pasternak.*

Ben Stanley outside the new house being built for him
by the U.S. government. *Photo by Judy Pasternak.*

Chapter 11

A Blind Eye and a Deaf Ear

As the latest round of unsettling reports from Navajo country filtered up higher, to rarer altitudes within the federal bureaucracy, the reaction was . . . nothing, really. Despite the fact that environmental consciousness was rising around the country, the disquieting news out of the Navajos' land was shrugged off, pushed aside. The drinking-water education program that Don Payne had urged never materialized.[1] Clippings from a physicians' newsletter about Rick Auld's stomach cancer study stayed in a folder belonging to the chief medical officer in the Navajo regional office of the Indian Health Service, and that was that.[2] A few years after government agencies listened to the passionate conversation at the University of New Mexico's "birth effects" conference, Ronald Reagan's Secretary of Health and Human Services (the department overseeing the IHS) assured Congress that there was no evidence that any new studies on the impact of uranium were necessary.[3] Likewise, Congress had finally passed a bill to deal with the mill tailings, but the funding schedule kept slipping; the Navajo piles were their lowest priority because so few people lived nearby. The frantic energy of the uranium rush, when red tape was easily ignored or sliced away and money was no object, had long since dissipated.

It was not only the emerging information about illness and exposure in the wider population that was ignored. Even the uranium miners often found their troubles dismissed by blasé bureaucrats, although by this time there was no disputing that their jobs, and their service to the country, had given them lung cancers. When an IHS lung specialist based in Shiprock asked for $125,000 for a mobile cancer clinic to visit the rising number of old miners coming down with the disease, the request made its way to headquarters, crossing the desk of the deputy director of the health service. The response was the written equivalent of a sneer: Go ask the mining companies for the money.[4] Needless to say, the project was stillborn. Wheezing and wracked by painful coughs that sometimes brought up blood, the ailing uranium veterans were forced to travel regularly for hours on end, across the reservation's rutted roads for check-ups at scattered IHS facilities and into the outer world for treatment at hospitals in Farmington or Flagstaff, even Phoenix and Albuquerque. They had trucks instead of Adakai's wagon and horses, but they were no more comfortable. Without those mining paychecks, the reservation's fleet of vehicles was not getting replaced and the desert was tough on aging shocks and tires.

Officialdom's prevailing attitude to the problem was summed up in a five-page memo that ticked off instances of neglect in a neat list, extraordinary for its equanimity. The writer was Charles Reaux, the chief industrial hygienist in the regional office of the IHS. He was attempting to get a handle on the whole uranium situation:

"Environmental radiation induced potential health hazards on the Navajo Reservation are from three main sources: (a) abandoned uranium mill tailings, (b) abandoned uranium mines and (c) radon daughters in homes. . . . An organized systematic research effort to define the radiation health effects on the Navajo Reservation has never been attempted."[5]

In assessing the various old mining areas around the reservation, Reaux noted that Red Valley and Monument Valley–Oljato "have airborne plus water exposure." Thus he matter-of-factly summed up the poisoned world where Clifford Frank and Mae John were living, and the tainted ground flanking Goulding's trading post: Oljato, to the west where the Holidays were raising their five children and by this time also sheltering a divorced niece's family, and Cane Valley to the east, the land of Adakai.

Reaux's recommendation, dated December 15, 1986, and addressed to his superiors in the Navajo Area Office, was equally bloodless: fixing the problem, even defining its scope, was too expensive to take on.

"The true risk assessment of the radiation problems may never be performed due to the vast cost of such appraisals," Reaux explained. The IHS, indisputably underfunded, "may be better off not to enter into an aggressive radiation health program," he wrote.

In other words: we'll never know for sure, and that may be easier for us.

As for studies of potential exposure risks, "the manpower requirements are beyond current ... means." And "radon in homes is another significant but resource consuming endeavor." He suggested keeping abreast of whatever the tribe was doing (that effort, of course, consisted mostly of Harold Tso seeking federal funds in vain).

In other words: Don't make a stink. Don't ask for money. Just stay out of it.

The Indian Health Service took his advice.

The IHS was far from the only agency to back away from the slow-motion disaster that was clearly unfolding in Navajoland. The *Navajo Times,* the reservation newspaper, had picked up the story of the Oaksprings houses in Red Valley. After this news got around, ten more chapters of tribal government asked for inspections of houses for signs of uranium contamination. The tribe didn't have the money to do them all. The few they were able to test showed more troubling results, so Harold Tso appealed to the Bureau of Indian Affairs and to the Department of Housing and Urban Development. He was certain that wherever there was a mine, there must be at least one or two houses with uranium inside. He wasn't sure how many of those might be dangerous. He wasn't even sure how many mines had existed; no one knew all the locations. His pleas for federal help were met with a resounding silence. He let the matter drop.

On another front, he didn't even try for aid. One spring day in 1981, two of Tso's staffers stopped by his office in Window Rock to alert him to yet another uranium-related problem.[6] They showed him some photographs they had snapped of the Cameron pits—Lois Neztsosie's lakes. "Water is collecting," they told him. Taking a cue from the way Joe Hans was attempting to take care of the uranium houses way out in Cane Valley, they suggested that Tso ask the Department of Energy to fill in the old pits when—if—DOE finally came through to cover the huge mill-waste piles. "We can't do that," Tso told the pair. "It doesn't qualify as mill tailings. It will have to go under the mines. The timing is wrong." The DOE was slow, but no one had actually agreed to accept responsibility for repairing the damage caused by the mining. The AEC's postwar decision to regulate mills but not the mines reverberated still.

Tso meant to head north and west from the capital at Window Rock to the Cameron plains to see the pits for himself. But he never got around to it.[7] He had a disaster on his hands far to the south and east, over in the Church Rock chapter.

The trouble at Church Rock, ironically, had taken root as the mining wound down in the rest of the reservation and, even more ironically, was the direct result of the new caution about tailings piles. Though the demand for the makings of atomic bombs had withered, after 1971 uranium could be sold on the private market. Mining companies didn't think it was worth the expense to keep working in the most remote quarters of the *Dinétah* without the government's price guarantee. But Church Rock was practically a suburb of Gallup, New Mexico, and nuclear power seemed poised to become the energy source of the future. The splitting of atoms could heat water, just as the burning of coal, oil, or gas could, and the steam could turn turbines and generate electricity. Twenty-two commercial nuclear power plants were operating in the U.S. by 1971, and two years later, utilities placed orders for forty-one more reactors, a one-year record.[8]

Sprinting like one of the desert coyotes to get in on this peacetime market was United Nuclear, a subsidiary of the venerable Union Carbide—just as Union Mines, the Manhattan Project's front group, and U.S. Vanadium, VCA's big rival, had been. The company paved a dirt road leading to a uranium-filled ridge in Church Rock, near a valley known

as Red Water Pond for the color of the small local lake whenever summer monsoons stirred up the thick clay soil. United Nuclear also ran
power lines to the top of the ridge (the Navajo neighbors, of course, got
no share of this electricity). Soon, four- and five-car ore trains rattled
underground. Buckets lifted up the ore and loaded it directly onto dump
trucks.

The trucks trundled the market-grade ore straightaway to United
Nuclear's mill, which lay just outside the reservation's eastern boundary
and was visible from the ridge. With Congress up in arms about tailings
piles, United Nuclear had hit on a solution—and it was, quite literally,
a solution: just add water. The mill waste was liquefied and stored in a
large pond—no muss, no dust, no potential as construction material. A
large earthen dam, said by the company to be state-of-the-art, held the
wastewater out of a dry gulch nearby. The arroyo led to the Rio Puerco, an
intermittent stream that marked the southern border of the Navajo Nation, as the San Juan did in the north.

About 5:30 a.m., on July 16, 1979, the Navajos of the Church Rock
chapter woke to the sound of running water, lots of it. They wondered
where it had rained to the north to cause this flash flood in the Puerco.[9]
But the torrents had nothing to do with rain. A twenty-foot breach had
opened overnight in the United Nuclear dam.[10] Some 93 million gallons
of radioactive liquid poured from the pond into the arroyo, and from the
arroyo into the riverbed. The water, filled with acids from the milling process, twisted a metal culvert in the Puerco and burned the feet of a little
boy who went wading. Sheep keeled over and died, and crops curdled
along the banks. The surge of radiation was detected as far away as Sand-
ers, Arizona, fifty miles downstream.

The IHS and the state urged Navajos not to drink the water nor enter
it, nor let their animals do so, anywhere downstream from the spill. But
the people by the Puerco didn't have many alternatives. United Nuclear
distributed six hundred gallon-bottles of clean water, but the Church
Rock chapter calculated that more than thirty thousand gallons a day
were needed.[11] The three community wells serving Church Rock, regulated by the IHS, were useless. One, at the Church Rock School, had already been closed, having been flagged just the previous month for high

levels of radium and alpha particles. The two others contained water with high iron and bacteria levels.[12] Then there were five shallow wells along the river owned and maintained by the tribe, marked by metal windmills that turned to bring the water up. These were in various states of disrepair and perhaps at risk. IHS asked the tribe to fix them and advised residents that these "are not expected to show any contamination, if at all, for several years."[13]

When it was all over—after the company was pressured to increase its water deliveries and build some livestock watering tanks—Harold Tso visited the Puerco and noticed many white crystals with a yellowish tinge along the bottom of the drying wash. These salts were new; they had never shown up after past flooding. Tso felt sure they were not a natural phenomenon. "It's okay if this stays in the bottom of the river," he thought. "It's not okay if it gets in the water."[14]

The Church Rock spill was the largest accidental release of radioactive material in U.S. history, larger even than the much more famous near-meltdown the following month at the Three Mile Island nuclear generator in Pennsylvania.

After the Superfund was created for EPA in 1980, the off-reservation United Nuclear mill went on the list to be cleaned up, but the Rio Puerco did not. The Superfund law demanded that EPA try first to fix responsibility for the hazard, so that companies could be sued for clean-up money. If the responsible parties, as the jargon put it, had gone out of business, EPA would pay for the environmental repairs out of its $1.6 billion trust. In the case of the Puerco, though, EPA found it impossible to find someone to blame for the conditions. EPA's consultants explained that no baseline testing of the river had ever been conducted, so there was no way to separate natural radiation and heavy metals from contamination by the spill, or for that matter, from the nearby uranium mines, which had been pouring water pumped from the tunnels into the river for years.

The state of New Mexico decided to find out if the local food was at least fit to eat, and conducted a study of Church Rock cattle with the help of the IHS. By the time Charles Reaux was writing his memo, the study's conclusions, and his interpretation of them, demonstrated anew the authorities' ignorance of the way Navajos live.

Reaux reported that the study "proved that health effects on humans eating animals grazing near/on the Rio Puerco/Church Rock area was not significant." But the researchers found markedly higher levels of radio-nuclides in cattle there compared to livestock grazing in nonmining areas. Their advice was that eating the meat would not pose a problem *as long as the people there didn't depend on the butchered animals for their everyday food over a long period of time.* That, of course, is exactly what the Navajos did depend on. When they butchered an animal, they ate each one down to the bones, which they sucked around the fire.

A few Navajo children were sent to the Los Alamos lab to be checked for radiation exposure, and some of the grownups went to the Indian hospital at Gallup, where they were assured their health would be watched closely in the future.[15] But there is no evidence that any long-term moni-toring took place, and health effects, of course, were not likely to show up right away. A local writer would later observe that the IHS expended more effort on finding out what happened to the livestock than on find-ing out what happened to the people.[16]

Back on the reservation, the mine stayed open for another two years. When it shut down, it was not a casualty of the spill but of the turn away from nuclear power in the wake of Three Mile Island. In the new, envi-ronmentally correct era, the company sealed the shafts over with cement. But United Nuclear left cables and equipment. And one more thing: a hill. The furor over tailings, and the switch to liquid storage, had not pre-vented United Nuclear from dumping the ore that didn't meet standards for sale. The trucks dropped loads of subpar rock right over the edge of the cliff, until the waste rose thirty feet high, as tall and as long as the ridge. After United Nuclear went away, sheep still climbed over the grit and dynamited chips as they searched for food. The winds roared off the ridge for hours at a time, raining dust from the huge pile over more than a dozen houses in Red Water Pond, the community right below.

In his inventory of risks, Charles Reaux made no mention of this.

The tribe decided to try a more aggressive tack to get the government's attention. The Navajo leaders had long recognized that their natural resources had been making companies rich for many years, and that those companies had paid royalties to the Bureau of Indian Affairs on their behalf. Why then was the tribe so poor? The Navajos had already gone to federal claims court, set up to deal with just such questions, and demanded an accounting of money due them for oil, coal, timber, gravel, and, not incidentally, the uranium secretly diverted from vanadium in the old Manhattan Project days.

In 1982, with the dimensions of their uranium problem beginning to dawn on them, the tribal leaders added a new demand to their lawsuit: $6.7 million to seal and clean about three hundred mines. The United States had come down on the wrong side of a conflict of interest during the Cold War, the tribe argued. On the one hand, America had a duty under the Treaty of 1868 to protect the Navajos. On the other was the desire to control the expense of making atomic bombs. The Navajos accused federal inspectors of failing to enforce safety and environmental standards in order to keep uranium prices low.

Tso gave an eloquent deposition. "Should the government shirk its obligations, it will be writing off the value of present and future Navajo generations," he testified.[17] No one called Howard Nickelson, who had been so concerned about the companies' profit, or any of the other inspectors for testimony, and in 1985 the judge rejected the claim, calling the allegations "entirely speculative."

That same year, Tso quit his job with the Navajo government and moved to Albuquerque.

Tribal leaders considered suing the mining companies, but a legal consultant reluctantly advised against it.[18] He found it hard to believe what had happened, but the firms had operated and departed with government approval. Blame was a circle game, and the tribe just couldn't win.

Stewart Udall was learning the same tough lesson. The crew cut of his Camelot days had been replaced by a shaggy mane with streaks of white, but he still had a hawk nose, thick dark eyebrows, and a supremely confident air. He was representing three different sets of radiation clients in separate cases—downwinders exposed to fallout from atomic testing, white widows of miners who had worked in VCA's Marysvale mine in Utah, and the Navajos whom Harry Tome had brought to his attention.

His research quickly led to bouts of fury. "How easy it was for the AEC to cow others in the government," he wrote in his journal. "49 out of 50 MD's are gutless. . . . They don't like to make waves, that is clear. It is also clear that public health MD's are all milquetoasts." [19]

Then he found Duncan Holaday, retired and living quietly in the small town of Patterson, north of New York City in the Harlem River valley. A few weeks after a preliminary phone conversation, the high-powered lawyer paid a visit. If Holaday had once had "milquetoast" tendencies, he shed them completely in Udall's company. Guilt-stricken and angry, he talked for hours, offering up important documents and pointing to a parade of witnesses that promised plenty of headlines. [20]

Udall was many steps removed from Holaday's experience, but he knew he'd face questions about his own role in the treatment of the miners. As a congressman, he'd considered himself a friend of the Navajos and an ardent environmentalist. He'd served as secretary of the interior, overseeing both the BIA and the Bureau of Mines. Why hadn't he found out earlier what was going on and done something about it? He told anybody who asked (and people did ask), "Because of the Cold War, we believed what we were told." [21]

Now he was coming face-to-face with the human toll; the price paid by American citizens for the policies of the government of which he'd been a part. One Navajo plaintiff in particular stuck in his mind. Betty Jo Yazzie had lost her husband to bladder cancer in 1962. Fifteen years' work in the uranium mines had hardly left Kee Yazzie rich. His estate, in its entirety, consisted of a belt, a bracelet, and some beads. Betty Jo scavenged for firewood to keep herself and seven children warm.

In 1969, she remarried, to another veteran of the mines. Three years later, her second husband died. Now she was a bladder cancer widow and a lung cancer widow, too. [22]

Driven by her story, and dozens more in the same vein, Udall made the case a family crusade. His daughter Lori moved to the Navajo reservation for a year. His son Tom, a lawyer, assisted with depositions. When Udall moved to Santa Fe, his son Jay, a poet, moved there, too, to help out.

Udall's wife, Lee, took charge of the books and raising money, since the clients had none and the tribal government rejected entreaties for donations. She persuaded a well-known Navajo artist, R. C. Gorman, to contribute one of his paintings to the cause. The $25,000 it fetched at auction financed travel for the witnesses.[23]

At long last, Udall brought the story of Betty Jo Yazzie and "Check" and more than eighty more widows and dying miners to a federal courtroom in Phoenix. The judge whittled the plaintiffs' list down to eleven, to make the case more manageable, but even so the trial took a three-week chunk out of the summer of 1983.[24]

Udall believed his evidence was devastating. He put Ralph Batie and Duncan Holaday and some of their colleagues on the stand. In addition, Udall's lead medical expert had impeccable credentials. He founded the biomedical division at Lawrence Livermore National Laboratory; he had analyzed data from Japanese A-bomb survivors and had also studied the health impacts of low-level ionizing radiation.

The expert's calculations led to a stunning conclusion: The Navajo uranium miners averaged cumulative exposures that were about forty-four times higher than the levels at Hiroshima and Nagasaki.[25]

Before an audience of mining company lawyers, supplemented by a handful of the plaintiffs and a couple of reporters, Udall hammered at the government's decision to study the miners without helping them. "It's like a physician at the scene of an auto accident: You don't just walk away from it," he told the judge.[26]

The Department of Energy attorney who led the defense hit back, pointing out that the federal government had shared information with the tribe all along (while ignoring how undermanned and outmatched tribal officials had been).[27]

The judge, William F. Copple, deliberated for a year. The mine radiation had caused the cancers, he concluded. "This tragedy of the Nuclear Age cries out for redress," he wrote in a fifty-three-page decision.[28]

Nonetheless, he was ruling against Udall and the Navajos. The U.S.

government could not be held liable for the dead and dying. Federal authorities had been within their rights to leave the question of mine safety to state and industry officials.

(The states were off the hook, because, as far as was known, none of the Navajos had filed for worker's compensation. Of course, they had not known that they were injured until long past the workers' comp deadlines. And a Udall case against the companies had been dismissed.)

Copple urged the Navajos to take their plight to Congress, right back where they had started.

In a spidery script, Duncan Holaday penned a short note of condolence to Udall: "Dear Stewart, I am profoundly disappointed by the decision in your case for the Navaho [*sic*] miners! National security did not enter into the AEC's decision at all—just a refusal to recognize a clear obligation." He also imparted some sad personal news. His wife, to whom he had been very close, had passed away just the month before. He was going to move. His house was just too empty. Watching her fade had been intolerable. He understood all too well now what the Navajo miners and their widows had endured, for lung cancer was the way that death had taken Mrs. Holaday.[29]

The Navajos appealed, of course, and hope flared for a moment when one of the three judges on the appeals panel in San Francisco interrupted a government lawyer in the middle of his argument that the United States had studied the miners in order to get the data they needed to establish a safe standard for radon in the mines. "I wouldn't dwell on that, counsel, you were using them as guinea pigs," snapped the judge. "We've won," whispered Udall's son, Tom, who was by this time New Mexico's attorney general. But the unanimous opinion of the panel mirrored Copple's and the Supreme Court declined to hear the case.

Udall dispatched a young Navajo lawyer who had assisted him out to Red Valley to explain to their clients that this was the end. He didn't go himself. He found that he couldn't. He felt humiliated. He had urged the Navajos to be patient and have faith, and he simply didn't know how to explain to them the concepts that had led to this outcome.[30]

This much was clear: Breathing in radon and its daughters was the way to get lung cancer. Rick Auld suspected that the stomach cancers he had found were caused by drinking contaminated water. Signs that other types of cancer could be caused by long-term exposure to *leetso* continued to appear. By the mid-1980s, a group of pathologists from Utah and Colorado had examined the tissues and bones of uranium miners and millers to follow the alpha-emitting variations of uranium and thorium. They found concentrations not just in the lung, but also in the liver, kidney, spleen, gonad, and heart. They also found the isotopes in ribs and vertebrae and sternum. The accumulations varied dramatically, from tissue to tissue, from bone to bone, and among the dead men.[31] Perhaps these distributions accounted for the disturbing findings in a review of 259 dead miners: As expected, lung cancer rates were fifty-six times as high as the general population's and stomach cancer, too, fit the pattern that Auld had discovered, at eighty-two times the rate for males fifty-five to seventy-nine years of age. But there was more: the mortality rates among these miners for cancers of the prostate were 45 times higher, of the pancreas seventy-eight times higher, of the liver 263 times higher and of the bladder, 68 times higher.[32] In addition to these, the New Mexico Tumor Registry expressed concern over possible associations of mining with pituitary and kidney cancers.[33]

Noncancerous, but nonetheless serious, health impacts were also a concern. The PHS linked high radon levels in the mines to an increased risk of lung diseases: tuberculosis, fibrosis, silicosis. Uranium was known, too, to damage kidneys, because of its chemistry as a heavy metal rather than its radiation. The March of Dimes funded a study of birth defects in the Shiprock area and found that the increase had a statistically significant association with the mother living near a uranium mine or mill.[34] But the author urged caution, because of the small numbers involved, and the need for more study.

When it came to Navajo neuropathy, the syndrome of hooked fingers and toes, with damaged eyes and livers, certain questions were never even asked. An IHS epidemiologist named Steve Helgerson led a team that concluded in 1990 that "no common environmental factors (i.e., water source, heavy metal exposure, toxin exposure, family occupation) have been discovered "among the afflicted children.[35]

There were certainly good reasons to theorize that the syndrome was hereditary. Multiple cases existed within families. The first Navajo neuropathy patient appeared in 1959. This was about the same time that mines were being abandoned, but the onset out of the blue also fit the pattern of a disease caused by the "founder effect." A "founder effect" begins with one person who develops a mutation in a recessive gene. When that person has children, the other parent's dominant gene suppresses the mutation. But the change is quietly passed along, from one generation to the next. The trait does not surface unless two descendants of the founder have children together, each contributing a recessive gene—usually generations later, among distant relatives.

But in giving short shrift to an environmental role, the IHS researchers did not fully explore the possible role of uranium mining. They ruled out a water source as the cause of the illness because no single well supplied all of the affected families—but they did not consider whether various water sources shared common contaminants. Patients were screened for exposure to various heavy metals, but not for uranium—which is not part of the standard panel for such screenings. The scientists rejected "toxin exposure" as a possible cause because they were thinking of pesticides, and nobody much used pesticides on the reservation.

Uranium did come up in regard to "family occupation." One of the researchers wondered whether all of the fathers had been miners and if so, whether their exposure might have affected their genes. That possibility was discarded because most of the mining had been done in the eastern part of the reservation, while Navajo neuropathy cases were five times more common in the west. It didn't occur to anybody that most of the mines in the east were tunnels, while those in the west were mostly open pits. Helgerson didn't know about the "lakes." He hadn't heard about Don Payne's water sampling or the frightening results.

The group noted the "familial pattern" among patients and concluded the most likely cause was "an inborn error" of metabolism. Because resources were scarce—that money problem, again—Helgerson counseled focusing all future research on genetics.[36]

Six years after Congress passed the Uranium Mine Tailings Remedial Action law, the Department of Energy finally began work on the Navajo tailings piles, tackling what Tso considered to be the worst environmental problem on the reservation. The last site that the DOE got to in *Diné bikeyah* was the one in Cane Valley. The soil underneath was so sandy and unstable that DOE geologists feared that it might not support the cap.[37] So they decided to truck Cane Valley's small mountains seventeen miles away to Mexican Hat, where they would be combined with the waste at that old millsite and sealed off. This was the only case on Navajo land where the department elected to remove the tailings, rather than cover them in place.

The DOE supervisor for the project was warned that medicine men in Mexican Hat had put a curse on his endeavor. They had had enough of white man's meddling. So he got innovative and fought back by their rules, hiring his own medicine man to bless the Cane Valley removal. The locals recommended Roger Hathale, who lived at the very top of Comb Ridge, in a small house with spectacular views: on one side Cane Valley, with a green film of vegetation floating over acres of red-tinted land, and on the other, Dennehotso and the world beyond, stretching into the blue. Hathale regularly traveled down the ridge's western slope, into Cane Valley, to haul water home. He patronized the same well that Lorissa Jackson and her cousins visited to fill their families' barrels, the old pump where they shrieked with laughter during their shower sessions.[38]

The medicine man had two things in common with their great-grandfather, Adakai: a penchant for clashing plaids, and an abiding belief that uranium mining had been responsible for letting a captive poison escape, allowing it to decimate their world. Before accepting $500 for the ceremony over the tailings, he carefully considered whether it made sense to further disrupt the mesa and Mother Earth. But he decided that getting the pile out of Cane Valley was a good idea.[39]

What followed must have been quite a sight. Energy Department officials from Washington and executives from the companies that had contracted for the job converged on Cane Valley for Hathale's two-and-a-half-hour ceremony. The medicine man instructed his out-of-town visitors to strip off their shirts and salt themselves with corn pollen. He had them down on their hands and knees, contemplating harmony and balance and renewal.[40]

Yet once the massive moving job began in May of 1989, the agency neglected some crucial details. First, there was the matter of the soil underneath the big Cane Valley heaps: Over the decades, the rain drove radiation and heavy metals from the tailings into the ground. The contractor scraped off the surface, but did not scoop out the dirt underneath and the toxics remaining there continued to make their way into the groundwater farther below.

Even more incredibly, the Navajo crews who were hired were not required to wear protection—despite the fact that the reason they were hauling the tailings away was their power to inflict harm on The People, despite the fact that the very first action taken with regard to tailings had been Joe Hans's halting of the tribe's heavy-equipment training at the Shiprock mill. Funding, and thus the work, stopped in February of 1990 and didn't resume for nearly two years. But by May of 1994, the crews had transported 1.3 million tons of contaminated material out of Cane Valley to Mexican Hat.[41] The truck drivers kept their windows up most of the time, but the dust came in the vents. Sometimes, the trucks got stuck in the sandy piles and the drivers stood waiting outside in the wind, coated by a blizzard of tailings, while bulldozers with chains slowly pulled their vehicles free.[42]

A small portion of their cargo was debris from three Cane Valley buildings and one haul road, repaired at last by the DOE after fifteen years of entreaties from Joe Hans, and twenty-five years of human occupation. The agency had agreed to fix so-called "vicinity properties" that had been provably polluted by the mills, whether from tailings blown onto the ground or from tailings mixed into a structure.[43] Cane Valley posed the toughest dilemma for subcontractors assigned to sift the eligible areas from those for which they had no authority. The presence of the mine complicated things. As Harold Tso had told his staffers about the mining-pits-turned-lakes, DOE wasn't about to push the bounds of the authority it had been given by Congress. Piping from the mill, or old lumber . . . that could be cleaned up. But the same material from a mine, or *leetso* ore in a house, was none of DOE's concern.[44]

There was enough reasonable doubt for six of the homes from Hans's list that DOE balked at fixing them. The agency sent letters explaining in complicated bureaucratic English the thin slices that DOE had cut as it narrowly interpreted its mandate. "Evaluation of your property identified above has not revealed the presence of residual radioactive material, from one of these sites, in excess of standards established by the Environmental Protection Agency," the documents said.[45] *From one of these sites* was the key phrase; it referred to the various abandoned uranium mills. This did not mean there was nothing to worry about. The letters went to Window Rock because, technically, the people of Cane Valley were all tenants of the Navajo Nation; they could not own land. If the residents received their own copies, it wouldn't have done much good. They couldn't even read English, let alone decode the wording that intimated their houses were safe without really saying so.

One of these letters referred to Vicinity Property MV013, the home of Juanita Jackson. Lorissa didn't see it or hear about it. She had been away at school when Joe Hans paid his visit. She had noticed small flat canisters in the house one summer—the DOE contractors put them there to measure radon—but had been too busy being a teenager to pay much attention. And she'd been busy being an adult ever since, pairing up at nineteen with a former Marine and bearing a daughter and two sons.

Eventually, she continued her education while her husband worked construction or, whenever he was laid off, watched the kids. In 1989, four years after the DOE sent its convoluted messages, Lorissa earned a degree at last. She was the first in her family to graduate from college. A convoy of relatives traveled to Cedar City, Utah, to watch her, gowned and robed, take a diploma in hand from Southern Utah University. Somewhere along the line, an advisor had suggested that she major in education, and she found when she took a few courses that she really liked it. Despite her pronouncements to her Oregon classmates, Lorissa was going to be a teacher. Juanita couldn't stop beaming.

Part IV

THE GREAT-GRANDCHILDREN

Death and Awakening

Chapter 12

"Hear Our Voices"

Juanita Jackson, like many Navajos, fiercely guarded her privacy. She never complained and she never talked about aches or pains. Better not to tempt the fates. But about six years after the Department of Energy declined to repair the house, she made an extraordinary revelation to Lorissa. Her daughter had come to visit from her first teaching job at White Horse High School in the Utah town of Montezuma Creek.

Juanita mentioned, offhandedly, that there was a bump on her neck. Doctors wanted to operate, to take a closer look.[1]

"What should I do?" she asked.

It started like that.

Lorissa made an appointment for Juanita at the Northern Navajo Medical Center, the IHS hospital in Shiprock, a three-hour drive to the south and east. Juanita had only been to a hospital to give birth, so Lorissa took her there. On the way, dread settled in. Lorissa knew enough to fear that this was cancer, but felt ill-informed about the disease and its treatment.

"Can this be controlled with a laser?" Juanita's modern daughter asked the doctor. "No, no, that's not an option," the physician replied.

Juanita's second visit to a hospital was for the biopsy. Yes, the cells were malignant. It had spread to the lymph node, the doctor said, but he wasn't sure where it had begun.

Adakai's granddaughter stopped spending her days at the loom and the cookstove, and spent them instead with the cold, sterile machines of the white man's impersonal medicine. She endured CAT scans, then radiation, then chemotherapy. Lorissa or one of her brothers accompanied her to Shiprock each time.

The incision from the biopsy kept oozing. Whoever had invented the Navajo word for cancer had gotten it just right: *Łood doo nádziihii*, "the sore that does not heal." The children had to clean their mother's wound. Some of them couldn't stomach the job and stayed away.

A day came when Juanita suddenly couldn't breathe. She sounded like she was drowning on air; she wheezed like an empty bellows. Lorissa happened to be there and drove her, fast, to the IHS emergency room at a clinic in Kayenta, about an hour away.

Juanita was transferred to a hospital off the reservation, in the border town of Farmington, New Mexico, yet another forty-five minutes east of Shiprock. The next time Lorissa saw her, she was getting oxygen from a tube and a tank. The cancer, it was now apparent, had started in her lungs and breast.

After this episode, Juanita stayed with her son Pete and his family in Kirtland, not far from Farmington. Her children wanted her to be close to the more up-to-date, mainstream hospital, even though it meant leaving the home in Cane Valley that Ben Stanley and her other relatives had built just for her.

Lorissa was training in the daytime as her school transitioned to a new system of teaching. In the evening, she would drive from Utah to New Mexico to see her mother. Juanita was restless, waking every four hours on the hour. She was hallucinating. She was fading.

Juanita, once so strong—she raised all those children, mostly as a single mom; she tackled all those chores—was all but helpless toward the end. Lorissa had been very young when her grandmother and her father died. This was her first close-up experience with a loved one's death. That last month was very hard.

Her brother Paul called Lorissa while she was in yet another meeting, "I think you better come," he said. She left immediately for Farmington. Her brothers and sisters had already gathered at Juanita's bedside by the time she arrived.

When Lorissa talked to her mother, Juanita's only response was to start breathing more deeply. After a while, Lorissa noticed that there was a longer and longer time between each breath. And then there were no more. It was July 24, 1992, just one day before her fifty-ninth birthday.

During the course of the illness that ravaged her, Juanita had made something clear. She did it in the Navajo way, an indirect comment here and there, all allusion. Lorissa and her siblings understood. They all knew that Juanita believed that somehow it was *łeetso* that killed her.

While Juanita Jackson slid away, other Navajos were also linking what had happened to the miners to what was happening to their families. Mae John, "Check," was one. She and the other Red Valley Navajos who had driven the Udall lawsuit finally found vindication when Pete Domenici, Jeff Bingaman, and Orrin Hatch—U.S. senators from New Mexico and Utah—added the uranium miners to their effort to win payments for "downwinders," their constituents who'd developed cancer after living near the A-bomb test sites.

The senators wrote into the introduction of their bill a muted acknowledgment of the pain the United States had inflicted upon all of the people affected by the nuclear-weapons process, at the beginning and the end of the chain. The Cold War that was at the root of that pain was by then winding down. Ordinary Germans wrenched apart the Berlin Wall. Polish shipbuilders ignited a rebellion that led to free elections. The mighty Soviet Union itself was spinning apart by the time a compensation measure finally passed into law in 1990. Called the Radiation Exposure and Compensation Act, it contained this clause: "The Congress apologizes on behalf of the Nation to the individuals described in subsection (e) and their families for the hardships they have endured."

It has to rank as one of the least gracious expressions of regret in history. And in the throes of victory, new suspicions were welling up inside Mae John. Because she had not owned a refrigerator while she was living near the mine where her husband worked, she had stored meat against the cool cavern walls. She ate that meat while pregnant. Did this explain her son's hip defect? She drank the cold mine water that her husband, Lee, brought home and after the mining stopped, she continued to get her water from a stream flowing down from the mountains that were filled with old uranium sites—the same creek where the women had gathered on Sundays to launder the yellow-stained clothes of their men. Did this explain her kidney disease? She had no way of knowing for sure, of course, but she was starting to suspect that Lee was not the only one in the family whose health had been wrecked by the uranium mines. There was no compensation for the others who had never worked in the mines, of course.

The Navajos reorganized their government into a three-branch system modeled after the Guardian's and elected their first president that same year. The voters chose continuity, installing the last tribal chairman as their new executive, and he shared Mae John's concerns. Peterson Zah, the former director of a legal services agency for the *Diné,* was intent on setting up a forceful system of agencies. His second priority was to get something done about those old uranium mines left out of the reclamation plans at the mills.[2] The sick miners were beginning the complex process of proving their eligibility for the new compensation program, which set $100,000 as the price of a miner's lungs. As they did so, Zah recruited Sadie Hoskie, a Navajo working in the Denver office of the U.S. EPA, as the inaugural head of the Navajo Nation EPA, the successor to Tso's old commission. It was too late to make the old mines safe for the men who had toiled there, but it was not too late to make them safe for the neighbors.

Hoskie took a leave of absence from her federal job, moved to the Navajo capital at Window Rock, and set her staff to analyzing the old mines, one by one, to see whether they could qualify for Superfund. Despite the fiasco over the Rio Puerco, Zah and Hoskie thought the Superfund law seemed tailor-made for the Navajo reservation. Superfund could force polluters to pay for much more than cleanup. It could fund health studies, clinics, maintenance, and monitoring, all sorely needed in the Home of the People.

Now, late in the twentieth century, two of Hoskie's staffers were driving near Haystack Mountain in the southeast, where the napping shepherd had woken to a great discovery some forty years before, when the radiation detector in their vehicle started beepbeepbeeping, even though the windows were closed. They discovered the source at two mining complexes nearby. It turned out that at least eighteen sheep had died mysteriously, after years of watering at an old abandoned pit, and of the 125 residents within a three-mile radius, at least five people developed stomach cancer, while another four had lung cancer.[3] The locals here had also built homes with ore and a family still lived in one of these.[4]

The Haystack mines were located in a complicated region. During the nineteenth century, in an attempt to continue "civilizing" the Navajo, and to teach them the white man's ways, the federal government had granted some of them private property in the eastern borderlands, now called the allotment zone. The experiment had failed and ended, but this was not part of the reservation proper anymore; virtually every section of land out here on the edge belonged to the heirs, sometimes dozens of them, of the original allottees, as they were known. In some cases, the property or simply the mineral rights had been sold by allottees to outsiders, as was their right with BIA approval. This had the effect of carving out private, corporate plots of land surrounded by Indian tracts. Other squares in this checkerboard were state or federal land. This would become important later on, but for the moment all that mattered was that the same Navajo culture held sway. More than fifty Navajos, who still came under the chapter system of government and voted in tribal elections, lived within a half-mile of the Haystack mines.

This time, with Zah and Hoskie pushing, there was action. Inspectors from the federal Centers for Disease Control were invited in from their base in Atlanta. The CDC declared a health emergency, which led EPA to invoke emergency powers granted under Superfund. Within two years, the mines were sealed. Two down, hundreds more to go.

Zah was convinced that the cleanup was so swiftly performed only because the two mines were off-reservation and within a few miles of white New Mexico towns.[5] One, in fact, was on an AEC parcel that had been leased out and the other was owned by the Atchison, Topeka & Santa Fe Railroad, which had formed a subsidiary to mine the claim. The Department of Energy, for the AEC, and the railroad each agreed to pay a portion of the cleanup costs. EPA did not pursue any other mining operators and ultimately paid the balance of the cleanup, about $500,000. Even though Superfund encouraged dunning the polluters, the companies that had performed the actual mining and left the rubble in place were not held accountable.[6]

Zah couldn't help but compare the activity in the checkerboard with the fate of more than two dozen abandoned mines deep in tribal territory. Hoskie's small staff, learning on the job, had painstakingly investigated forty-two abandoned mines and found twenty-eight that were hazardous enough to make the cut for Superfund. At King Tutt No. 1, the relatively small Tutt-Shorty claim near Oaksprings, the Navajos' health physicist recorded 16,380 cubic feet of mine waste still heaped at the site. Testing showed that the mound was rich in uranium, radium, thorium, lead, selenium, and arsenic, all damaging to human health for various reasons. But neither King Tutt No. 1, nor any of the other old mines, had made the national priority list.

Zah sent Hoskie to Washington to complain. She told members of two House committees, who held a joint hearing in 1993, that the Navajos wanted "speedy, thorough and permanent remediation of all sites." The problem was Superfund's ranking system. The reservation's low population density worked against the Navajos, even though they lived with mining's legacy every day in a manner that non-Indians could never imagine. The process "has proven a failure and must be changed," Hoskie charged.[7]

The congressmen before whom Sadie Hoskie aired her grievances agreed that she had every right to be upset. Rep. George Miller, a California Democrat, criticized the "piecemeal and uncoordinated approach" that "fails to eliminate the radiation health hazard." Rep. Bill Richardson, a Democrat from New Mexico, said the work at Haystack was "all well and good," but "there must be a final and complete way to address the problems of cleanup."[8] They asked EPA to get a move on, to come up with some overall plan of attack.

But EPA officials were angry. They complained to each other that Hoskie—one of their own, after all—had blindsided them on the Hill. Those mines had to compete with toxic waste sites from all over the country; they simply weren't the worst of the worst.

So Hoskie tried lumping mine sites together; there were two hundred just on the old King Tutt grazing lands. Perhaps the entire mesa, considered as one location, could qualify? Still steaming, EPA agreed to consider the proposal. But when the two governments tried to hammer out a plan for the mesa in 1994, they quickly got bogged down in disputes. They couldn't even agree on the minutes of their meeting. The Navajos thought the United States had committed to pursuing "responsible parties" (including VCA, now Foote) early in the process, and listed this as an "action item" in their summary of the discussion. After getting a copy, the EPA shot back: "Please delete as an action item . . . USEPA did not agree." [9]

Two more years passed before the EPA concluded that the King Tutt Mesa mining complex was indeed dangerous enough to merit a Superfund cleanup. But the federals still hewed to the ranking system. With only nineteen homes within three miles, chances for making the priority list were low.

There was one guaranteed way on. Every state governor was allowed to place one hazardous site on the priority list, and the president of the Navajo Nation, as head of a sovereign government, had that right as well. The letter for the King Tutt Mesa Aggregate Site was duly drawn up. All that was needed was the president's signature. [10] But by then, the EPA was urging the tribe to consider a different path.

Long before the Manhattan Project and the Cold War, miners had dug for coal in Navajo country. Hundreds of spent coal mines dotted the reservation (many of them created for the BIA to heat the boarding schools). By the 1990s, the tribe had a department devoted to filling and sealing these holes. The work was paid for with fees collected from coal mining companies across the country and distributed by the Interior Department. The EPA pushed the Navajos to use this coal money to close off the uranium mines as well. Buried in the fine print of the program was a clause that said Interior could disperse money for noncoal mines once work on all the Navajo coal mines was complete.

Hoskie had been first to raise this possibility, in her testimony to Congress, and she had been kicking herself ever since. [11] Upon reflection, she much preferred Superfund. The coal-fee program would not permit a thorough job. It was not designed to deal with radiation or with the rest of the many-layered problems surrounding the uranium sites.

Superfund gave EPA the power to clean polluted groundwater that had spread beyond a mining plot. The coal money couldn't be used for that. Superfund could remove and replace the uranium homes. The coal program couldn't do that, either. And the coal-fee program did not give the tribe authority to go after the mining companies to pay for anything that the Interior Department wouldn't. If the tribe turned to this funding source, the uranium companies would get off scot-free. In fact, it would be the *coal* companies who paid fees to Interior who were underwriting the cleanup and, while they were hardly innocents when it came to the environment, they had had nothing to do with this particular mess.

But the coal-fee money had one advantage: it was readily available. The Navajo coal mines had been finished up in 1994. The Interior Department certified that the tribe could now tap the fund to fill uranium mines. EPA pointed out to the Navajos that even if the tribe put King Tutt Mesa on the Superfund priority list, pursuit of the polluters could be tied up in court for years. The hundreds of other Superfund candidates on the reservation faced even longer waits, if they made the list at all, because the tribe would have used up its freebie.

In the Navajo capital at Window Rock, the time had come to make a choice. The tribal unit that had sealed off the coal mines stood ready to start work on King Tutt right then and there. The Navajo EPA had been waiting and the residents had been waiting. A partial cleanup trumped none at all, tribal officials decided.[12]

The pit-lakes still rippled in the western desert in 1992 when a form letter arrived in the Neztsosie household. Who knew that a simple business solicitation arriving at their cinderblock home would loom so large over the rest of their lives? A Colorado attorney named Cherie Daut announced that she would soon visit the chapter house in nearby Tuba City. She was seeking clients among the former miners who were now eligible for compensation, charging a 10 percent commission to help them navigate the paperwork.

The Neztsosie sons and daughters who had been to boarding school could read the advertisement. They thought maybe they too could use a lawyer. Maybe this *bilagáana* lady could push the IHS to offer more aggressive treatment for their little sisters, the clawed and suffering girls. Maybe she could find them doctors who could cure this Navajo neuropathy.

On the appointed day, Daut appeared in the Tuba City chapter house to answer questions. She had expected the handful of wheezing miners who appeared, but soon enough she was faced with a surprise. The door to the chapter house opened and Laura Neztsosie entered. She struggled toward the lawyer in leg braces. Plump, pleasant Linnie followed in a wheelchair. Last came their older brother, David. They needed him to drive to town, but they didn't need him to speak.

Laura slammed her frozen fingers on the table where Daut had set up shop. "Please help me!" she cried in her high, thin voice.

The sisters' appearance shocked the lawyer. Daut was reminded of a photograph that she'd seen years before in *Life* magazine of a Japanese mother tenderly bathing a youngster with twisted, shriveled limbs. This deformed child, with hooks like Laura's and Linnie's, lived in Minimata, where the bay was contaminated with methylmercury. The American photographer W. Eugene Smith shot the tub scene and others like it while staying in Minimata, igniting scandalized reactions around the world.[13]

As the Neztsosies talked about their way of life, they mentioned the blessing of water from the pits. Once she realized that they were talking about old uranium mines, Daut leaped to a connection. Could the pit water have caused the warping of the figures before her, the way that Minimata Bay had sickened thousands? Soon she was seeking help from lawyers in Los Angeles and New York with experience in environmental litigation. She pried a registry of probable Navajo neuropathy cases out of the IHS. The list had forty-four names.

The Navajo Nation, the name that *Diné bikeyah* took when the new government was set up, included a system of tribal courts. Lawyers had to pass the Navajo Bar to practice, and they could appeal to the justices of the Supreme Court in Window Rock. In 1995, Cherie Daut filed suit in the tribe's Tuba City District against El Paso Natural Gas Corporation, which had acquired Rare Metals.[14]

The other lawyers she consulted had recommended experts, and the experts tested the pits, for they had no idea that Don Payne and Steve Cinnamon had preceded them. Their findings were similar to Payne's. The toxicologist in the group calculated that for each day in the desert that Lois drank three liters from the "lakes," she was exposed to uranium at levels nearly one hundred times the standard the U.S. government would impose. The water also contained high levels of arsenic, cadmium, and radiation. The heavy-metals expert on the team was aghast. "Lois Neztsosie," he thought, "was pumping a witch's brew into her womb." [15]

Doo shiłbeehozindalá ("I didn't know!"), Lois cried out when she heard this news.

In Cane Valley, the age of boisterous families with ten or twelve kids apiece had long since vanished. As the Jacksons buried Juanita in an inconspicuous plot in the community graveyard, Lorissa mourned her mother and mourned the empty spaces too.

With no jobs and no roots to hold them, her brothers, sisters, and cousins had scattered, just as she had, and they seldom visited. Only eighteen houses were still occupied at the foot of Yazzie Mesa. Befitting a ghost town, its few residents were wraiths. Cecil Blackmountain, once a legendary storyteller, now choked and spit and rasped his words when he tried to talk too long. Ben Stanley walked and stopped, walked and stopped again, chronically short of breath. He hired Cherie Daut and got a compensation check; he paid her $10,000 and shared the remaining $90,000 with his eleven children and bought himself a truck. The compensation program also opened a window into the fate of the outsiders who'd come when the mining revved up and disappeared once it ended. Over and over, young Navajos showed up in Cane Valley, asking Ben to take them to the sacked and ruined mesa. "My father worked up there," they'd say, and their fathers were all either dying or dead. The visitors sought scraps of information that would help them fill in blanks on the endless forms.

Ben's mother, the aging Anna Adakai Cly, had finally understood after seeing the DOE work on the neighbors' houses that the problem described by Joe Hans on his visit years before was truly serious. Even though she didn't qualify for Energy Department aid, she had the uranium stucco stripped off her outer walls. But she didn't have the money for a new exterior, so the wind and winter cold rushed right into her rooms.

Wrenching as it was to witness the decline of Cane Valley and the few who had stayed there, the place tugged at Lorissa. She chipped in with her siblings to renovate Juanita's house; they weren't thinking of Joe Hans but of the wear and tear of a large family over many decades. Someday, one of them could live there again. She, in fact, kept moving closer. In 1997, she joined the faculty at Monument Valley High School, down the paved road from Goulding's, which was now a full-fledged lodge-restaurant-grocery store-gas station-tour guide operation. The old mining road nearby was now a highway, and the tourists came in droves.

Lorissa was assigned to teach business education and technology courses and she rented a trailer conveniently located right on campus, where most of the faculty lived. She threw herself into her work, driving many weekends to education conferences in Phoenix or Salt Lake. She served as a negotiator for the teachers' association. She spoke as much English as Navajo these days, but she remained extremely proud of her native heritage. She decorated the walls of her spotless living room with beautifully carved wooden cradleboards from many different tribes that she'd collected on her trips. She draped one of Juanita's weavings over the back of a chair, and displayed an old burlap sack for Blue Bird Flour, the brand of choice at the trading posts for many years, and the source of many a batch of frybread. During the summer breaks, she was director of a special program at the school called *'Ndahoo'aah,* which means "re-learning" or "new learning." She recruited elders from around the region to teach traditional crafts to students, who used graphics programming on computers to produce their designs.

Lorissa was leading her classes, raising horses with her husband, and mothering her children when pain pierced her quiet life anew. She heard that Navajo uranium was attracting attention yet again. The news was in the papers, on the Navajo radio station KTNN, on local TV. It was happening far to the east, in Church Rock and one chapter over in Crownpoint, which sits on the largest known undeveloped uranium deposit in the United States.

A new, small business from Texas called Uranium Resources Inc. was trying to launch another uranium boom. Union Carbide was once more exerting its reach through the years. The original scout for the Manhattan Project had been the parent company of U.S. Vanadium, VCA's rival—and later of United Nuclear, which spilled the Church Rock tailings. URI was not a subsidiary, but it had been formed by Union Carbide alumni. They said they had a new, safe, clean way to harvest uranium. They had slipped through the opening afforded by the allotment lands, sewing up mineral rights with the signatures of private Navajo landowners in chapters just across the reservation line. They promised $10,000 signing bonuses, a hefty sum to the allottees, and a string of royalty payments in the future.

Where uranium was bound tightly to rock that ran through pockets of subsurface water, URI would loosen it with a benign scrub of carbon dioxide and water—seltzer, basically—that the mine operators would inject underground through wells. This procedure would of course grossly pollute what had been near-pristine water, but they would pump it up to the surface, filter out the uranium and send it right back down. No tailings piles, no crackable dams, no radon-filled caverns, no pits.

The URI men worked out of their homes in the Dallas area while they got their business off the ground. They were already running one of these so-called leach mines near Corpus Christi. They flew Navajo property holders down to look at the operation. Look how clean, they said. And because this was technically processing, not mining, they would have to pass muster with the Nuclear Regulatory Commission before they could even get started. Look how safe, they said.

But the way wasn't so easily greased as it had been in 1942. Plenty of the Church Rock and Crownpoint locals were up in arms. They want to make uranium soup *right in the water*? In Church Rock, scattered private wells tapped the same aquifer that URI wanted to go into for uranium. The stakes were even higher at Crownpoint. Six municipal wells, famous for their sweet water, were within a few miles of the proposed leaching zone. Some fifteen thousand Navajos depended on the supply for their drinking water. They came from miles around to haul from the pump at the chapter house.

Lorissa, watching from afar, applauded the protesters. Enough was enough, she felt. Church Rock and Crownpoint should not be allowed to become next-generation Cane Valleys. Her ache turned to resolve. She wanted to help.

If she could do nothing else, she could *teach*. As it turned out, the youngest generations of *Diné bikeyah* knew as little as most Americans did of what their elders had endured, were still enduring. This became apparent in the spring of 1998. The tribe had set up a compensation office to help uranium workers, whether or not they chose to pay a lawyer. The director of the office and a medical school professor teamed up to lead workshops at the schools in Monument Valley and on the reservation side of the river at Mexican Hat; the students were meant to pass word on to their parents. The visitors were shocked when they realized that the pupils at Mexican Hat did not recognize that the white pile across the road from their grade school, so different from the rest of the red-rock landscape, was made of uranium tailings. They were amazed to discover that the students at Monument Valley High School were aware that many of their relatives had died from diseases of the lung but the teens had never learned of the link to uranium and indeed did not know about the mining that had permeated the region.[16]

Afterward, they held a public meeting for adults and asked why the children had never been informed about the uranium boom and its deadly aftermath. Ben and Lorissa offered a suggestion: someone should videotape the elders' stories while there were still elders to tell them. "The students should do it," Lorissa thought to herself.[17] They were the ones who needed to know.

Her principal, Pat Seltzer, steered her toward the Utah Arts Council, which agreed to underwrite expenses. The council also hired a consultant: a real, professional director named Trent Harris. Harris had returned to his native Salt Lake City after trying to make it in L.A. He liked to joke that he'd been thrown out of Hollywood for committing the sin of losing money, but he had acquired a devoted cult following. He was best known for *Rubin and Ed*, a quirky and darkly funny film starring the actors Crispin Glover and Howard Hesseman. The story revolved around a frozen dead cat; a long-haired man who loved striped bell-bottoms and high platform shoes; and a polyester-clad buddy who spouted sales-force bromides. *Details* magazine gave it this rave review: "More psychedelic fun than a barrel of monkeys on mushrooms!"

This was hardly the sort of production that Lorissa had in mind. And when it came to working with kids, Harris's credo was: "Not if I can help it."[18]

Still, the Arts Council gig offered decent cash and he was dimly aware of the uranium miners' saga that had been twinned with the more familiar tale of the downwinders. Like John Ford before him, he loved the reservation's dramatic scenery and the fresh air. And he quickly came to admire Lorissa. She was as serious and reserved as he was offbeat, but they were both passionate about their work. As the school year began, she hand-picked six students who had family ties to uranium mining. One of them was her daughter. Her own children had much to learn about this painful part of their past. Juanita had never talked about those days much, except to say that the valley was busy. Now Lorissa wanted to know what had happened, but she could no longer ask her mother. She made her crew research the topic and write papers. They looked up the uranium decay chain, read about atomic bombs, and learned about mining companies. They completed this assignment after school in addition to their regular classes. The teenagers discovered the history and the peril all around them. "Even I have played on the mill tailings hill and it has only been within the last five years that they have put up signs and a fence," wrote Leontine Oliver, Lorissa's daughter.[19]

In the John Ford films, the Navajo extras had almost always been silent. In this movie, the Navajos would speak out.

The academic in Lorissa had led her to title the project "A Volatile History: The Continuing Effects of Uranium Mining on the Navajo at VCA." She decided that she needed something catchier. She came up with "Hear Our Voices."

As the students mapped out their production plans, an interview with Luke Yazzie, the "founder," topped their list of must-haves. But they never got the chance to capture him on tape.

Like his father, Luke didn't talk much. But when the topic of *leetso* came up over the years, he had denied the contamination. When the flurry of deaths among the miners made that impossible, he'd boasted that uranium would never get him. After all, he was in really top-notch shape. He was outside all the time.[20]

Occasionally, *biligáanas* still showed up to examine the mesa. Luke's house was the closest to the old Monument No. 2, and they always stopped in. *Leetso* was generally on their minds, but nothing ever came of their inquiries. "I already been told lies about it," he would tell them. "I been cheated on."

An elderly white woman and man, along with a driver, arrived in the valley sometime in 1993. They were about Luke's age, in their early eighties. Like the others, they walked around on Yazzie Mesa and then showed up at Luke's place. But this set of visitors was different. Luke was clearly glad to see them. He said in Navajo to his daughter, Mary Lou, "What is her name?" He was trying hard to remember, remember, remember.[21] He told his daughter, who spoke English, to offer coffee to their guests.

They introduced themselves: Mary Elizabeth and Page Edwards. It was the couple who had accompanied Denny Viles to the mesa fifty years before. Oh yes! Luke knew them now. After the VCA-Foote merger, after supervising the shutdown of Monument No. 2 and of Shiprock, Page had moved to head Foote's Denver office. He had closed that one down, too, and long ago retired in suburban Lakewood. Though Page and his decisions had been hugely important to Luke's working life, it was Mary Elizabeth, Mary E. for short, whom he recalled. She was frozen in his mind as the vivacious woman in the old photograph he still had on hand. Page was just the lanky man who had snapped it with his camera. They had had a great time doing the paperwork, everyone teasing each other. Denny Viles and all those people.

With Luke's daughter translating, the Edwardses stayed for half the day. Mary E. cocked her head, appraising the sunken version of the young man in the black cowboy hat who had guided VCA to such fortune. In his old age, he had come to closely resemble Adakai. One thing was different: his hair, unlike his father's, had turned white. But there was something else. "He looks to me like he's getting sick," she remarked.[22]

Indeed he was. In the opening months of 1994, Luke spent several weeks in a hospital. He was dying of lung disease. And June had fallen ill, too. She had gall bladder cancer. It was spreading and no operation could save her. "We've got this uranium inside us," they suddenly began to tell their children. After swallowing decades of their father's denial, the children didn't want to hear it.

Several of them went nonetheless to the tribe's uranium workers office in Shiprock to inspect the list of compensation lawyers. They passed over Cherie Daut in favor of Stewart Udall. He too had entered the business that he'd had such a hand in creating. They drove Luke to Santa Fe, where Udall had a respiratory testing center all lined up for his clients. The old man's lungs were so dysfunctional that the doctor cracked, "I can't believe you're still standing." In due time, the check came from the Department of Justice. The family collected it in Santa Fe, Udall shook Luke's hand, and back went the Yazzies to Cane Valley. Luke had his payment at last, in exchange for his life.

The Indian Health Service sent Luke and June for treatments at the Tuba City hospital. On the long drives, Luke repeated his instructions to whichever son or daughter was at the wheel. "You guys need to take care of this land, because there's a lot of uranium here. And it's a really good place. It's nice and beautiful. Even if I go, just take care of the place."[23]

On the night of September 11, 1998, Mary Lou Yazzie left her father's bedside to go check on her house, a two-hour trip. Upon arrival, an indescribable feeling came over her. It was well after midnight by then, but she felt compelled to get in the truck again to retrace her journey.

The weather turned foul. Thunder boomed; lightning crackled through the dark. Hail pelted the windshield. Mary Lou had to slow down so much, she felt like she could have made it to Tuba City faster if she hiked there.

She was in the brightly lit hospital again, exhausted and walking down the corridor to Luke's room, when a niece ran out to greet her. "Oh, you made it back!" Something in her face made Mary Lou rush in and grab her father's hand. He took two shuddering breaths. Then the founder slipped away, a victim of his own betrayal. The mesa had exacted its revenge.

Two months later, Lorissa's students trekked with their equipment to Cane Valley. It was too late for Luke and June Yazzie to star in this documentary, but Ben's mother, Anna Cly, had something she wanted to say. Anna was Adakai's daughter by his first wife, and with Luke's death she assumed the mantle of her generation as the last of the patriach's children. In her bare-bones house she sat upright, clad in a velveteen blouse of rich burgundy clasped at the neck with a traditional brooch of filigreed silver and turquoise. Her pulled-back hair had stayed as dark as her father's, and silver loops hung from her ears. She looked directly into the lens and made her statement in Navajo, the only language she knew. The translator picked up her rhythms, the quiet power of her words:

"Before the mining, we lived in harmony and everything was well and beautiful. . . . Now people come and take pictures and they tell us that the foundations of our houses test positive for radiation. We're told that our water is contaminated so we haul in our water from Bluff City and Monument Valley. . . . Everyone has walked in it. It is the same with our neighbors.

"Yes, it is like that," she said. "What will become of it?"[24]

Next, the group traveled to Crownpoint, a four-hour drive along dirt and paved roads to the east. They taped an executive from URI working to start up the uranium mining anew. He could bring good jobs to the Navajos, he told them, and they found him persuasive. Lorissa said nothing. She wanted them to make up their own minds.

Then they talked with a Crownpoint elder who was around Anna Cly's age. The old man would not consent to an interview on camera, but he addressed them as "my children, *shiyázhí, she'awéé', sha'alchíní,* my babies." He told them Mother Earth is sacred and should not be disturbed.

One of the students, a girl named Tisha Charlie, began to cry. "I don't know why I never asked," she sobbed.[25]

Chapter 13

Under Scrutiny from Every Angle

efore the arrival of Trent Harris, Monument Valley High School owned two video cameras. Neither one worked. Harris took the parts from one and used them to fix the other. He visited for a week at a time, teaching the student crew about storyboarding, and how to mix music and voice. He doctored the script. Mostly, though, he stood back and let the students do their own work. Twenty-two hours of footage boiled down to thirteen minutes and twenty-two seconds. At long last, "Hear Our Voices" was ready for prime time.

Lorissa screened the documentary at an assembly at the high school. She showed it to the PTA and to the school board. Twenty-three years after Joe Hans set up his projector in Cane Valley, the subject was the same, but this time it was better understood. The groundwork had been laid, of course, the hardest way of all, through disillusionment and death. Only after people had begun to die did someone publicly cast the problem in Navajo terms.

For many years, tribal officials and federal scientists had tried to figure out how to explain radiation to the many Navajos who had never graduated from high school, let alone college, who spoke no English and read no words at all. *Łeetso*, "yellow dirt," was part of nature, so how to convey the perils it posed? A discussion of the chain of uranium's breakdown, of alpha, beta, and gamma decay, was clearly out of the question. Harry Tome had recognized immediately when he was told that radiation was a dangerous smoke that the analogy would never make sense. Way back in Joe Hans's time, in the 1970s, the translators equated radon gas with steam. Both were vapors, true, but Navajos associated steam with water hissing off the heated rocks in the sweat lodge. Steam softened and purified. Steam was relaxing. Steam was only good.

Lorissa and the six students took a different approach. As part of their reading, they had come across an essay in an obscure magazine called *Indigenous Woman* that introduced the concept of *łeetso* as a monster.[1] Monsters are a key piece of the Navajo Way mythology, the tales that make sense of life and living for The People. *Naayéé'*, the Navajo word for "monster," translates roughly as "that which gets in the way of a successful life." *Łeetso* certainly fit that definition. To control a monster, according to Navajo lore, one must name it, and one must understand it. In the opening of "Hear Our Voices," the teenagers offered a parable to their elders. The names of Adakai and Luke Yazzie, of Harry Goulding and Denny Viles, went unmentioned. Instead, they recounted the story of holy Changing Woman and her sons, the Hero Twins, who learned through many trials how to slay monsters. "The first monster they killed was *Łeetso*. He was the worst of all monsters . . ."

A narrator told the story while a series of what the students called "mist" shots unrolled. The familiar contours of their landscape, the round sun behind rock masses and turrets, dissolved into a roiling shroud of twisting color blocks. Now *this* was steam. This was the feel of the sweat. The fog put the *Diné* in a frame of mind receptive to long heart-to-heart talks, for stories of the Holy Beings and for instruction in the ways of the world.

The students, and Lorissa, too, introduced themselves on screen, first in English and then in painstaking Navajo, informing their viewers of their maternal and paternal clans. The People knew who was talking to them and why they should listen.

"Hear Our Voices" also struck a chord far outside Monument Valley in the *bilagáana* world. The video garnered praise and honors at film festivals around the West. At lunch during the twentieth annual Utah Short Film & Video Festival, Lorissa ran into Trent Harris. His "Wild Goose Chronicles" was named Best of Festival. "Hear Our Voices" won Best Young Media Artist. The students' handiwork appeared in Flagstaff, Santa Fe, even in Portland, Oregon. The showing at the Northwest Film Center, in 2000, brought something special in the mail: certificates for everyone and a $100 prize. Lorissa used the money to take the kids out for a raucous, happy dinner at the only restaurant for miles around—Goulding's, of course.

The students, five girls and a boy, were all changed by their project. The making of the movie bolstered their confidence and helped them discover talents they hadn't known they had. But it had also helped them locate a passion for the story they had told, and for their people. They would go on to college, and burst out in discussions to tell their classmates about *leetso*. They would write fervently about it in class papers.[2]

Lorissa's life was changing, too. Part of her transformation was unrelated to the film. She and her husband decided to part ways; she took her old name back. But "Hear Our Voices" did two things: It made her feel even more deeply the harm that uranium had done; she kept replaying in her head the teary-eyed speech of "grandmother" Anna Cly about the way things used to be. And it brought Lorissa to the attention of a wider world.

She was in demand. Elderhostel, a lifelong-learning tour group aimed at affluent senior citizens who wanted to stay sharp, hired her to lecture a roomful of graying *bilagáana*s over at Goulding's lodge. White Horse High School, where she had taught first, asked her and the students to speak at a conference on Navajo culture. The Environmental Education Outreach Program at Northern Arizona University asked her to write a summary of the project for its "Hear Our Voices" web page, as an example for other educators. The NAU program also wanted to hold workshops at Monument Valley High for elementary and secondary school teachers. Could Lorissa please help?

The primary group resisting renewed uranium extraction, and URI in particular, also sought her assistance. The organization was called ENDAUM, for Eastern Navajo Diné Against Uranium Mining. Mitchell Capitan, a utility technician and rodeo rider, had started ENDAUM with his wife, Rita. The new process—*in situ leaching* it was called, or ISL—had been percolating for decades. Page Edwards had filed away notes and papers about the water-filtering approach back in the 1970s. Mitchell Capitan had worked for Mobil in a local pilot project. He recalled that the company could get the uranium into the water, and extract a goodly amount, but it couldn't get the water clean again. He didn't want that happening in Crownpoint, his hometown. Another member of the ENDAUM board was Larry King, a rancher from Church Rock who lived near the old mines and across from a second group of URI sites. He had been a surveyor for the United Nuclear mine and remembered being asked to go take a look at the tailings dam over by the mill in the weeks before it burst. He had noticed many six-inch cracks, had chalked it up to dryness, had reported his observations, and returned to his job mapping underground tunnels on the ridge.[3] Enraged still by the big spill that followed, he no longer trusted anybody's word that new technology was safe. He'd had enough of experimenting, and he'd had enough of being asked to have faith in the new.

The ENDAUM leaders asked Lorissa to be available when a television crew or newspaper reporter was on hand to document the growing conflict. Her presence could show that opposition to uranium mining was not confined to the allotment checkerboard. She could bear witness to the excesses of the past.

She drew the line there. She had never liked being the focus of attention. One night, principal Pat Seltzer happened to be eating dinner at an off-reservation café when Lorissa and her family walked in. She was impeccably dressed, in a jacket made from a Pendleton blanket and in her finest turquoise and silver. The entire place looked up; conversation ceased.

"I hate it when people stare at me," Lorissa told Seltzer later.

"Lorissa," the principal answered, "they were staring because you were so incredibly beautiful!"[4]

It was getting easier to speak out, but mostly Lorissa wanted to learn more. Her weekends were soon filled with uranium-mining conferences almost as often as they were with teaching seminars. The movement was going national, across the *Dinétah*. She didn't think of herself as an "activist," just as "active." She wasn't driving the efforts, but she was lending the weight of Cane Valley's collective memory to the cause.

———————

Meanwhile, Sadie Hoskie's storming of Capitol Hill was bearing fruit. Mary Holiday could see this in the open sky. Late in the summer of 1997, long after Hoskie had returned to her regular job in Denver and just as Lorissa was beginning to dream of "Hear Our Voices," a helicopter repeatedly rumbled low and loud on the other side of Goulding's above the Holiday compound. The U.S. EPA had arranged for these flights over many of the old mining districts to chart the extent of the problem. Onboard, a portable scanner sought out unusually high levels of radiation. This had never been attempted before. Charles Reaux had told the IHS it would be impossible. But the helicopter was a good first step.

The agency showed some sensitivity as the mission began, conferring with the local chapter officials, tacking up flyers, and making announcements in Navajo over the tribe's radio station, so that the *Diné* would not be unduly alarmed by swooping rotors so close to their homes. The word had reached Mary, so she took little notice as she moved about her bustling family camp, where the old *hooghan* with the nice, smooth floor had been joined by an assortment of earthen, frame, metal, and stucco dwellings. The front entrance to each faced east toward dawn, in accordance with Navajo tradition. Behind them loomed a mesa with a pale green uranium stain that started at an old mine and pointed down the cliff. With the mine so near, the helicopter's presence made perfect sense.

Mary did not give a second's thought to the portion of the mine that had been invited inside her *hooghan* more than twenty years before. She didn't live there anymore; in the late 1970s, she and Billy Boy had moved about fifteen feet away, into a two-room house that they painted a bright teal. But a parade of kinfolk had passed through the original place since then. Mary allowed her niece, Elsie Begay, to move in to the *hooghan* with her seven children after Elsie's marriage broke up in 1978. Three years later, the Begays switched to a smaller *hooghan* on the Holiday property. Next came two of the Holidays' grown children, who had left the reservation for a while, but had married and wanted to return. The two couples and, soon enough, three children lived together under the shingle roof.

From the front door, they could watch the setting sun behind them wash Monument Valley's sandstone formations in vivid red.

In 1989, Elsie's son Lewis died of a brain hemorrhage caused by a tumor. He was twenty-five. The next year, Billy Boy died, suffering from lung disease in addition to his diabetes. He was in his early sixties.

During the 1990s, Mary's daughter Daisy and her husband had bought a trailer, moved it to the camp, and hooked it up to electricity, a nice twentieth-century touch. They even got a TV. Lorissa taught some of their children over at the high school.

Mary's son, Robert, and his family slept in the old *hooghan* one weekend a month; they spent most of their time up in Salt Lake City, where he had found work installing air conditioners and heaters. Though everyone called it "the rabbit house"—one of the toddlers pronounced "Robert" that way—the Holidays also used the *hooghan* to store cans of beans, sacks of flour, extra blankets, and toys, along with garden tools and plastic water barrels. The door was padlocked, but the children liked to stand on one another's shoulders and climb through the windows.

Under the copter's whirling blades, Mary Holiday went about her daily chores, clad in the "grandma" uniform of velveteen blouse, long skirt, thick socks and dusty shoes. She chopped wood for the stove, cooked tortillas, brewed tea. She set up her loom outside to weave in the shade of a juniper while the grandchildren played dress-up for hours inside the old *hooghan.* The radiation flights were an annoyance, with the insistent whupping noise so loud and harsh, breaking the morning hush, but they were nothing more than that. After a week or so, the copter moved on to a different part of the reservation, and was soon forgotten.

The lands around Goulding's were under scrutiny from every angle. Lorissa and Trent Harris were not the only ones roving the area with a camera crew. "Hear Our Voices" and the government helicopter would help to change the course of yet another film, and in the process, open yet another Navajo family's eyes to the true meaning of *łeetso.*

Jeff Spitz, a tall white man with close-cropped hair, an earring, and an Emmy, was also drawn to *Diné bikeyah* and the notion that Navajos should tell their own tales. He lived a world away, on the north side of Chicago, where he made documentaries. His subjects tended toward the urban, from a racially integrated university in segregated Chicago to the immigrant experience in public libraries. He had grown up in Beverly Hills, but had landed in the Midwest for graduate school, and he stayed.

Spitz's path to the reservation began when his father-in-law asked him to talk to a friend of his, a real estate developer named Bill Kennedy. Kennedy's father had studied filmmaking. The father had died and Kennedy wanted Spitz, who knew movies, to help him decide what to do with with a silent short that his dad had produced with his film teacher during a trip to the reservation in the early 1950s. *Navaho Boy: The Monument Valley Story,* it was called, with the old-fashioned spelling favored in those days. Kennedy's father had fallen in love with the intense light falling on the rugged landscape, and the son too seemed obsessed with the American West. Even in his office, at the far edges of the heartland metropolis, he wore a broad-brimmed hat, a bolo tie, and boots.

For a time when he was younger, Kennedy's father had shown the film to small audiences, providing his own narration to the events depicted on the screen. The real estate man thought the film must be too valuable to stay hidden away in some attic or junk drawer. He asked Spitz to take a look and offer some advice. He had no idea how to bring it back out into the world.

Spitz popped the suburban cowboy's twenty-eight-minute tape into a recorder and was immediately captivated. *Navaho Boy* was very different from the John Ford epics from the same era. Some of the Navajos in the movie, it would turn out later, had actually been extras for Ford, but this time they were the center of the action. The plot revolved around a young boy being sent off on a donkey and returning with a medicine man who proceeded to perform a ceremony, complete with sand paintings and chanting, for two patients. There were many scenes of routine tasks. Originally shot with Kodachrome, the movie was still as bright and sharp as a desert sunrise.

Through some creative detective work, and many twists and turns of fate, Jeff Spitz was able to find a second copy of *Navaho Boy,* a different version with a voice-over by the film teacher who had accompanied Kennedy's father. He also confirmed the name of a central Navajo character and discovered that her children were likely still living near Goulding's. He flew to Albuquerque, drove six hours, and in the morning set out with a handful of stills to track down the cast of *Navaho Boy,* still unsure what he wanted to ask of them.

After a couple of days, he ended up shaking hands with a graying woman in whom he could recognize the cheerful girl smiling infectiously onscreen while her mother brushed her hair. It was Elsie Begay, Mary Holiday's niece, who had grown up to seek sanctuary in the old *hooghan.* She lived in a newer one now, made out of drywall, at her aunt's compound. She was still warm and friendly. She remembered the making of *Navaho Boy,* though she had never seen the finished work. She told Spitz that her parents had appeared in many films; John Wayne had even suggested naming her baby brother after himself and it was done. Because of their proximity to Goulding's and their friendship with Harry, they had also posed for countless calendars, fine arts photographs, paintings, and postcards. They were famous anonymous people.[5]

An idea was forming. All the Navajos Spitz encountered asked to see the movie. What if he went home to Chicago and had Bill Kennedy come back with him to the reservation, bearing *Navaho Boy?* What if he filmed the adult characters watching their young selves and their family? What if he had them explain in their own words, without the filter of a white narrator, what the original movie was about and what they thought of it? It could make a fine documentary.

At first, all went as planned. Kennedy was amenable and the pair showed up at Elsie's with *Navaho Boy.* After delivering a little speech, Kennedy ducked into Elsie's new *hooghan,* right by the old *hooghan,* to show her his father's work for the first time. Elsie said something in Navajo to her family inside. Only later, when he hired a translator, would Spitz discover that she was urging the others to "Make room for the white man!" Neither Spitz nor Kennedy talked to any of the Holidays. The movie wasn't about them, after all.

On a later trip for more filming, Spitz heard about the helicopter. His cameraman was spooked. He wanted to leave. He didn't want to be exposed to radiation. At the same time, Elsie and her family kept swinging the conversation toward the plight of the miners. Her brother was having a hard time prying compensation out of the government, even though his lawyer was Stewart Udall.

He wasn't there to make a film about uranium, Spitz kept reminding himself. But he couldn't quench his curiosity about the situation. One of the family members worked over at Monument Valley High School, so Spitz was spending time there. Somehow he learned of "Hear Our Voices." He took a look at the video and, like so many others, he was moved. He loved hearing the students express themselves. He was impressed by how they worked as a team during their interviews and by how far they'd traveled in their quest for answers. Clearly, a tragedy had occurred in the Home of the People. He decided to make space after all in his full-length documentary for the mining experience of Elsie's family, weaving it together with the chronicle of their movie days.

Seeking money to finish up, he applied to the native division at Robert Redford's film institute. He got no funding, but he received something just as precious: an invitation to screen the movie at the legendary Sundance Film Festival; arrangements were made for a showing in early 2000. Back in Chicago, he started preparing for this big break when thoughts of his cameraman's reaction to the copter came to mind once more. Since uranium had made its way into his project, he decided he should try to find out what, if anything, the aerial scan had uncovered.

The EPA didn't want to tell him. His contacts mumbled about "jurisdictional issues." It took volunteer help from a lawyer to wring the information from the agency. After many weeks, the response arrived in the form of a poster-size map, with magenta-colored lines and blotches denoting elevated radiation superimposed over the terrain.

Spitz unrolled the page on the wooden table in his sunny kitchen in Chicago. He had spent enough time in and around Goulding's to know what he was looking at. There was a reddish-purple mark over the old mine that had stained the mesa, and another curious splash of color just to the east.

For a moment, he couldn't believe his eyes. But there was no mistaking what he saw. "Holy shit! Look at this! That's Elsie's house!" he couldn't help blurting out loud. What he knew no one in the *Dinétah* knew. Something in the Holiday compound that was home to his main character, a woman who had become his friend, looked to be as hot as the mine.

About the same time that Spitz had this terrible epiphany, the tribe's Abandoned Mine Lands unit reached Cane Valley. In 1999, fifty-six years after VCA opened its big, hot Monument No. 2, and thirty years after Foote Mineral withdrew, the gouges and slashes on the mesa were due for recovery and balm—at least as much as could be managed within the limits of the coal-fee money they'd chosen over Superfund. With eleven years' experience at mine reclamation, five years of it with uranium mines, the AML, as it was known, enjoyed an excellent reputation with its supervisors at the Department of Interior. Every year when it was time for the annual evaluation, the tribe received top ratings for honesty, competence, and creativity, the equivalent of straight A's. The tribe's technicians and contractors sprayed foam or stuffed rocks inside openings to block mine portals. Sometimes they had to hold on to safety ropes to do the work on cliffs, like window washers at a city skyscraper—a radioactive skyscraper. They bulldozed and terraced the land to make the steep cutaways walkable again for animals and people alike. They dumped clean soil over fields of uranium rubble to put it back under the earth where it had been before the mining started.

The AML faced a big job at Monument No. 2. The sheared-away mesa had become, in essence, a giant radioactive pit. The artificial bowl contained thirty portals, seven vertical shafts, and sixty-five acres of radioactive waste.[6] A mining consultant who observed the project had his worries about how long the cleanup would last. He watched the crew carefully place the mine waste at the bottom and cover it over with forty or fifty feet of dirt, but it was clear that the harsh climate could undo all their work. When he inquired as to how they planned to prevent erosion, the answers were vague.[7] They did scatter seeds over the new land, but the consultant was dubious that the plantlings would take hold strongly enough in the bone-dry surroundings. He thought they would be scattered by fierce winds and seasonal monsoons.

Ben Stanley had qualms too. He tried to tell them they were missing some hot places. Back when Monument No. 2 was a busy mining site, he had seen the laborers toss low-grade ore into the deep gully between the North and South Rims. He knew that the heavy rains, when they came, poured right through the toxic leftovers.

"This is going to affect us," he told the workers.

"It's too hard to go down there," one of them answered.[8]

The AML team did descend from the mesa to the Cane Valley floor. The technicians and contractors thoroughly tamped down a new layer of clean, reddish dirt over a large mine-waste pile standing right next to Jesse Black's. The light-colored, single-story home was one of the structures on Joe Hans's list that the DOE had declined to repair.[9] The AML workers did not investigate the likelihood that the construction of the house had been connected to the proximity of the low-grade ore a few yards away. Simply put, it wasn't their job. There were no Joe Hanses among them.

The outside observer and Ben Stanley may have had their doubts, but the Interior Department was impressed. The Navajos' effort at the yawning pit won the department's award for the best mine reclamation in America in 1999. Interior Secretary Bruce Babbitt hailed the Navajos for "setting new standards for the industry." This was not difficult to do—because there were, in fact, no federal standards for restoring old uranium mines.

"The site is free of sources of water pollution, soil erosion, sedimentation and radiation emission and is once again open to the community for livestock grazing," trumpeted the press release for the award—not that it had ever been closed since the mining stopped.[10] The monolith of uranium ore on the mesa was still standing; it was naturally occurring, after all—even though it would have remained inside the butte if the mining had never come along. The consultant thought the monolith and other exposed deposits should be cleaned up; he worried that these oddities would attract the herders and their flocks.

There was one other development that the AML workers had either not noticed or not cared much about. As they prepared to seal up the mine as best they could, Jesse Black's daughter Nina decided that she and her husband had better rush to collect some ore while it was still available. The young couple used their last-minute haul to build one more Cane Valley uranium house, right under the cleanup crew's noses.

For some reason, Nina never thought about her father's house, where she grew up, in connection with the breast cancer she'd been diagnosed with when she was twenty-seven years old. Her dad had mentioned Joe Hans's findings once or twice, but never made it sound all that important. She moved her things into the new place that she felt lucky to have, lucky that she could build with the final load of waste from Monument No. 2.

The next year, though, in 2000, before she and her husband could actually take up residence, her father fell ill and was diagnosed with lung cancer. He had waited quite a while to let them know that he wasn't going to make it. He kept things close. This was tradition.

Her father's sudden death—sudden to her, if not to him—shocked Nina into recognition of the danger she had faced once before and the harm she was preparing to risk once more. She and her husband left Cane Valley and their unused home behind. They moved more than eighty miles away, to Crystal, New Mexico, a reservation town on the other side of Canyon de Chelly.[11]

In the meantime, Foote Mineral, which had swallowed VCA, was in turn swallowed by the mining giant Phelps Dodge.

Past the reservation line, up in Colorado, two federal agencies were acting on their worries. The U.S. Bureau of Land Management and the U.S. Forest Service owned property in remote canyons where VCA had operated ten uranium mines. Soon after Phelps Dodge took over in 1999, the BLM and the Forest Service approached with a request: please clean up your predecessors' mess. They were concerned for the safety of the occasional hiker or camper who might wander across the old mine sites, or stay there overnight. Phelps Dodge asked for proof that the mines had indeed been VCA's, and when that was forthcoming, the conglomerate started dispensing millions of dollars to seal off the radiation and heavy metals.

The BLM and Forest Service were divisions of the Interior Department, sisters to the Bureau of Indian Affairs. The firm did not, however, take any steps at all to cleanse Monument No. 2 or King Tutt Mesa or any of the other properties that VCA had managed on Navajo lands. There was a reason for that: no one asked.[12]

Cherie Daut's legal team had come up with a Navajo neuropathy study that looked to be a bombshell. She was taking a back seat—she had been diagnosed with lupus and was filing for deadline extensions, but she missed so many on her compensation cases that her license was suspended.[13] The other lawyers, plugging on, had hired James W. Justice, an apple-cheeked University of Arizona researcher, based in Tucson, who had formerly worked as an epidemiologist for the Indian Health Service. He interviewed relatives of forty-one Navajo neuropathy patients and he was not told which were plaintiffs and which were not. As he assembled the mundane details of their histories, habits, and lifestyles, a clear pattern emerged: When these mothers drank uranium-polluted water while pregnant, they bore children with Navajo neuropathy. When they were away from the old mines during their pregnancies, they bore healthy children. Lois Neztsosie, for instance, had avoided the mines because of the blasting when she was pregnant with her older children. After the mining ended, she spent another pregnancy housebound during a year of deep blizzards while a relative cared for the herd. The family's drinking water that season came from melted snow. She drank from the "lakes" only while pregnant with Laura and Linnie.

But the Neztsosies and their fellow plaintiffs were dealt a double blow. The Navajo neuropathy lawsuit, which started in the tribal judicial system, had wound its way, startlingly, to the stately white columns and solemn black robes of the U.S. Supreme Court in Washington. The reason had nothing to do with the evidence; at issue was a point of law that would determine whether the case had to move from Navajo to federal jurisdiction. Daut ardently wanted to stay in the tribal courts, where she felt the jury would be sympathetic. Her target, the parent company of Rare Metals, just as ardently wanted to play by *bilagáana* rules. The business, El Paso Natural Gas Co., argued that this was a nuclear-materials matter and as such was governed by a Congressional law that limited liability for the industry.

The Supreme Court agreed with El Paso. The case passed from tribal to federal court. The federal court appointed a mediator.

By the time El Paso offered in 2000 to settle for a total of $500,000 with no admission of wrongdoing, Linne Neztsosie was dead. Drained, the four families who had sued agreed to take the payment. Cherie Daut wept at the small size of the sum that she had won for her clients.[14]

Deprived of a trial, Justice wanted to get his findings out. In 2001, he presented his results at a conference of the Public Health Service Commissioned Officers Association. The IHS had people attending, but the focus of its research did not change.

After the helicopter came men holding vials of glass. EPA officials, maps in hand, decided to move from air to ground. The agency requested help from the U.S. Army Corps of Engineers. The Manhattan Engineering District had launched the poisoning of the *Dinétah*. Now the Los Angeles Engineering District was charged with figuring out how much damage remained.

The Corps picked a veteran toxics specialist named Glynn Alsup for the job. He was a portly, jovial man with more than a hint of his native Tennessee in his twang. Alsup assembled a small group to roam the *Dinétah* with him, and he started with water. He asked permission from chapter officials each time he wanted to collect a sample and disarmed the locals by putting up with their gentle teasing and giving as good as he got. When one of them told him to beware of bears because they find white men especially tasty, he merely smiled. When a flat tire led his guide from the chapter house to announce that they could be marooned for days, Alsup piped up, "I've got a whole box of energy bars. I think I'm going to get rich!"[15]

But he was not so jolly when it came to the numbers that were streaming in from the lab. Alsup was taken aback by the results, as Don Payne and Daut's experts had been, and he was ranging over a much larger area.

He checked the lake pits, but he also visited Red Valley, Monument Valley, Tah-chee—more than two hundred springs, wells, and washes in all. One of every five water sources was contaminated with dangerous amounts of uranium, other toxins linked to its decay chain, or radiation—or a combination thereof. The Corps man was convinced by the locations that the pollution was related to mining.

He took to warning the neighbors when he found unsafe water, which did not endear him to the new leaders of the Navajo Nation EPA. The latest director, Derrith Watchman-Moore, felt that Alsup was boxing her in. When the Guardian's researchers did pay attention to the reservation, they produced glossy reports that looked nice sitting on shelves. But over and over, they had shown themselves unwilling to do anything about the conditions they were documenting. Watchman-Moore could predict what would happen next. Frightened Navajos would be coming to her, crying, "What are you going to do about it, Navajo EPA?" And if the U.S. government couldn't find enough money to solve the problem, the Navajos sure didn't have the cash on hand.[16]

The last straw came when Alsup branched out into testing houses. Somehow, the movie director, Jeff Spitz, had located him in the bureaucracy. Spitz had told Elsie what he saw on the map and she was upset but didn't know where to turn. Spitz found himself transformed into her advocate. On the phone, Glynn Alsup told him that he had to respect the Navajos' authority, that he could only check the area if he were asked to, and only if chapter officials gave him the go-ahead. So when Alsup made it to the Oljato chapter house on his rounds, Elsie was waiting there for him to make her request.

Spitz was up at Sundance on the January day in 2000 that Glynn Alsup kept his appointment at the Holiday compound. He told Elsie that the chapter would allow him to sample anything she wanted him to. What she wanted was a look at her aunt Mary's *hooghan*, where she and her family had stayed for three years. She knew the history of its concrete floor.

Alsup held his radiation detector up to an outside window. The needle jumped to the top of the scale. The instrument was reacting as it had at the entrance to uranium mines. His voice quavered as he circled the *hooghan* calling out numbers. He ducked inside and tried to make it fast. Radioactive emissions there reached 1,000 microroentgens per hour, seventy-five to one hundred times the levels deemed acceptable by the EPA.

Mary Holiday and her daughter Daisy stood and watched. Daisy called her brother to break the news about the "rabbit house." Elsie's son, Leonard, and his wife, Sarah, also came out of their trailer nearby, drawn by the hubbub. They had a secret. Leonard, a handsome carpenter, had been losing weight, and they knew why. Three different doctors had confirmed the diagnosis. He didn't smoke. He had never worked a day in a uranium mine. But he had lung cancer. He looked at the nervous man taking readings at his former home, and a sudden suspicion took hold.

Derrith Watchman-Moore and her staffers were enraged. Alsup, they thought, should have also consulted with *them,* with the tribe, not just at the local level, before he stirred up this whole new pot of trouble. The Navajo Nation EPA demanded Alsup's ouster from the reservation. He was gone within weeks and the sampling program that Sadie Hoskie had beseeched Congress to start suddenly ground to a halt.

Mary Holiday's *hooghan* was left standing. Six months later, Elsie wrote to the EPA to inquire about its fate. The kids were still going in it. Three more months passed before she got a reply. "We recommend that people stay out of that hogan [*sic*]," wrote Sean P. Hogan, an EPA official. "We also recommend that the hogan [*sic*] be removed from the area so that no one is exposed to those levels of radiation." Treading carefully after the blowup with the tribe, he added that his agency would not take any action unless the Navajo government requested it.

Alsup had also discovered a previously unknown structure with dangerous levels of radiation over in Teec Nos Pos. After much maneuvering, the tribe finally authorized the EPA to "eliminate this risk." In April of 2001, federal wrecking crews tore down the two homes.

The United States of America gave Mary Holiday a corrugated-metal shed to compensate her for the loss of storage space.

———————

On December 7, 2003, two days after his lung began bleeding profusely, Leonard Begay collapsed and was flown to University Medical Center in Tucson. "This patient lives in Monument Valley, Utah, near the uranium mines," the attending physician noted in his records.

Leonard knew what to expect. Sarah's father, a veteran of the mines, had died of lung cancer the month before.

He kept hugging and kissing his family and asked his wife to squeeze onto the narrow hospital bed beside him. He instructed her to build a house—a good house, a safe house—for their two kids.

On December 19, at 2:50 a.m., he died. He was forty-two years old. His wife told the children that they all had something in common: She had lost her dad to uranium and she was certain they had lost theirs to uranium, too.[17]

Chapter 14

Resistance

nly nine days after George W. Bush took the oath of office for his first term as president of the United States, his vice president convened an elite task force. Through the winter and spring of 2001, drivers in black town cars periodically delivered Cabinet secretaries and top political strategists to an enormous gray columned office building on Pennsylvania Avenue. From next door at the White House, from the State Department, from Energy and Transportation and Commerce, from the EPA, the president's people came when summoned, each one permitted to bring a single aide. The "principals," as the bigwigs are labeled in capital parlance, took the same seats every time around a long polished-to-gleaming wooden table. The room had the requisite trappings of power—the fireplace, the swagged floor-to-ceiling windows—setting the scene for posterity (most of the work in the building got done in a different kind of classic D.C. décor: small, verging-on-shabby rooms with furniture that was merely old, not antique). The invited staffers stood mute along the walls while Vice President Dick Cheney held forth from his chair at one end, dominating the discussion with their bosses. The mission: a strategy to produce more electricity and transport fuel for an energy-hungry America. Bush and Cheney had definite ideas about how to proceed. The two men at the top both had backgrounds in the Texas fossil-fuel industry. In fact, during the campaign their ticket had earned a nickname: the "Houston Oilers," a play on the name of that city's departed football franchise.

So the emphasis on nuclear power came as a bit of a surprise. About one hundred aging reactors were generating electricity in the United States, using the same basic science as the atomic bomb—split a nucleus, liberate energy. But this fleet was scheduled to start going dark within several decades. No new licenses had been granted since 1976, thanks to Three Mile Island, Chernobyl, and a slew of billion-dollar cost overruns and construction delays. The end of commercial nuclear power in America was a distinct possibility.

A few months into Cheney's task-force process, though, the Energy Department submitted a briefing paper to the vice president's office. Use more nuclear, the report urged. Build scores of new reactors. Under "pros," the department noted that this policy would be "a bold step." Cheney liked bold steps. And it would show that the "Houston Oilers," push as they might to drill more for dirty petro-products and dig more for dirty coal, could still do something helpful about global warming, which threatened massive upheaval around the planet in the future. Nuclear, after all, emitted very low quantities of carbon dioxide, a major by-product of oil and coal, and a key contributor to the changes in Earth's atmosphere—yet unlike wind or solar power, nuclear had proven itself as a consistent producer of large amounts of electricity. Under "cons," Energy noted that this change of course would be controversial, given the frightening accidents.[1] Cheney had no problem with that. The safety recall was good overall, and he seemed to enjoy confrontation. Nuclear power went on to win a place in the report that he issued as "a major component of our national energy policy."[2]

In response, the price of uranium was soon rising, rising, from $7.10 for a pound in 2000 to $14.50 in 2003 to $20 in 2004. And in response to *that,* the men of Uranium Resources Inc. renewed their charge to get at the Navajo deposits underneath Church Rock and Crownpoint. They had a jump on the future, it seemed.

URI, through a subsidiary called Hydro Resources Inc., had a license from the Nuclear Regulatory Commission to use the new water process in the allotment territory. But this time around, outside environmental groups leapt into the fray, helping ENDAUM and others get organized and offering legal help. The opposition had filed an appeal and snarled the whole process in paperwork and testimony.

And this time, a candidate for the Navajo presidency was campaigning on a pledge to stop URI and anyone else who wanted to mine uranium again where it could place the *Diné* in harm's way. Joe Shirley, Jr., was a traditional, raised by his grandparents in Chinle, a central Navajo town near the Canyon de Chelly. On special occasions he liked to wear a bolo tie with a silver clasp, intricately carved with a gold *hooghan* superimposed over a frieze of the canyon. It was a declaration of where he kept his heart. Shirley had left the reservation long enough to attend two small Christian colleges and then do graduate work at Arizona State. His bachelor's degree was in business and he held a master's in social work, but he was well versed in public policy, having risen in both tribal and white-world politics. He served simultaneously as a Navajo council delegate and an Apache County supervisor in New Mexico.

Shirley's reverence for the Navajo Way led him to take what was a provocative stand at the time. The issue of new uranium mining was tearing families apart in the vote-rich checkerboard. The debate pitted royalties, jobs, the potential of a different way to mine against the pain of the past and the toxic legacy remaining in the present.

Joe Shirley won election handily in 2001. Still, making good on his promise would not be easy. Pete Zah had tried a ban by executive order when URI first made approaches, back in the 1990s, but the council had split with him for economic reasons. At the time, however, the scope of the damage from the first round of mining had been far from clear. The ever-taciturn Navajos seldom shared their health problems with each other, and the federal government was only too happy not to delve too deeply.

In the first months of his term, the new Navajo president grew even more convinced that he was taking the right stance. The more he heard about the long lags in cleanup and the dangers that remained on the land, the more his position hardened.

In the spring of 2003, he strode into a chandeliered conference room at a funky Spanish-decor hotel in downtown Albuquerque. He was there to address several dozen Navajo and federal officials. The audience in khaki pants and loose-fitting Oxford shirts, shifting in their folding chairs, was all that was left of the short-lived effort that had begun with the helicopter and the water sampling and ended with finger-pointing and recrimination. It had come to this: a quarterly meeting on uranium issues where the agenda always seemed to be the same and nothing ever got done. Glynn Alsup was in attendance, but he had not been allowed to fill a single water vial since his crew was kicked off the *Dinétah*. No one else had, either.

Shirley stood at the lectern, gray hair swept back, posture slightly stooped, eyes glaring though he did not raise his voice. "I'm glad that we are talking," Shirley told the group. "But how long have we been talking? Decades, I think." And then he left for Window Rock. He saw no reason to stay.

This gathering was my introduction to the uranium issue. I was then a reporter for the *Los Angeles Times,* a member of the paper's national investigative team. After making some preliminary inquiries about the subject from my base in Washington, D.C., I had been invited to come west to hear about the various communities where problems were still cropping up. I felt totally lost. The conversation seemed to center on an alternate universe. Where was Oaksprings? What was Cove? A discussion of Middle Earth or Narnia would have included more familiar place names.

The only thing that was clear was that the president was not the only one who was fed up. Some, in fact, were upset with Shirley himself; they saw him as all stinging words and no action. Others wanted to show him that he had support. Whatever their motives, Navajos around the tribal homeland were doing something remarkable for such a patient people. Over and over, in the early years of the twenty-first century, they got tired of waiting for their Guardian, they got tired of waiting for their tribe, and they took matters into their own hands. They were following the lead of the widows of Red Valley, but this time, the rising up took hold at communities in all quarters of *Diné bikeyah*. Like Lorissa Jackson, they wanted, needed, to make their voices heard. They concluded, further, that words were not enough. It took numbers to catch the attention of those who could implement change. I returned to Washington to work on another project that would take many months, but I resolved to visit the Navajos' country and some of the rebels as soon as I could.

I met Milton Yazzie at the Albuquerque conference. He explained that he lived in the western part of the reservation, south of Cameron by the Little Colorado River in Arizona. The place where he lived was called Black Falls. Yazzie was a plug-shaped veteran of Los Angeles's Skid Row (including Indian Alley, where homeless Native Americans gathered to drink too much in familiar company). He had returned to his parents' ancestral home in his mid-forties to change his ways. To reach community college classes in the white resort town of Flagstaff, he commuted an hour each way over dirt roads from the family's wooden dwelling, a typical setup with an outhouse in back and a basketball hoop in the front.

The nearest neighbors were seven miles in one direction and thirteen miles in the other. It took a while to catch up with everyone, but soon after he came back, Yazzie started hearing about a host of ailments among the scattered populace of Black Falls. Too many seemed to have eye or kidney disease for this to be based on mere coincidence. Was it, he wondered, the water? And did the water change after the mining companies blasted the land in search of uranium?

He started bringing plastic barrels in his pickup truck on his trips to Flagstaff, to fill them up there for his parents. He wanted them to drink from a safe supply. But that didn't take care of the neighbors, and it didn't answer his questions. For years, he pestered both the tribe and the EPA, beseeching them to test the wells and springs around the Black Falls countryside. He was rough around the edges and he misspelled words and sometimes his cell phone service was cut off because he couldn't pay his bill. His government contacts brushed him off, offering soothing words and sympathy but nothing much in the way of action.

In 2002, he persuaded EPA officials to hold a meeting at his parents' to talk about the hazards of uranium. The next year, the agency's regional office honored him as an "environmental hero." He drove to San Francisco to receive a plaque, the first award he'd received since he was given a shovel in high school as a joke, because he "ditched" so much. The EPA even issued a press release heralding the importance of his efforts. "Despite approaching numerous agencies, the area remains without clean, regulated water," the release said.

Yet six months later, the EPA denied an application from the IHS for a grant to bring clean water to Black Falls. The project was ineligible, EPA officials ruled, because there was no evidence that the locals were drinking polluted water.

At his wit's end, Yazzie approached researchers at Northern Arizona University, based in Flagstaff. A half-Navajo, half-white chemist, Jani Ingram, agreed to help. She was pleasantly surprised to get funding through a Native American cancer project at the university, and she was able to sign on a half-Navajo, half-Pomo graduate student to assist. The surprise was less pleasant when she got the results from her six testing spots: high levels of uranium and other mining by-products showed up. At one spring, both uranium and arsenic were present in such large amounts that she felt compelled to advise the tribe that no one should drink from it. This was a loaded combination; uranium can damage DNA and arsenic can inhibit the body's ability to repair that damage. The tribe's solution? Shut down the pump. The neighbors, of course, were outraged. In a desert, the only thing worse than contaminated water was no water at all. Talk of marshaling the National Guard to bring in bottled water came to naught. The watering station stayed open.

I tagged along with Ingram and the grad student during a three-day weekend in the winter of 2004. My editors at the paper thought the Navajo story might merit an in-depth series if there was scientific evidence that uranium mining had caused health problems. Ingram wanted to see whether her summer results might be affected by the change in seasons. Milton Yazzie would guide them back to the water sources they had previously visited. Three horses craned their necks in the paddock as our vehicles pulled up at the Yazzies' at 8:30 in the morning, just as we had arranged. Strangely, a host of cars and trucks were parked in the dirt by the house. "Usually, there's no one here," Ingram said, her brow furrowed. A white teepee in the yard pointed to the sky. Traditional Navajos live in eight-sided or rounded *hooghan*s, while the tall tents are associated with the Great Plains tribes.

It turned out that clan relatives of Milton's had responded to a call he had issued for help. He was dispirited by the cold reception he'd gotten from both governments, which he saw as uncaring, and from the neighbors, whom he saw as ungrateful. The relatives had come from another settlement to hold a ceremony. One of them was a holy man in the Native American Church, which borrows from the customs of many different tribes, hence the teepee. They had started the day before and they weren't done. We were asked if we wanted to take part. Ingram wanted to get back to town (and pavement) before a predicted snowfall. She muttered to herself: "Be flexible."

Inside the sloping teepee walls, flaming oak branches were arranged in a triangle, with a mound of molded ashes in the middle. An old white enamel coffee pot snuggled into the ashes. Behind the fire, someone had laid out Tupperware containers filled with pita breads, turkey, dressing, and creamy, shockingly colorful concoctions of marshmallow and canned fruit in gelatin. One was light green and the other bright pink. We helped to carry even more food from the Yazzies' front porch to the teepee. But before we could eat, the interrupted ceremony had to be completed.

We newcomers took seats, as the others had, on piles of Indian blankets and mats arranged in a circle (as the participants with the least knowledge, we should have sat closest to the entrance, but we didn't even know enough to do that, and no one mentioned our faux pas). The group had been up all night, meditating and praying for Milton to succeed in his campaign. They talked for hours about the mill tailings and the dust and the wells.

Now it was time to pass a silver-colored bucket of water and a silver cup around the circle. In turn, each person dipped the cup into the liquid and drained the draught. "Where did this come from?" I whispered to Milton. He smiled tightly and answered, "Flagstaff." Using *biligáana* water for the ceremony had to hurt.

One of the relatives got up to prod the fire with a tool shaped like a hockey stick. It was made of cottonwood. The embers glowed. Sage and evergreen flavored the smoke. The service was over.

We scooped mutton stew into Styrofoam bowls. Some of the relatives prepared plates with the Tupperware bounty and passed them down the line. A boy made the rounds, clockwise as tradition demanded, asking, "Orange, strawberry, Pepsi, or Dr Pepper?"

The holy man's nephew, sitting cross-legged, told amusing fables, one about a man who catches crows with his bare hands and another about an old Navajo lady on a plane. His listeners chuckled appreciatively. Then he suddenly changed the subject. His words flowed through the fragrant cloud in the center to Jani Ingram on the other side. He wanted to know about her work.

"We need this research," he said. "A lot of people drank from the pits and from the wells." He pushed his hand forward and pointed. "There needs to be a medical study. There needs to be research."

Ingram agreed. "That is what they need, hard information, instead of just people complaining."

"The children, the families, we need the research," the nephew said. "Nobody's doing it."

Afterward, Ingram, the grad student, Milton, a *Times* photographer, and I headed out for a cold, muddy day of roving between distant wells, recording locations in log books and collecting specimens. We said goodbye to Milton Yazzie and left for Flagstaff as the first snowflakes drifted down. When Ingram got her samples' analysis back from the labs, it showed that heavy-metal concentrations were even higher then they had been the first time.

Half a year later, I found myself on the opposite side of the *Dinétah*, in Red Valley. The residents there were making plans to bring a modern touch to the quiet plain between the Carrizo, Lukachukai, and Chuska mountain ranges. They wanted to build a new ballfield, a senior center, a high school, a convenience store, an auto repair shop. But after being seared by the miners' deaths and the shock of the uranium houses, they wanted to make sure that they didn't place new construction in contaminated zones. The EPA and the Corps of Engineers had been banished. The tribe wasn't answering their calls. They networked with everyone they could find until they reached a young chemist far away in Illinois.

Berlin-born Franz Geiger was an expert in soil and water, an assistant professor at Northwestern University. He was a big fan of author Tony Hillerman's mystery novels; the protagonists of the popular series were Navajo tribal police officers who solve murders all over the reservation. Geiger had even taken a Tony Hillerman vacation with his brother, visiting the settings from the books. He also happened to hold grants from the National Science Foundation that required outreach work of some kind. This fit the bill. He pored over Glynn Alsup's sampling data—these were available on a CD-ROM and in slow-loading files online, formats that few Navajos would be tempted to investigate. It was clear to Geiger that there was a problem, a big one.

He and one of his students flew into the small airport at Farmington and spent three days commuting onto the reservation and back. Much of the first day was consumed by a presentation at the Red Valley chapter house to anyone who cared to listen. When Geiger arrived, a meager but eager audience had already been waiting for an hour and a half. The chapter president apologized for the turnout of only a dozen people; many who had wanted to be there were out with their herds. On the second morning, the community land use planning committee and other influential locals gathered at a picnic table outside the chapter house to plot the day's itinerary. Among them were Fred Begay, a Los Alamos physicist who had been one of the charter members of the tribe's environmental commission; Harry Tome's brother, Marshall, a rancher and former general manager of the *Navajo Times;* and Rex Kinsel, of the Red Rock school district board, who was specifically recruited to serve as peacemaker.

Kinsel knew so many young people and their parents that he was judged the best-equipped person in Red Valley to defuse tension if someone drawing water at the test sites objected too vociferously to the presence of the white professor—not to mention the white undergraduate and the white reporter. He was more than willing to take on this role. He felt strongly that the deaths of his father, a foreman in the mines above Cove, and his mother, who washed the coveralls by hand in steaming water, and his brother, who had birth defects, could all be blamed on the contamination. But there was no evidence. He wanted this project to succeed. "The school nurse will sometimes talk about uranium, but nobody has come out saying which places are safe and which aren't. Nothing," he told Geiger.

The professor's plans were actually more ambitious than merely identifying bad water, as so many others had before. He was going to test pitchers containing filters, the kind anyone could buy at the store, to see whether they could remove the toxins. If it worked, maybe companies like Brita, Pur, and General Electric could be persuaded to donate their wares, so Navajo families would not have to choose between thirst and safety.

"The filter is probably good for a lot of the metals, but there are some it probably won't be good for," Geiger told the group. "It will only be good for two or three months. But it will be something and it's available on the reservation. And hopefully, it will be free."

"Good," said Marshall Tome. For the first time ever, instead of balking at the cost of clean-up and looking the other way, someone was actually trying to find an easy, fast solution.

The first stop was on Roof Butte, the highest point in the Chuska Mountains. No houses were visible, but Kinsel said plenty of people were around. This was a popular place to camp with herds in the summer because the weather stayed cool on the heights. Under a cerulean sky, in the heart of a pine forest, a duct-taped pipe funneled a thin but steady stream into a concrete trough. A member of the Navajo entourage, a former tribal-council delegate, had downed the fitness drink he carried, but he was still thirsty. He filled the empty plastic bottle from the trough and took a swig, then held it out to Geiger, who hesitated. "I don't know . . ." he said, his voice trailing off. Then the professor grabbed the bottle, tilted it up, lowered it again, and wiped his mouth. "Drinking a little is not going to be bad," he said in his light German accent. He could see the appeal. The water was really cold. And it tasted good.

At stop two, Kinsel's assistance was needed. A Ford pickup pulled up behind the water-sampling party at a faucet in a pine glade partway down the mountain, at the edge of a small meadow where sheep and goats grazed peacefully. A man with large, wire-rimmed spectacles and a long ponytail slung over his left shoulder emerged from the driver's seat. He had come to fill several containers. The blue plastic barrels were for water to drink. A battered tin drum that had once been white was for water to use for washing dishes. He would bring the brimming barrels home to his wife, his six children, and seven grandchildren. After a short discussion in Navajo, he turned to me and to Geiger. He would talk with us, though he was obviously none too pleased by our intrusion at his well. "I honor my elders," he said in English.

His name was Davin Joe. He taught Navajo culture at a local school. He was forty-two. He had worried about the water quality for all of his adult life, he told us. Clearly, evenly, he recounted the deaths of his father and three younger siblings from lung cancer. "Mr. Tome raised his voice," he said, referring to the miners' fight. "Now you're hearing my voice. It becomes another generation asking questions. We pray and hope that it's not contaminated. I get concerned because I go through this hacking cough."

He looked straight at Geiger. "If you find uranium in here, what's the solution? It's got such a long half-life."

I offered what turned out to be a misguided attempt at empathy. "You must be angry," I said. His face stayed expressionless, but he was quick to put me in my place, to show me how little I understood. "As far as anger, you take care of it with prayer," he replied. "I can't change the circumstance, but I must stay in harmony."

He turned back to Franz Geiger. "In the 1960s, where were they? Where were you guys?" His tone was totally calm.

A workable plan turned out to be more difficult to fashion than Geiger had foreseen. Like Jani Ingram, he stressed the importance of monitoring the water through different seasons. Glynn Alsup's samples were a snapshot. The groundwater, a subterranean river, kept on moving. Conditions could change, for better or for worse, as they had in Black Falls. To save time, trouble, and money on water pitchers, he thought, The People would need constant updates on their local pumps and windmills. He wanted to recruit high school students to make monthly water collections; a girl from Shiprock High had come along on the sampling trip and then started a water chemistry club. Geiger thought that the kids could send their vials to his lab, which would then post results online in an easy-to-decipher format for those who couldn't read. He'd mark the locations with colored dots on Web-based maps that included photos of the wells in question. A green dot would mean the water was safe, a yellow dot would mean there was some cause for concern, and a red dot would trigger use of the water pitchers. Geiger estimated that $5 million a year would cover the cost of pitchers for all those who needed them at one time or another in Red Valley and beyond. He was prepared to ask the private companies to help out. Think of the marketing opportunity, he would tell them. You could say that your filters are helping the Navajos clean their once-poisoned water and live a healthy life on their sacred land.

But asking Navajo elders, living without electricity, to check their water quality each month was, to understate it, not a practical idea. Every chapter house had a computer, but it wasn't likely that the people most in need of the data would ever make the effort to consult the machine.

Geiger himself strongly believed that this cumbersome two-step would be at best a temporary fix to protect the Navajos while they waited for the EPA, the DOE, *someone* to finish the job. But some of the Red Valley committee members feared that the filter system would give the federal government an excuse to put off a thorough cleanup indefinitely.

In the end, though, the biggest problem of all was the limitations of the filters. They removed 95 percent of the uranium, but they didn't take out the arsenic, which often was also present in the mined ore. Geiger would not in good conscience be able to assure the Navajos that their filtered water was safe.

Most of his samples—including one from the faucet where Davin Joe had filled his barrels—showed good-quality water, technically, at least for the date of June 23, 2004. Nothing exceeded EPA standards, though several contaminants came close. But he was concerned about the interplay of pollutants that were present, even though each one by itself came in under the federal safety limits. His greatest worry was a chemical cocktail that showed up in a well serving the Red Rock Day School and its two hundred students. Children, smaller than adults, and still developing, were the most vulnerable of all. But there was no proof of harm.

One evening, unwinding over beers on the back patio of the Farmington hotel where the out-of-towners stayed, I asked Geiger what it would take to truly shield the *Diné* from the uncaged *leetso* in their country. He paused for what seemed like a long while. "You have to remove the top-soil," he said at last. "The government would have to remove the soil all over the reservation."[3] But that would cost billions and take decades.

Church Rock was yet another flash point, all the more so because URI, and other firms too, had set their sights on the uranium still there. The clashes over new mining placed a magnifying glass on the continuing legacy of the last round. Church Rock chapter was planning to build more housing and, like Red Valley, wanted to avoid new development on dangerous ground. The Puerco river bottom was still a bed of salt. Those who lived along its banks blamed continuing stunted harvests on the big spill, which may or may not have been the cause. No scientists ever tried to find out. The unreclaimed United Nuclear waste pile stirred up bad feeling every day. Elderly people on oxygen offered the most unnerving reminders of all.

Through the 1980s, the families at the chapter's Red Water Pond settlement by the big waste pile had lobbied their Church Rock chapter leaders and dignitaries visiting from Window Rock to complain to the EPA about the waste. They even traveled to neighboring Pinedale and Coyote Canyon chapters to beg for help. But their pleas never reached Diane Malone, the tribe's liaison to the Superfund program. She learned about the waste pile in the mid-1990s by chance, when she was invited to tour the Superfund operation at the old mill, just across the reservation border, where the dam had breached. Malone glimpsed the huge heap on the Navajo side and inquired about it. Every time after that, when she visited the mill site, she asked company and federal officials: "Why is that pile still sitting there?" They never gave her a straight answer.[4] She thought that the pile was on state land, that she had no authority over it. But she didn't check the location for sure.

As for drinking water there, no one had tested it. Glynn Alsup had not made it as far east as Church Rock before his project was halted at the tribe's command.

Enter Chris Shuey. For a white man, Shuey knew Church Rock well.

As a young reporter, he had covered the tailings spill. He wrote a piece about the mining widows, too. The plight of the Navajos moved him so much that he went back to school and earned his master's degree in public health, and from there he plunged into activism. Rumpled and intense, he was given to lengthy monologues made up of equal parts scientific jargon, bureaucratic acronyms, and indignation, delivered in an urgent, ever-louder staccato. He was advising ENDAUM, the main group opposing renewed mining, and he couldn't bear how often he had to confess ignorance when asked about past, present, and future. "Are our houses safe?" "I don't know." "Can we drink the water?" "I don't know." He was so sick of not knowing. Shuey was both persistent and precise, and he knew the power of information. He wanted to get real answers, and if it helped ENDAUM's cause, so much the better.

He came up with the Church Rock Uranium Mining Project, CRUMP as he liked to call it, and helped the local chapter officials win a $90,000 grant and a $20,000 contract from the state. Quickly, CRUMP accomplished something that the tribe had never gotten around to. The group proved that the big waste pile was on Indian land. They laid plans to investigate further. They would conduct the testing that no one else had ever taken on.

That much money and ambition in the hands of the locals set off klaxons in Window Rock and San Francisco. Wary tribal and federal officials decided they'd better keep an eye on these people, and the best way to do that was to help. They should make sure at least that the data was collected correctly. Suddenly, the elusive EPA was offering technicians and a van with radiation-scanning equipment. The previously unresponsive tribal government donated detectors and training.

Diane Malone joined the Navajos who walked through Red Water Pond near the waste pile on an October morning. They lined up and halted every few steps, like police officers searching for evidence. Each time they stopped, they took readings at waist and ground level and logged their measurements. The wind whipped in from the direction of the hill of rubble, carrying so much dust along that at times the technicians could hardly see. The instruments confirmed that the sand stinging their faces was radioactive. Now that Malone was finally visiting the pile she had seen from a distance, she wanted to get away quickly.[5] Forced to face the numbers, the EPA concluded in 2006 that chronic exposure to the radiation levels at Red Water Pond could lead to bone, liver, and breast cancers.

The new partnership also visited thirteen livestock-only wells in Church Rock chapter. The designation was a misnomer and everyone knew it. People drank the water there, too. That was life in the *Dinétah*. The tour showed the limited options available. Eight wells had water that tasted unpleasant, but was not dangerous. On the other hand, a crystal clear well, with water so delicious that it could have claimed a taste-off blue ribbon, contained twice as much uranium as the maximum permitted by the EPA in drinking supplies. All told, four water sources—about a third of those tested—came up hazardous for human health. One had recently been abandoned, but the surrounding community had used it for twenty-seven years. It had been installed for The People by Kerr-McGee, which operated a nearby mine at the time. The well had a name, Friendship I. The water contained arsenic and radium.

At the Church Rock chapter house one day, I ran into Ed Carlisle, who held a position that is roughly equivalent to a city manager. I asked about the chapter's plans to build one thousand new houses on an open tract near the paved road. "That project is dead," he said. I asked why. "Because of the uranium problems," he answered.

The new waves of evidence from so many quarters of the Navajo homeland gave Joe Shirley the political groundswell that he needed. The tribal council overwhelmingly passed a ban on further uranium mining "in Navajo Indian country."[6] The council delegates had not only placed the tribe's communal land off-limits, they were also asserting their authority to nullify the leases that URI held in the allotment checkerboard territory of Church Rock and Crownpoint. They called their measure the Diné Natural Resources Protection Act of 2005.

On April 29, 2005, Shirley signed the bill into law. He traveled to Crownpoint for the ceremony, a defiant shot at URI. As Chris Shuey and the mining critics had hoped, the president linked the attempts to mine again to the excesses of the past. "I believe that the powers that be committed genocide on Navajoland by allowing uranium mining," he told his audience.[7]

The price of uranium that day was $24 a pound. URI had already invested $25 million in its bid to mine in Church Rock and Crownpoint, with an eye toward making billions in the end. The fight was on.

The way the uranium men saw it, they were suffering the consequences for history that had nothing to do with their safe new process—wash uranium into the water off the stone where it was bound, pump the "pregnant" solution up, filter the uranium out. Their opponents were wielding blatantly emotional arguments that would deprive the United States of a mineral that could help free the country from the political clutches of Arab oil sheikhs and African despots and Russian oligarchs. This argument was national security redux. It would have carried more weight if URI had not teamed up with the Japanese conglomerate Itochu, which was expected to tie up the bulk of the uranium produced at Church Rock and Crownpoint.

URI was soon joined by more small startups wanting to get in on the game. They played the way URI did, the way most any business would, attempting to build local support with all manner of enticements: How about a scholarship at New Mexico Tech solely for a Navajo student? You are cordially invited to a conference of chapter officials at an Albuquerque resort hotel. We can donate thousands of dollars for local improvements once the mines get rolling.[8]

They saw the "checkerboard" as the gateway to the reservation proper. They made no secret of their hopes to get past the ban. Phone calls to the Navajo mineral office came so thick and fast that Shirley issued Executive Order 02-2005, instructing all tribal employees: Don't answer any questions. Report all contacts to the Navajo attorney general.[9] The directive infuriated the mining executives. What kind of democracy was this?

Robert McNair, the director of capital projects for a Canadian energy firm, decided to try an end run. He called the state of New Mexico seeking help. He wound up on the phone with the state's deputy environment secretary, who was none other than Derrith Watchman-Moore, the former head of the Navajo Nation EPA. She still had no financing to clean up the old mess, but this time, instead of blocking surveys of damage, she would use that as leverage. She told McNair that she would not support new uranium mining of any form until her homeland was purged of its poisoned past.[10]

McNair knew how extensive the problem was. He also knew that, despite URI's boasts about the efficacy of leaching uranium from water, the process was as much art as science. He believed that the recovery rates were far from certain. This was not worth the trouble. His company, Dejour Enterprises Ltd., decided to pass and trained its sights instead on a massive deposit in Saskatchewan.

I met McNair at a huge convention in Manhattan for investors in hardrock minerals. In the past, the Hard Assets Investment Conference had been known among fund managers as "the gold conference." But the 2006 version was fixated on uranium. The price had reached $43.50 a pound and the fever was high. The line for registration snaked across an entire floor of the immense and slightly cheesy Marriott Marquis in Times Square. Slickly coiffed young men in European suits, *yarmulke*'d Chasids, retirees of both genders in expensive stone-washed denim and white sculpted hair, all clutched plastic bags filled with business literature and stock newsletters. A tall sign near the check-in alerted the crowd in red letters: DON'T MISS! URANIUM PANELS. One tipsheet editor, James Dines, had a booth in the main hall with a large banner overhead: THE ORIGINAL GOLD BUG. THE ORIGINAL URANIUM BUG. He gave a hyperbullish keynote speech on uranium's prospects to a packed auditorium. In a room tucked off a side corridor on the floor above the big bazaar, editor Lawrence Roulston addressed a subscribers-only Q&A. The door was open; I could see and hear the discussion from the hall. "Can you recommend any small uranium companies?" asked the first to raise his hand.

Through Dejour, I snagged an invitation to a small lunch with four mining-company presidents, including one who was pressing hard in the vicinity of Navajoland. I grabbed a grilled vegetable wrap and a seat with a good view of the panel. I was on Broadway, after all, and I was eager to take in a show.

I wanted to hear from Strathmore Minerals, which had acquired mineral rights on several properties near Grants, New Mexico, moving closest to the reservation at a Church Rock tract near those that were being developed by URI. Strathmore estimated that it could recover 15.3 million pounds of yellowcake from the Church Rock plot alone. On the day of the lunch,[11] that much uranium would have grossed $665.5 million on the open market.

Strathmore's CEO, David Miller, could barely contain his enthusiasm. "We know uranium. We've been in uranium. We're gonna make a lot of money in uranium," he told the group. A geologist who served in the Wyoming state legislature, Miller's twangy voice served as windup for his folksy delivery. "I like to put rocks in the box," he said.

His firm was the largest property owner in Canada's Athabascan Basin, the same region where Dejour had decided to focus. "But guess what? There's gonna be no production for twenty years." The deposits hadn't been completely charted yet. Of the parts of the world where uranium had been more thoroughly scouted, the United States was definitely the place to be, he declared. "Politically stable. We can get the permits. Environmentally, you've got to jump through the hoops forward and backward, but we know how to do it."

He didn't mention the Navajo resistance to new mining. After the audience filed out, I approached and told him that I was a reporter for the *L.A. Times.* He waved me over to sit next to him and we talked for a while in the empty room. A shock of hair hung down over his forehead, and even though it was gray, it gave him a boyish look. He seemed open and blunt. "There were problems in the past. The radon gas did kill people. It's a different game now," he said. His Church Rock leach mining operation would hire fifty to seventy-five people, he told me, paying them anywhere from $20 an hour to $100,000 a year. Navajo technicians would likely be at the low end of that scale, but this was still a very good wage for the area. At another site nearby, he thought Strathmore would have to open a conventional underground mine and he wanted to build a mill.

But he agreed with URI that Church Rock was a prime candidate for the solution-mining process.

"There's actually less radionuclides when we are done," he said. "We're going to improve the water quality." He couldn't guarantee that he'd get out every speck of the uranium he loosened from the rocks, but he could get the water clean enough to meet standards for whatever it had been used for before. As a URI vice president, Mark Pelizza, would ask me later, "How clean is clean enough?"

"Regulators," Miller said, "are sometimes real sticklers."

As for the Navajos, he wondered if Shirley really represented the will of the people. He wished he could give them a royalty bonus and get access to their deposits "right now." Someday, perhaps, a different president would take another tack. "They say there is more cancer. I think my facts are right. Their facts are wrong. A poor economy takes more years off your life," he said. "Do they want jobs or not?"

Abruptly, he shifted gears. He interrupted himself and squinted at me. "Are you a reporter for that Southwest Center?" He meant Chris Shuey's environmental group. "You're not a reporter for them, are you? You're not a surrogate for them, are you?"

I was truly nonplused. I was hardly in Chris Shuey's pocket. Indeed, though I had explained to him that I was working on a series and it would take a long time, Shuey often complained that I wasn't writing articles about every twist and turn in the saga of the uranium ban—and the next year, when my stories finally did run in the newspaper, he would complain that I gave too much weight to the industry point of view. But soon after the conference, I understood what Miller was implying, and why. He seemed to suspect that I might be lying about working for the *Times*—I noticed that he relaxed a little when I handed him a business card—and that I might be some kind of spy. This made more sense when I realized that he himself had employed others to peddle his side of the story. In a rack in front of Strathmore's display space were printouts of articles from a website called StockInterview and packets from a consultancy called Cohen Independent Research Group. I took some with me to look over when I had more time. The StockInterview site, which frequently quoted Miller and quoted others complimenting Strathmore, wrote about sending "undercover" reporters to talk to Shuey. I followed a link on the website that led to a disclosure of payments from the companies touted there. Strathmore had spent $20,000. Buried in the fine print of the "independent" research group's report was a similar admission. Strathmore had paid $28,000 for the glowing assessment it was proudly distributing at the fair. When I asked Miller about this, he answered my question with a question: "It's not illegal, is it?" No, it wasn't, but he sure had been worried that someone would try those same tactics on him.

Strathmore and URI and other uranium interests were paying lawyers, too. They knew they couldn't overturn the uranium ban on the reservation itself, but they wanted to save the investment they'd already made in the checkerboard territory on the Navajo Nation's eastern flank. The companies had already been arguing for years that the tribe had no control over nontribal property just because it happened to be owned by Navajos—nor did it have control over private property that just happened to be surrounded by Navajo land. From their standpoint, the mineral rights on the allotment tracts and the strictly private squares of property were none of Joe Shirley's concern.

The long-standing dispute over who was in control in the checkerboard had begun, as this kind of dispute often does, with a technical issue. URI held a license from the Nuclear Regulatory Commission for its solution-mine process, but the firm still needed a permit to inject the fluids into the ground to strip the uranium from the sandstone running through the aquifer and pull it into the water.

The company had applied to the state of New Mexico for clearance. URI wanted an exemption from the Safe Water Drinking Act. Company executives estimated they could filter one million pounds of uranium each year from the "pregnant" Church Rock water and had high hopes that they could prove to the Navajos with this operation that solution mining was effective and safe, safe enough to proceed in Crownpoint and elsewhere.

The state had agreed with URI that the Church Rock aquifer was not likely to be used for drinking water and had granted the injection permit back in 1994. But the tribe had stepped in to challenge New Mexico's right to do so. The state didn't have jurisdiction, the tribe argued, because Church Rock was in "Indian country." Even though it was just outside the reservation border, the chapter participated in the Navajo government system, had a Navajo population and a Navajo culture. The federal government, the Guardian, should make the decision on the permit.

After years of fitful legal activity, the Tenth Circuit Court of Appeals sent the whole mess back to the EPA, ordering the agency to decide whether it should decide. In the fall of 2005, the EPA finally got around to seeking public comment, an important step on the road to drawing a conclusion.

By this time, the Navajo Department of Justice had added a new lawyer. David Taylor was hired to concentrate on the interconnected legal intricacies around the issue of new uranium mining. He had a strong background in toxics law. As an assistant attorney general for the state of Missouri, he had represented state interests when the small town of Times Beach was found to be so contaminated with dioxin that the whole place had to be erased, wiped right off the map. Times Beach looked pretty straightforward compared to the various kinds of uranium exposures all across the Navajo Nation, which covered a much larger territory and tens of thousands of people. Given the tribe's painful Long Walk history, the outcome at Times Beach—relocation—seemed out of the question even if the logistics could be managed.

Taylor wanted to figure out how to get the mess cleaned up, but first, he thought, the Navajo Nation needed to prevent any more pollution. He was not persuaded by the claims that modern mining techniques were environmentally sound. He vowed to wage "a knockdown, drag-out legal battle" to stop a new round that might impact Navajo communities. The companies pledged to work just as hard to get up and running.[12]

With the passage of the uranium mining ban, the arcane battle over who should regulate an injection permit took on added meaning. If the answer was the federal government, because the Church Rock land was "Indian country," then the Navajo tribe might argue that its executive branch was empowered to enforce the council's laws—including the ban—in the entire allotment zone. Attorneys for the tribe and for the companies could all see the implications.

URI was confident that one 160-acre square of the Church Rock checkerboard would prove its case. The U.S. Supreme Court had held that "Indian country" was land set aside for Indians and under federal superintendence. But the company owned this property outright.

The issue before EPA was this: should the definition of Indian country depend on the single tract in question, or on the character of the larger locality?

Strathmore, the National Mining Association, the Uranium Producers of America, and others all weighed in on the side of URI. Private land was private land, they contended.

But the Tenth Circuit had recommended that EPA take into account the "community of reference." In 2007, the agency announced its finding: even the URI-owned Church Rock tract lay in "Indian country," because 78 percent of the land in Church Rock chapter was Navajo tribal or allotment land, and virtually all of the population was Navajo.

"I hope this means that there will be no more uranium mining on Navajoland and in what we regard as Navajo country," Joe Shirley said. "I'm happy for my people residing in the eastern portion of Navajoland and very happy for my government."[13]

URI appealed the decision. Everyone trooped back to the bench.

The most impassioned Navajo supporters of URI were the owners of allotted lands near Crownpoint who had agreed to lease their mineral rights. One of them was Bessie Largo, a droopy-lidded widow who made ends meet by weaving rugs. Her scrubby allotment acreage was not suitable for farming. The mineral lease, she believed, was her birthright. She was supposed to make a living off the land and that was exactly what she was trying to do.

She approved a ten-year contract in 1992, swayed in part by the promise of royalties down the line but just as much, if not more so, by the

$36,800 signing bonus the company pledged to pay right away. Even if the company never mined an ounce of uranium, this money would be hers.

Fourteen years later, when I visited her trailer, she had yet to see a dime. I was escorted by Ben House, a former Navajo council delegate who had been working as URI's local liaison for a decade. Largo had a burning question for House. "Where is my signing bonus?" He sighed, translated the query into English for my benefit, and told me, "She asks me that all the time." He answered in Navajo and then explained in English that he'd said they were working on it, they were trying.

I don't know whether Ben was aware, but although that had been true at one time, it was no longer. Even URI agreed that allotment land was "Indian country." The Guardian held sway there. The only difference was that the United States held title on behalf of individuals rather than on behalf of the tribe. So URI could not pay the bonuses directly to allottees like Bessie Largo. The company did deposit a total of $367,200 with the Bureau of Indian Affairs for the bonuses. But the BIA never distributed the money.

The reason, apparently, was that the BIA had not yet approved the leases. And the reason for that was the long delay the company had run into in getting its license and permits in order—even though the bonuses were not for mining, but for agreeing to rent the rights.

By the time I watched Ben House offer reassurances to Largo, though, URI was no longer acting to get the bonuses to the people. Quite the opposite, in fact. With the ten-year terms of the leases running out, the president of URI wrote to the BIA in 2000 and again in 2003, seeking refunds, parcel by parcel, until he had asked for all of the cash.

The government, so slow to distribute the money to the people it was charged to protect, promptly sent checks to the company, and even paid interest.[14] The first round of economic benefits that was supposed to flow to Navajos from the new uranium boom had utterly evaporated, and no one was telling the people who still expected payments.

Chapter 15

Ghosts

Mark Madden, a dogged researcher in the Washington bureau of the *L.A. Times*, handed me a thick sheaf of clippings and papers in the late spring of 2005. One of them was Joe Hans's report about Cane Valley. When I read it, it looked like it might be disturbing but I wasn't sure what it meant. So I arranged to speak to a high-ranking official at EPA headquarters. He agreed to talk to me about the findings, but only on background—he could be quoted, but not by name—because he hadn't been employed by EPA when Hans filed his document.

I wanted to know whether the measurements were worrisome. "Some of the numbers were high and looked alarming to me," he said.

He could find only a few skimpy memos about Cane Valley in the files. "I think it was our community affairs people who told them to advise residents that there was uranium there and it was potentially dangerous and they should abandon those homes," he said. "EPA did its part by advising the tribe that these were some things to be concerned about. That was their responsibility."

"So what about the houses? What about the people?" I asked. "Where are they now? Did they get sick?"

"Nobody's gone back to see," he replied.

I had nothing to say to that.

Neither did he, for more than a minute. Finally, he came up with this: "I share your concern that this has happened."

I called Pat Seltzer at Monument Valley High School and asked if there were any students there from Cane Valley who might relay messages from me to their parents. I told her why I was looking for contacts. "We have a teacher from there," she said. She offered to put me in touch with Lorissa Jackson.

Yes, Lorissa told me on the telephone, she was willing to take me to Cane Valley.

For my first trip out there, in June of 2005, we met at the high school, on the paved road to Goulding's that intersected with the highway. The bleachers at the stadium had to have the most breathtaking view of any athletic facility in America. Just east of the scoreboard loomed a backdrop of long buttes and high red pinnacles. In the sky, a world of blue, a thin line of clouds floated like a reflection right over the sandstone formations.

Sheep were grazing on the field, which was irrigated to a startling, almost painful green compared to the the surrounding landscape. Crops grew alongside the driveway, and a complex of faculty apartments and trailers looked out on the modern campus. Lorissa was waiting in the parking lot. She had long, dark hair, glasses that tended to slide down her button nose, archway eyebrows, and a round face—Juanita's features, too, though I didn't realize that yet. On this day, she was quiet, very earnest, and not sure what to make of me. She seemed braced, girded. I showed her Joe Hans's handiwork, which she had never heard of. There in dispassionate print was her mother's name, a diagram of the house that Lorissa grew up in, numbers that showed how much unseen risk her family had faced. Her mother's death shifted into clearer focus, but she didn't let on, not then. Outwardly, at least, she remained in *hózhǫ́*, harmony.

Lorissa was willing to help me, and she was eager to learn what else I might be able to add to her family lore. But she knew it would be a long, sad, taxing day. She knew that she'd have to be patient, translating culture as well as language for the *bilagáana*. We would be driving for forty-five minutes, but we were going farther than that.

When we turned off the highway onto the dirt road leading to Cane Valley, we could see the famous rock towers and high tapered cones, but

this time they rose to the west and the lineup was reversed from the familiar arrangements on the postcards at Goulding's gift shop. Goulding's and
the school football field lay at the front gate to Monument Valley. I was
staring, across a flat expanse of tumbleweed, at the back door.

We kept on going, crossing from Utah into Arizona, though no sign
marked the border. On our right we passed a faded blue house—it had
been Juanita's—and continued to Ben Stanley's, where my education
about this special place would finally begin. I had no idea then that the
old mine on the top of the mesa behind these homes was one of the most
storied of the Cold War uranium boom.

Ben was suspicious when Lorissa introduced us. He was tired of non-
Navajos poking around. But I carried a radiation detector and he was curious about what it might reveal. He got in his truck and led me in my
SUV past a group of rusted truck and auto hulks, dated by the sharp metal
fins in back and rounded curves in front. They had been abandoned when
the mine closed. We passed the wash on the north end of the ridge and
climbed the old mining road. Lorissa tried not to laugh in the passenger's
seat as I veered and rocked up the slope. When we reached the monolith
at the summit, we stopped.

First, I measured the background radiation level. It showed 30 microroentgens per hour, about three to five times higher than the averages I'd
picked up down in the valley.

Animal and tire tracks crisscrossed the dirt by the old pillar. When I
set the detector against it, the sound of artificial crickets filled the air: 180
microroentgens per hour. I backed away, stopping every seven feet to take
readings—100 . . . 300.

That night, a monsoon swept through and upon our return the next
day to the mesa, we saw at once that the uranium veins on the dislodged
rocks stood out in stark relief. In the rain-brightened landscape, telltale
stripes of green and yellow were everywhere: 400, 380, 900, 1,000. In one
natural tent, formed by two tilted slabs of stone, the needle moved off the
chart, past 5,000.

"Let's get out of here," I said.

Lorissa suggested that I talk to Hoskey Sloan. Like Ben Stanley, he was a grandson of Adakai, and Adakai's younger wife had lived with his parents after her husband died. His father was Oscar Sloan, the translator and café proprietor at Monument No. 2.

Hoskey's parents were both gone by this time. Oscar died in 1995 of heart and respiratory problems. Lillie, Adakai's daughter, died in 2000 of complications of diabetes, but she had lung damage too. Anna Sling, Adakai's wife, died soon afterward of pneumonia at a nursing home in another reservation town. Like his two brothers, Hoskey had long ago left for school and had stayed away to work, but he felt strongly that a Sloan should be living at the precise spot at the head of the valley where his father and mother had settled. The family still had a permit from the tribe to live there, and he cherished the location. So despite the ninety-minute commutes to and from his welding job, he had set about building a spacious new house on the site of the dwelling where he had grown up.

As a practical man in the Navajo way, Hoskey Sloan thought perhaps he could preserve the old foundation. But he had a dim memory of helping his father mix sands from the tailings pile into the concrete, back when he was small. And he remembered his mother telling him later that they'd been told the place was radioactive. (When I looked, there it was in Joe Hans's report, though Hans listed it as "unoccupied." "It was occupied," Hoskey said, irritated. "It was always occupied.") The Sloans should have moved, he guessed. But it was the only home that they had.

Hoskey Sloan thought back to the respiratory diseases that had plagued the older generations in his family, the ones who stayed in Cane Valley while he went out in the world. He wondered if the foundation would be bad for his small sons, who liked to crawl on the floor, or whether he was making too much fuss.

By chance, he spied an old friend one day in 2004, out at the old mill site. Carl Holiday had gone to work for the tribe's Abandoned Mine Lands unit and was inspecting the DOE's work. Hoskey went over to ask for his advice.

Right away, Carl Holiday took his detector to Oscar Sloan's foundation. He took one look at the readings and knew exactly what Hoskey should do. "Get rid of this stuff," he said.[1]

After that conversation, Hoskey tore out the foundation with his own hands and dumped the debris by the old mining road, near the old auto graveyard. He took me to the pile that once supported his family's home and I scanned it with the detector. All of the seven chunks that I checked were emitting radiation at least two times above the background. Two measured 100 microroentgens per hour. The following month, I talked to Craig Little, who had advised DOE on which Cane Valley houses should be cleaned up—and which should not. Little told me that long-term exposure to the hottest pieces of Oscar's house might increase the chance of getting cancer by 10 percent.[2]

When I telephoned Carl Holiday to corroborate Hoskey's story, I also mentioned that I had been up at the mine on the mesa. I told him about the high numbers that my detector had registered, despite the prize-winning reclamation that the tribe had installed six years before. Holiday made sure that inspectors headed back out to Monument No. 2. When they saw how much of their clean topsoil had eroded, they buried the chunks of uranium again under a brand-new load of dirt.

At the processing site, of course, the uranium tailings had been carted away by the time I arrived in Cane Valley. But the huge heaps had left an invisible calling card behind. Beneath fields of tamarisk and prickly pear, Indian ricegrass, snakeweed, and Russian thistle, a plume of contaminated water stretched for a subterranean mile.[3] The stream, half again as wide as it was long, contained about 4.5 million polluted gallons from the ore itself and the various chemicals that VCA poured through it to draw the uranium out. Nitrate was the worst offender—this was essentially fertilizer water—but elevated levels of radium and uranium also showed up in pockets. The source, the government thought, was ammonium that had been used to leach uranium from the ore. Sulfate, too, was high.

No one was yet drinking the plume water, the government believed. It hadn't reached the wells. But if it did, or if someone drilled a well into its present location, and if it was given to an infant, the nitrate could interfere with the blood's capacity to carry oxygen. Indeed, during the five years that the government continued sampling the water, EPA determined that nitrate was more toxic than had previously been believed. The sulfate could cause severe diarrhea, which can be life-threatening to a baby. The uranium was not present in high-enough levels to produce kidney damage. But when the Energy Department sank new monitoring wells, they revealed that the concentrations had increased. The cancer risks were high enough to cause concern if people drank it for years on end.[4]

The DOE staff had recommended setting up a treatment plant to distill the water—a method akin to the back end of URI's solution-mining process, except that in this case the water was already tainted. The distillation would not take any water away from the aquifer, no small consideration in the desert; it would simply be cleansed and sent back down. It would take twenty years and $8.6 million, and was judged the best option for making sure that the plume never reached the parched or hungry of Cane Valley.[5]

In the end, though, the department chose a different course. DOE had sprayed herbicides on the tailings piles to eradicate black greasewood and four-wing saltbrush at the site. These native plants sent roots far into the aquifer and over time they could have sucked the toxins out. Now the agency proposed to replant the same two types of native brush that its workers had stripped away, using extensive irrigation drips, and persistent weeding and monitoring. The outcome wasn't clear, and even if it worked, would it be safe for the animals to eat the poison-laden vegetation? Prime grazing areas would have to be fenced off for twenty-three years. The staff had called this option "very problematic," but with a $3.6 million price tag, it was considerably cheaper than distilling.[6]

At this news, two of Lorissa's cousins, daughters of her "grandfather" Tony Yazzie, took up the resistance.[7] It was their portion of Cane Valley that was going to be affected. Tony's house was one of those that DOE had fixed in the 1990s, but the decontamination came too late for him. He had stayed in his place for nine years after Joe Hans's warning, until he died in 1984. He was fifty-nine years old. He had a brain tumor.[8] And now his children were going to lose their grazing land? One daughter, Suzy Taylor, was a paralegal working in Farmington and knew how to wield lawyers' terms. The sisters were not just out for themselves. They insisted that DOE build bathrooms to replace the outhouses of Cane Valley, to help make up for the residents' inconvenience. DOE complied. And in 2003, under the sisters' continued pressure, the tribe used some of its coal-fund money to build a pipeline for the Navajo Tribal Utility Authority. Tony Yazzie's daughters and the tribe, too, were using uranium as an excuse to bring Cane Valley into the twentieth century, now that the twenty-first had begun. This was controversial, to say the least; one former AML official criticized the tribe for spending on this type of project rather than on maintenance of the eroding mine caps, which clearly required constant repair work.[9] But the locals, at least, felt more than justified. For the first time, Adakai's descendants could flush toilets or wash their hands or fill a pot from the faucet to boil on the stove in Clay Springs, A Rough Rock. They would get utility bills—so strange to pay for water—and many continued to haul from wells for their livestock. But they could have faith that their new drinking supply was sanitary, much safer for most of them than their walls and their floors.

More ghosts haunted the reservation. New sightings popped up everywhere. At Church Rock, contaminated water from the Superfund site where the dam had broken was heading for the Navajo border. At Shiprock, a plume from the capped tailings pile was moving toward the San Juan River. At the old Tuba City mill, DOE was using the distilling method it had rejected for Cane Valley. But before he was banished, Glynn Alsup found a tainted well and informed the DOE that even its most expensive process was failing to contain the groundwater pollution from the tailings.

A new Navajo EPA employee had come up with yet another disturbing piece of information—a totally unexpected source of Cold War pollution. When she moved in to her office, she found that some previous occupant had left behind a massive document, a good five inches thick. The report had been produced in 2000 by a consultant for the Hopis, the Navajo's neighbors and sometime rivals. The Hopis had never allowed uranium mining. At the Navajo-Hopi border near Tuba City, there was no natural deposit. Yet when the smaller tribe's consultants set out to check the groundwater quality on their side of the line, their monitoring wells had picked up dangerous levels of uranium, thorium, and radium-226. The consultants thought the poisons must be coming from Navajo. More specifically, they suspected the abandoned Tuba City town dump. The bad water had not yet reached the Hopi drinking wells, but, not unreasonably, the Hopi tribe wanted to stop the impure stream and cleanse it before it ever arrived.

The new Navajo hire, Cassandra Bloedel, had never expected to become a uranium detective when she signed on to work with solid waste. Old refrigerators, automobile oil, glass bottles, the more prosaic leavings of everyday life . . . that is what she'd thought would occupy her time. To the solid waste department, exotic meant the rumor that a circus passing through the reservation had once left a dead elephant at the Tuba City dump.[10] The raw fuel for atomic bombs mixed right in with the trash . . . this was beyond Bloedel's wildest imaginings. But she knew she had to find out whether someone had hauled radioactive material to the dump, so one day in June of 2003, she drove her tribal-issue pickup from Window Rock to the Tuba City chapter house for some sleuthing. And that's when things got even worse.

A lady approached, overhearing that Bloedel was with Navajo EPA and asking questions about the municipal landfill. She wanted to know what the tribe was going to do about the other dump, the secret one in the desert. When she was young, the woman explained, she had habitually herded sheep on a stretch of sand across Highway 160 from the Rare Metals mill. She had often watched bulldozers and heavy equipment coming across the street. They dug holes and they filled the holes with . . . *something*, she wasn't sure what. Her cousin saw it too, the woman told Bloedel.[11] His name was Ray Manygoats. He could show her the spot.

Ray Manygoats took Cassandra Bloedel to the place that very day. The field was nearly barren, but some patches were conspicuously and completely devoid of any plant life at all. Each empty space seemed to be a rectangle, roughly nine feet across. As the two Navajos walked closer, they could see metal barrel fragments, some stamped with numbers, protruding from the surface. Eight years of drought and fierce wind had swept off the soil that once concealed the drums. They were literally emerging from the grave.

Her guide explained that as a boy he brought lunch to his dad, who worked at the mill. Manygoats identified objects in this strange stretch of desert that seemed familiar from his daily deliveries more than four decades earlier. "I saw this type of gravel, these gears and chains, this cable," he said. "This is what I saw on the equipment in the mill." He and his cousin had watched all through the late 1950s and early '60s as the convoys left the Rare Metals compound and came to their family grazing grounds to make their furtive deposits. No one had ever asked the family for permission, as would be required under tribal law.

Two apparent instances of illegal *leetso* dumping! Bloedel's supervisor called the Department of Energy in Grand Junction, once the local headquarters for the AEC's Western uranium market. Grand Junction now served as home base for a DOE division with a spectacular name straight out of Orwell's *1984*: the Office of Legacy Management. The staff there said they had no records of any mill dumping in unauthorized locations. Of course they didn't, Bloedel thought. Who would keep records of that? Besides, the DOE added, the department had conducted a gamma-radiation survey back in 1981 that showed natural background levels at the location across Highway 160. Of course, it did, Bloedel thought. Just as the Navajo sand and clay had blocked emissions from unmined uranium, the dirt packed atop the waste had hidden its rays from government detectors. If Ray Manygoats and his cousin saw what they thought they saw, the mill workers had pulled off a literal undercover operation.

Nobody believed the Navajos, or perhaps nobody wanted to believe them, or perhaps ill feeling lingered from the halt the tribe had called to Glynn Alsup's water surveys. But this time, they kept pushing. Bloedel and her supervisor even marched unannounced into a federal EPA office at the regional headquarters in San Francisco. Not until May of 2004, nearly a year after Bloedel's first trip to the scene, did a team from the U.S. EPA show up to check the field at Highway 160. When they did, they found hot spots of radiation that measured as much as 1,000 times higher than the scans of 1981.[12] But the EPA still wasn't sure that the only possible explanation was the mill.

Four and a half months later, the two sides faced off at a conference table at a congressional office building near the Capitol. Rick Renzi, a congressman from Arizona, had invited them there. President Joe Shirley had asked for his help in cutting through a whole thicket of uranium issues, and Renzi, running hard for reelection, was trying to drum up Navajo support. He set up a session, aiming for a real conversation, most emphatically *not* a hearing. This was not to be an inquisition. Renzi wanted to herd the various sides into agreement wherever he could. Along with various federal and Navajo officials, he invited Stewart Udall's son, Tom, who had won a seat in the House, from New Mexico; and Jim Matheson, a third House member, from Utah. All three congressmen represented districts that included slices of the reservation.

Despite the imposing setting—under a brass chandelier and an arch-shaped mural depicting angels and airplanes and the words "on earth peace"—this was the Washington version of an "informal" meeting. The lawmakers didn't publicize it on their websites. They didn't grandstand into microphones. They grabbed chairs alongside the participants.

After Bloedel presented a rundown on the toxics in the neighborhood of both dumps, Donna Bergman-Tabbert, from DOE, argued that there was still no evidence that any of the problematic material came from the Rare Metals mill. And even if it did, she said, she had no right to do anything about it. As far as the Hopi wells went, Congress had given DOE the power to decontaminate groundwater, but only where the pollution originated at the millsites themselves. The town landfill wouldn't qualify. And where the radiation at Highway 160 was concerned, it may have once fallen under the category of "vicinity properties," but the department's work at Rare Metals had been finished long ago. It wasn't her fault that no radiation showed up in the scans way back when. DOE had tried its best and now it was too late. The authority for surface cleanup had expired in 1998. "The law is very clear," she said.[13]

The Navajo neuropathy trial, despite the settlement with El Paso, also would not rest. Cyprus Foote, the company that had absorbed VCA before being absorbed itself by Phelps Dodge, sued James Justice and the lawyers that Daut had brought into the case, alleging that they had made up false exposure claims. (Strangely, this action came from a company that had been cut from the defendants' list by the neuropathy lawyers, who certainly weren't perfect. They thought that VCA ran a mine where a neuropathy mother drank, but it turned out that this particular mine was operated by a different company. The lawyers said they had relied on a federal document and that they canceled the case against Cyprus Foote as soon as they realized their mistake.)

Justice was very distressed. He strongly denied any wrongdoing himself and he didn't believe that anyone had tried to fool him. He had notes from his interviews. He had spoken with 140 people; surely they hadn't all lied. He thought the company was trying to scare off anyone else who might have thoughts of filing similar cases. The after-suit was dropped, but I decided to probe further as a matter of due diligence.

I called the attorney who had represented Cyprus Foote and asked him what evidence he had. "I'd like to help you, but I can't," he said. I had met Lois and Laura Neztsosie by then, and had heard the tale of the "lakes." I had met two of the other plaintiffs, a sister and brother, whose mother said she drank spring water in mining districts in Monument Valley when pregnant with the girl, and water from a Cameron pit while caring for a relative with gastric cancer and pregnant with the boy. I had met Susan Stanley, whose son died of Navajo neuropathy. She lived off the reservation, in the Colorado town of Cortez, but had gone back on weekends to help her mother with the livestock throughout her pregnancy, and at those times she drank natural water from the vicinity of a mine. I had met Helen Nez, who told the same story twice, a year apart, with different people translating, about her trips away from the old mine by her home at Tah-chee during the pregnancies that produced healthy children. She drank from a reservoir fed by groundwater near the mine during the pregnancies that produced children with the syndrome. Likewise, she repeated the same tale about the uranium warning that Dr. Snyder had delivered as her little Euphemia lay dying. I called a chiropractor in Gallup who had treated one of the other sick children. I wondered about the mother's character. "Helen Nez is a saint," he told me.[14]

I had lunch with the Navajo translator who sat in on the Justice interviews and she told me that every mother had talked about their exposure to water from uranium mines, and relatives and employers had confirmed their whereabouts at various times. She told me about visiting one family who lived hard by an abandoned mine; the children had various birth defects and the mother had breast cancer. "I was crying when I left there," she told me.[15]

And I talked to Steve Helgerson, the epidemiologist who had concluded that no environmental factors were at play when he investigated for the IHS. His time at the health service had overlapped with Justice's stint. He had never seen the Justice study, so I mailed it to him. He was impressed. He didn't think it necessarily provided the sole answer, but he did think that it raised questions that needed to be explored. I asked whether I should be concerned that the paper was produced for the plaintiffs in a lawsuit. Most emphatically not, he replied. "There are some scientists writing for a medical journal who might have motivations. There are some working for a [lawsuit] who might have motivations," Helgerson said. "Jim Justice, he's such a straight shooter. His goal in life, his whole life, is to help improve the life of Indians, the health of the Navajo people."[16]

From the beginning, I had turned for guidance to Richard I. Kelley, a geneticist at Johns Hopkins University who had worked with "founder effect" diseases in the Amish. My editor knew him and made the connection. When Kelley reviewed the medical literature for Navajo neuropathy, he said it sure sounded like the work of a genetic mutation, and because Navajos tended to marry other Navajos, a "founder effect" made sense; two descendants carrying a recessive gene would be more likely to match up and have children.

Still, he was intrigued. He helped coach me on questions to ask, helping me prepare for interviews with both sides, the genetics researchers and the advocates of the exposure theory. As I sent him more and more material, he began to doubt his original opinion. If Navajo neuropathy resulted from the "founder effect," then the number of cases should rise, then level off and keep coming at a steady pace. But Navajo neuropathy cases had all but stopped—about the same time that the biggest pits were finally covered up by the tribe with coal-fund money.

Kelley started wondering whether the scenario might be more complicated: Maybe a genetic syndrome existed, but the Neztsosie girls had been misdiagnosed. They had been exposed to such high levels of contamination and he believed that their symptoms could be explained by the exposure, and they didn't have the liver damage that accompanied most of the Navajo neuropathy cases. Then, after he read Justice's study, he came to a conclusion that was the opposite of his starting point. He grew so convinced that the mining by-products were the prime suspect that he started refusing to call the illness "Navajo neuropathy." His e-mails to me bore the subject line: FCN . . . for Four Corners Neuropathy. It wasn't the people, but the location of the mines, he had come to believe.

A team of researchers at Tufts and another from Columbia University examined three genes that they thought might cause the disease. They reached a dead end each time. But then the Columbia group found a clue in liver tissue from three Navajo neuropathy patients. The scene of the crime appeared to be the mitochondria, organlike structures within the cell that are responsible for converting food to energy. The mitochondria contain their own special form of DNA, separate and apart from the genetic code in every human nucleus—and in these three livers, the levels of the mitochondrial DNA were greatly reduced. That condition could lead to progressive organ damage like the kind that the Navajo neuropathy children endured.

An Indian Health Service researcher was coordinating the Navajo neuropathy work, but his supervisors refused to give him permission to talk to me.[17] Richard Kelley, however, happened to be acquainted with the head of the Columbia lab that was working on the project. He contacted the scientist, Salvatore DiMauro, a neurologist and renowned expert on mitochondrial disorders. Would he consent to be interviewed by me? He would, so I got on a train to New York. Like the epidemiologist Steve Helgerson, DiMauro had been unaware of Justice's paper before I sent it to him. He pronounced it "quite nice." We were joined by another professor in a small study off his main office and the two of them launched into a philosophical discussion, which ended with them agreeing that everything is genetic and everything is environmental, too. DiMauro suggested that I close my article by quoting Francis Collins, the eminent geneticist.[18] "Every disease is genetics except maybe the person crossing the street hit by a bus," DiMauro paraphrased. "Wait, even that. Because genetics is what made the person absentminded." Added his colleague: "The reality is that of all the people who smoke only a very few have lung cancer. But of the people with lung cancer, so many smoke."[19]

Which was all a long way of saying: maybe there is a genetic predisposition to Navajo neuropathy. But maybe something in the environment triggers that gene. "The two hypotheses are not necessarily incompatible," DiMauro told me.

DiMauro's group announced a breakthrough in September of 2006. An Italian scientist had found a previously unknown mutation in a recessive gene—a mutation that caused mitochondrial disease of the brain and liver. Testing DNA samples from six Navajo neuropathy patients, the Columbia lab found the same mutation in the same gene.[20]

This still wasn't a tidy solution. For one thing, Italians with the genetic mutation suffered liver disease, but they did not have the curled hands and toes, nor the loss of sensation, that afflicted the Navajos.

For another, the researchers had not discovered a common ancestor among the various Navajo patients. In Kelley's work with the Amish, he was able to discern exactly which person, generations back, had developed the mutation that caused a "founder effect" disease.

Kelley wasn't persuaded that the great discovery was correct; for one thing, it wasn't clear whether the mutation occurred in many Navajos who did not develop the disease. But even if the genetic change turned out to be linked definitively to the syndrome, there was no doubt that an environmental factor could convert an otherwise silent mutation into a lethal disease. Kelley saw this in many of his patients. Indeed, he spent much of his time figuring out what caused a mitochondrial disease to surface in a previously well child—a change in diet, perhaps, or smoking—so that he could devise an effective treatment. In the case of Navajo neuropathy, he still believed that mining's effect on the waters was the likely trigger.[21] Otherwise, he wanted to know, "where are the cases?"

The Columbia group had collected no information about the patients' exposure to contaminated water, in the womb or afterward.[22] When I asked DiMauro about the questions Kelley raised, he said, "There are still things to be explained."[23]

Of course, there would have been no mystery if the pits and mines had been securely cleaned and covered in the first place. Either there would be no Navajo neuropathy, or the role of mining would never have been put into play.

My series ran in the *L.A. Times* in late November 2006. Some of the paper's readers were in a position to help the Navajos. One was John C. Hueston, a Southern California lawyer in his early forties who had just returned to private practice after a celebrated career as a federal prosecutor. In twelve years, he'd never lost a count, much less a trial. On loan from the U.S. Attorney's office in Santa Ana, south of Los Angeles, he had lived in Houston for two years, eating courthouse cafeteria food and doing late-night chin-ups to keep awake while he prepared for the largest fraud prosecution in U.S. history. He won the conviction of the chief executive of Enron, the energy giant. The verdict came after Hueston reduced the usually affable CEO to stutters and confusion on the stand.

Hueston's wife happened to be Navajo. The couple met at Dartmouth at an anti-apartheid protest, married at her aunt's *hooghan,* and made it a priority to take their four children on regular visits to the reservation. She was from Navajo Mountain, an isolated spot that was not part of the uranium belt, but she was aware of the sad history of *łeetso* and The People.

Hueston was touched by the *Times* series, interested in the tangled trail of money and documents that impeded progress, and, not incidentally, certain that he'd pile up brownie points at home if he got involved. He resolved to make a complete uranium cleanup his next big effort, and then he went after the job. One of the most sought-after litigators in the country faxed a letter to the tribe, offering his services. That letter made its way to David Taylor's desk at the Navajo Department of Justice.

Taylor didn't recognize the name, but it didn't take much research to figure out that this was a good person to get on the team. Hueston wasn't volunteering, but he persuaded his new firm to let him propose a substantial discount in his fees. Ambitious as ever, he brushed aside skepticism born of previous Navajo judicial defeats, pledging to work toward a historic settlement. It was time to get the companies, who had always,

always slipped off the hook, to kick in for repair of the damage they'd caused. It was time for Congress to give the EPA, the IHS, and the rest of the alphabet agencies the money that they lacked. No more excuses for anyone, he declared.

In February of 2007, Hueston was hired. Within months, he got United Nuclear to pay for removing radium from the soil at Red Water Pond, the community in Church Rock chapter at the foot of the old mining waste pile. Although the huge heap remained in place, the families got some temporary relief while the United States, prompted by the tribe, initiated Superfund proceedings to end the hazard once and for all. The agency started talks with United Nuclear and its parent company, General Electric. It was the first time ever that the United States government flexed its Superfund muscles to hold a private company accountable for any abandoned uranium mine within the reservation borders.

Hueston persuaded El Paso Natural Gas, which had purchased Rare Metals, to start lobbying in Washington to get the old Tuba City dumps cleaned. Get the federal government to do it, or we'll make you do it, was his unstated threat. Next in Hueston's sights was Kerr-McGee, and then the successor company for VCA. By this time, the federal and tribal governments had waited so long that Phelps Dodge, which had been willing to entertain discussion about King Tutt Mesa and Monuments No. 1 and 2, had been swallowed up yet again. The new owner was the gold mining firm Freeport McMoRan.

One step at a time, Hueston figured, until he met resistance, and then he'd head for court. He was hungry for a trial.

Congressman Henry Waxman of Los Angeles also read the series. He was incensed. But he was incensed about a lot of things—the conduct of the war in Iraq, White House editing of federal documents to downplay the threat of global warming, a dangerous diabetes drug, the government's laggard response to Hurricane Katrina's devastation of New Orleans. The list was long and Waxman was in the unaccustomed position of being able to deal with whatever caught his eye. He was a Democratic pit bull, a diminutive figure with outsized aspirations. He had not wasted time chafing under years of a Republican majority, which gave the other party control of the flow of legislation. He had become skilled in the art of congressional investigations and had managed to wield influence that way. But this was truly his time. The parties' fortunes had reversed and Waxman was a committee chairman at last, with the power to call hearings and issue subpoenas. And oh, what a committee he chaired. The jurisdiction of the House Committee on Oversight and Government Reform was "everything," he boasted.[24]

He had a lot on his plate, though, and he was sure that representatives or senators from New Mexico or Utah or Arizona would jump on the L.A. Times series and use it as a springboard for change. Months passed, and they didn't. Like so much else about the Navajos' relationship with the government, their representatives were overwhelmed with a huge and complex agenda, and the tribal lands were split among many districts. Their delegation was also consumed with a typical congressional grab bag of higher priorities: Renzi faced a criminal investigation. Senator Pete Domenici was helping the uranium producers and was unlikely to focus on an issue that might impede a new round of mining. (As a staunch champion of nuclear power, he helped slow down a DOE plan to sell uranium to reactors from national stockpiles. These were expensive to maintain, but drawing them down would have decreased uranium prices.) Sen. John McCain was busy running for president.

Tom Udall had worked on bite-sized pieces of the problem since he got to Congress. He tried to smooth out the compensation program his family had done so much to create and he fought federal subsidies that could have benefited URI. His strategy had been to take on only the battles that constituents brought to him. He wasn't prepared to launch a larger war.[25]

Waxman found the contamination and the toll that it had taken nagging at his thoughts. He was embarrassed by it, and since he had the power to help solve it, he decided to forge ahead.

Gentle prodding was not his style and, in any event, it hadn't worked. He ran into Udall in the House gym and told him he was planning to take action. "I want to be part of it," Udall responded.[26]

In October of 2007, nearly fourteen years after Sadie Hoskie's visit to Washington, the chairman hauled senior officials from four federal agencies before his committee. The members of the panel sat on a two-tiered dais in yet another stately room, this one in the Rayburn House Office Building. The power of the chairman was implicit in the oil portraits lining the walls, portraying past congressional leaders who had held the seat, and the gravity of the occasion was not lost on those whom he had summoned. The Indian Health Service, the Bureau of Indian Affairs, the Nuclear Regulatory Commission, and the Department of Energy had never paid such high-level attention to the issue and had never sat down together to be called to account.

"This morning, we are looking at an instance where the government has never worked effectively," Waxman said in a clear tenor as he opened the proceedings. Room 2154 Rayburn was packed with mining lobbyists, federal aides, and congressional assistants. Waxman told them, "It is hard to review this record and not feel ashamed. What has happened just isn't right."

The witnesses sat below, as if they were in Harry Goulding's bull-pen. From the long table where they were lined up behind microphones, George Arthur, a tribal council delegate, spoke on behalf of the tribe. Arthur was a chairman, too, of the Navajo legislature's resources committee. He had been instrumental in getting the mining ban passed. Long gray hair curled against the shoulders of his black suit jacket. He was Waxman's *Diné* peer, but he looked different. He *was* different. He tried to explain the difference.

"The Navajo/federal relationship is based on two treaties, the second one signed in 1868 after about one-third of my ancestors died in a federal concentration camp," he told the people facing him from their seats on high. English was obviously his second language; he pronounced the treaty year with a Navajo accent: *eh-teen-six-teh-eight.* He was approaching Congress as an emissary from his country-within-the-country, but he was serving notice. His would not be the spun-sugar words of the practiced diplomat. Neither would they be the words of a passive populace under the federal thumb.

"Navajo land is blessed with mineral resources, but the Navajo people have not benefitted much from these minerals until recently, because the Navajo reservation has served, in the words of a government study, as an 'energy colony' for the United States. Navajo warriors have served the United States with distinction in all major conflicts since World War I.

"The Navajo Nation is not a rich tribe. Because of federal neglect and historic discrimination by the states . . . we have few paved roads, few hospitals or clinics, and substandard schools. Many of our people lack running water and electricity. Unemployment remains at about 50 percent.

"The Navajo Nation has no casinos, nor the surrounding affluent population needed for substantial gaming revenues. We rely on the land and the scarce water resources available to us. We live, and will continue to live, within the four sacred mountains.

"We have maintained our language and traditions, including one where the umbilical cords of Navajo babies are buried in the land of their parents. The Navajos' ties to the land where they are born is profound. We don't just move when conditions become difficult . . .

"Uranium mining and milling on and near the reservation has been a disaster for the Navajo people. The Department of the Interior has been in the pocket of the uranium industry, favoring its interest and breaching its trust duties to Navajo mineral owners. We are still undergoing what appears to be a never-ending federal experiment to see how much devastation can be endured by a people and a society from exposure to radiation in the air, in the water, in mines and on the surface of the land. We are unwilling to be the subjects of that ongoing experiment any longer."

After George Arthur's eloquent turn came a neat parlor trick. Waxman's senior health counsel had suggested it to the Navajos: Bring some waste from the reservation with you and wave a radiation detector over it with the sound on. The Navajo EPA filled a small plastic tub with soil from the rectangles across Highway 160 from the Tuba City mill. The latest tribal environmental director, Steve Etsitty, had alerted Capitol security that he was bringing in hazardous waste. Police hovered nervously and soon after clicks filled the hearing room, officers whisked the container away.

Next, Edith Hood, a neighbor of the Red Water Pond waste pile, testified haltingly about participating in the community monitoring program that had brought similar radiation there to the government's attention. She revealed something to the power-suited panel that she had been keeping to herself: she was diagnosed with lymphoma in 2006. Her father, she told them, had fibrosis, scarred lungs. Her mother had stomach cancer. Her grandmother and grandfather died of lung cancer. As the next speaker began, she reached under her wire-rimmed glasses to wipe away a tear.

This time around, the Navajos spoke up with specific demands that they had thought out beforehand: A federal mining moratorium to match their own ban until "the human costs of past activities" are "adequately addressed and compensated," and the tribe and EPA together have determined that the poison is purged from the land. They wanted funding for twenty more technicians so that they could fend for themselves, instead of waiting for responses that never came. They thought $500 million devoted to the cleanup might be a good start—but just a start.

The members of the committee, Republicans and Democrats alike, were riveted and, soon enough, infuriated by the bland responses the bureaucrats gave to their biting questions.

Yet they held on to their tempers. Then Tom Udall took the floor. Waxman had invited all of the representatives with constituents in Navajo country to join in the questioning, even though they weren't members of the committee. Udall usually displayed a mild demeanor, but he had watched his father fight, he had helped him in that fight, he knew that the compensation program that resulted was just a thin slice of redemption that had caused as many problems as it solved, he had felt powerless to take on the whole panorama of troubles that uranium had visited upon the reservation, and now he had his chance to tear into those who looked away. He turned his wrath on Jerry Gidner, director of the BIA, the squirming embodiment of the Guardian.

"Do you think that you have fulfilled the trust responsibility, the Federal Government? How do you feel about that?"

"I think that is hard to say," Gidner answered.

"Hard to say?"

"Well, sir, I think . . ."

"I would hope you would be outraged," Udall interrupted. "I would hope that you would stand up and say, we are supposed to be protecting these people. We are supposed to be out there on the line. Have you asked, have you asked any of these agencies to put money in their budget? Have you asked them to put money in their budget to remedy these contamination and cleanup problems and radioactive homes . . . ? Have you asked them to do that?"

"No."

On this day, Udall could not even try to stay in *hózhǫ́* as his father's clients might have. Past and present merged in the rush of words as his composure cracked.

"Guess what? The entire Federal Government is just like all of you, sitting there, oh, going along merrily. And they let this tragedy happen. And if the BIA had spoken up then and said, we have innocent people that are working in uranium mines . . . If one agency had stood up and said that, maybe, maybe we would have prevented all of this tragedy, and all of these folks here who have lost loved ones and breadwinners and it has put them further into poverty. But your version of the trust responsibility is what? I don't understand it. What is your version of the trust responsibility? Why haven't you been out there saying something about this?"

Gidner: "Well, I think . . ." He didn't finish.

Udall: "I give up, Mr. Chairman." His time had run out.

To the Navajos, the committee members spoke words long in coming. "I want to apologize to each and every one of you, that in the year 2007, we would still have to be dealing with this issue," said Chris Shays, a Republican from Connecticut.

"I have to say that I feel enormous shame that the Federal Government has treated the Navajo Nation as poorly as it has," said Waxman.

Then he took one more step, an extraordinary step, given the many years that the government had turned away from its allies and charges, the Navajos. Waxman directed the agency officials to return in two months for a meeting with his staff, with lawmakers present, too, and then again six months after that. Tribal officials would be present and involved as well. "We are going to pursue this issue until we get it right," he said.[27]

Chapter 16

Beginnings

Four is a number holy to the Navajos. Four mountains mark the borders of the land given to the People by the Creators. Four colors—white, blue, yellow, black—correspond to each mountain. Four precious substances—white shell, turquoise, abalone, and obsidian—correspond with each color (the yellow was most assuredly *not* uranium). Four directions: east, south, west, north. Four seasons, four original clans, and a creation story through four worlds: the Black World, the Blue World, the Yellow World, and this, the Glittering World.

In four generations, the cycle of *łeetso* played out at Monument No. 2 and across the *Dinétah*. From Adakai to Luke, from Luke to Juanita and Ben, from Juanita and Ben to Lorissa, a family passed from instinctive dread to betrayal, from betrayal to unwitting destruction, from destruction to a modern understanding, closing the circle. The place names told the story: from Clay Springs, A Rough Rock, or White Streak of Reed Coming Out, to Yazzie Mesa, to VCA, to Cane Valley.

Over four generations, two governments in Washington and Window Rock groped their way to a relationship with more balance. Both the federal Guardian and the Navajo Nation began to see that failing to act was an action in itself.

But the story was not ending with a set of loose ends neatly wrapped. The scars were too deep and the healing was far from complete. The gift to the fourth generation was instead a chance at redemption, an opportunity to build a future, a path toward harmony, the dawn of hope.

Henry Waxman stayed true to his word. His staff kept calling the agencies and the tribe back to Capitol Hill, again and again and again, so many times that the Navajos complained a little among themselves about the expense of all the trips. Mostly, though, they cheered on the committee and the new respect that they were granted as full participants. Waxman himself, and some of the other lawmakers, too, sat in on some of the meetings. When he moved over to chair a different panel, Energy and Commerce, he took the Navajo issue with him, just as he brought along his staff. He had sworn to see it through.

Forced into working in concert for the first time, the agencies came up with a five-year cleanup plan. No one thought that by 2012, its end date, the plan would restore the land to *in as good condition as received,* the promise that the mining companies had signed so long ago, the pledge that the Guardian had failed so spectacularly to enforce. But precious momentum, lost in the squabbles of 2000, was regained. Everyone's perceptions were shifting. And it wasn't as easy to pass the buck when the other agencies were sitting right there.[1]

The members of the group knew from all of the previous false starts that they *had* to do something about the water. In 2008, nearly one-third of Navajo households were still unconnected to a public water system. EPA and the Centers for Disease Control tested 149 wells and springs; twenty-two of them contained hazardous levels of radionuclides. These served seven hundred families: some four thousand people were dousing their thirst with a tide of harmful particles.

Once again, this was not news to the Navajos. Four of the flagged wells were in Black Falls, where Milton Yazzie had spent a frantic decade seeking help. Yet here was a difference: at long last, dismaying news and sympathetic words were accompanied by action. An extension of a public water line was built; it didn't reach all the way to the homes, but neighbors could converge on a central faucet to haul water that they knew was safe. For the most isolated families, EPA started paying to truck in bottled water.[2] Signs went up in the chapter house and at the watering holes themselves: *Díí tó baa'akonosin!* WATER IS NOT SAFE TO DRINK. URANIUM AND ARSENIC EXCEED DRINKING WATER STANDARDS.

If anyone needed a reminder that delay has consequences, Milton

Yazzie's sister provided one. Before the new pipe was laid, she died of kidney cancer. Her brother was consumed with grief and remorse. When a tribal official sent condolences, he e-mailed a choppy response: "There isn't a day that goes by thinking, what if I had done things differently, maybe, something would have been accomplished, in order for my community to have hope and believe there are people out there with heart and not only dollar signs, and offer more understanding and prayer for Mother Earth, to return it to its natural state first. The elders were right, greed will unbalance what was right with nature in the first place."[3]

The testing also singled out the pump, just above Cane Valley, partway up Comb Ridge, where Lorissa and her cousins had once splashed and shouted while filling water barrels for their families. By this time, as a result of the efforts made by Tony Yazzie's daughters, Cane Valley residents were connected to treated water. But a federal employee had to make the jarring, rumbling drive to warn the occupants of the house at the summit of the Backbone, which was not hooked up to any pipeline. *Don't drink that water at that well.* Again, the information came too late to save a life. Dina Hathale, the widow of the medicine man who had blessed the removal of the tailings pile, was suffering from kidney cancer. By August of 2008, she was dead.[4]

Down in the flatlands between the Backbone and the gutted mesa, Juanita Jackson's house was occupied once more. Juanita had decided that once she was gone it would be Lorissa who held the grazing permit for the family, and thus responsibility for their share of the tribe's communal land. Lorissa allowed her oldest sister, Eunice, to take up residence at the old homestead.

After Juanita's death, Eunice had gone adventuring off the reservation for years, which is how her daughter Starlite came to be named for a Las Vegas casino. But she longed to return to the Home of the People. Eunice's grown son up north in Blanding objected. He asked how she could possibly live in the very place that quite likely had killed her mother. In fact, Eunice wondered whether the home had claimed a second victim, her own baby boy, who died at four months of age for no apparent reason.

Little Alonzo had slept in a room built with mine rock, an addition to the original house. Eunice had also stayed there during all nine months of her pregnancy. The room had registered the highest radon readings of any part of Juanita's house way back in the Joe Hans era.

Yet Eunice responded with the reply that Navajos so often give: she had nowhere else to go. "Mom, I guess it's your decision. If you want to commit suicide, go ahead," said her son, but he refused to visit her there.[5]

On my first trip out to Cane Valley, on the day after I handed Lorissa a copy of the Hans report, I met Eunice moving her possessions inside. At least the family had torn out the mine-rock section when renovating the house during the 1990s. The siblings spruced up the exterior for Eunice with a new coat of olive green paint. Lorissa approved. She liked the way it made the house blend in with the setting.

At the time, Lorissa didn't know how much Joe Hans had worried, or how hard he had tried to get a new house for the Jacksons. She hadn't seen the ambiguous language in the letter that DOE finally sent. I didn't know yet, either. When I got this information, I passed it along to her, but by then, many months had passed and Eunice was all settled in. The arrangement was comfortable. With a caretaker back on the premises, Lorissa's ex brought her horse down from Colorado to Juanita's corral (an animal she loved so much that the Utah license plate on her silver Corolla read "SHILLII"—Navajo for "my horse").

Even Lorissa, college-educated, tech-savvy, so driven to learn about uranium, so heartbroken by the way mining had crippled her valley, sometimes had doubts about her doubts. It was hard to believe that peril really lurked where nothing at all looked to be amiss. I sympathized. When I was at home in Washington, I often found myself thinking, "This couldn't really have happened, really be happening, could it?" Every time I collected another set of documents, I was shocked anew by what I read. And whenever I visited the Navajo homeland, I saw how easy it was to be lulled by the stillness, the quiet, the sky and desert flowing out to forever in all directions, the stark land forms that managed somehow to be at once forbidding and serene.

After Waxman's hearing, though, the EPA returned to Navajo country with more instruments that could ferret out what humans could not see or taste, hear or smell. As part of the new cleanup plan, the agency promised to check one hundred buildings every year, a total of five hundred, for dangerous levels of radon and radiation. This time, the tribe promised to let it happen because this time, the United States pledged to follow up, doing whatever it took to fix any problems right away.

The EPA readied a new tool, built in the Navajo fashion from materials at hand. Out in San Francisco, in a warehouse at the regional headquarters, technicians took the latest in detectors down from the shelves and attached it to an extremely sturdy baby stroller. On the navy blue awning, they sewed an official EPA patch. They were very proud of this contraption.[6] They would be able to roll it along to get continuous measurements on the ground.

The work crews took the scan-buggy out for a ride on the first batch of houses, concentrating on those that were already suspected, for one reason or another, to contain some sort of *leetso* material. Of that initial one hundred surveyed, they came up with thirty-nine properties that were hazardous enough to merit clean-up.

Not surprisingly, one was Juanita's old house. Thirty-three years after Joe Hans first identified it as dangerous, sixteen years after Juanita was buried in the local graveyard near the Sloans, three years after Eunice moved back, the EPA classified the dwelling as a "time critical" emergency.

Hers was not the only one. Ben Stanley, Jesse Black, Cecil Blackmountain, Anna Cly, Luke Yazzie. All told, twelve homesites in Cane Valley were suddenly classed as dangers. The names on the list in 2008 were the same as the names on the list in 1975.

The People in Cane Valley—and at the other new-old emergency locations in Red Valley, Teec Nos Pos, and Tuba City—were told that the government would demolish their homes. But they would not be left without shelter, as had happened in Oaksprings. They were given a choice: a payment in the $50,000 range to help them get a home elsewhere, or a new house that EPA would contract to build at the same location, with the surrounding soil purified.

The agency was hoping that most would take the money; it would mean less time, trouble, and cost overall for the government. But that option would also speed up the exodus from communities that were already withering.

Six families with contaminated Cane Valley houses opted for the check; all had left and put down new roots in Tuba City, Farmington, Salt Lake. They were transplants by now.

Other exiles felt the pull of Adakai's choice. Lillie Lane, an outreach worker from Navajo EPA, drove north to a nursing home in Blanding and interrupted the patriarch's last living daughter at her bingo game. The wintry blasts had driven Anna Cly out of her bare-walled abode. "What will become of it?" she had asked in "Hear Our Voices," and she was overcome with emotion to hear that the answer could well be "return." Sitting in a wheelchair, she received Lane with joyful tears in her eyes and many happy questions. Lane, who knew well the limits of Navajo elders who had never been to school, habitually carried an inkpad. She took it out so that Cly could sign up for a brand-new house. The old woman had dealt with *bilagáana* documents before and knew exactly what to do. She pressed her thumb against the pad and then pressed it again on the paper.

For Lorissa, too, there was really no decision to make. Her great-grandfather had chosen this valley for his people. Her "grandmother," her mother's aunt, another daughter of Adakai, had wanted Juanita to live in Cane Valley so much that she had sent for her to come home, had picked for her that very spot, with the rocks in back and the sweeping vista of Comb Ridge. Here the Jacksons would stay.

She went to work to ensure that there would be a place in Cane Valley not only for Eunice, but also for her. The tribe granted a homesite to her sister across the dirt road from Juanita's place and agreed to build a residence for Eunice. From the EPA catalogues, Lorissa selected a log cabin made of pine to be built on the family's original tract. She thought that within a few years, well before she retired, she would finally complete her journey back.

Eunice's Starlite was gone, enlisted in the Army. Lorissa's son, Darren, had moved in for a while but hoped to enroll in art school far away. Her other son, Warren, lived in Farmington. Daughter Leontine was living in

Oregon, where she had presented Lorissa with her first grandchild, a boy she doted on. Lorissa dreamed of having everyone back to recharge their roots, to a place that they knew they could always return, and do so safely. Eunice had been traveling to Blanding when she could to see her fearful son; now finally he would be able to come to her.

The cleanup influenced even those who did not qualify for new government-issue houses. Anna's daughter, Pauline, started to talk about moving south from Colorado to take care of her mom.

And the last house where Luke and June Yazzie dwelled together was still standing and certified safe by EPA's scan-buggy. Son Lewis, hearing about neighbors returning, thought of pulling up stakes from Kayenta and joining the migration home. He retired from his dual jobs as coal miner and union official and laid plans to reoccupy his parents' cottage. He took me out to see its weathered boards, painted blue, and the white lace curtains that June had hung in the windows.

The Luke Yazzie family had been avoiding the valley, Lewis told me, out of bitterness and fear. He displayed both in abundance on the day we met for breakfast at, of all places, Goulding's. (The setting was his idea.) After our meal, we walked a few short yards from the restaurant toward the little museum at the old trading post, the same building where his father had brought the *leetso* chunks that changed history. Lewis referred to that occasion as "Doomsday."

Outside, near the door, stood a sandstone slab engraved with a memorial to Harry and his wife. Lewis read the words out loud, his voice loaded with scorn. "The Great Spirit has accepted their souls . . ." Lewis ad-libbed his own coda: ". . . where they are being chased by Luke Yazzie to get what should be his." The Yazzie family joke, or half-joke, was that the Goulding's empire—lodge, gas station, grocery, campground, tours—rightfully belonged to them.

Lewis was definitely his father's son. Moving back to Cane Valley, he confided, offered a long-shot chance at recouping the fortune that fate and VCA had denied the Yazzies. Others in the extended family network had kept hinting that Adakai knew of something else on the mesa that the white man might want, but they always clammed up when I asked what it was. Lewis Yazzie leaned across his steak and eggs to volunteer the secret, without any prompting from me. "I think there is also oil up there," he said. "I used to see black liquid. Sometimes it would shoot out."

It was hard to know what to make of this. It could be big talk. It could be another case of mistaken identity, as when Adakai thought that *leetso* was gold. Or if oil was really on the mesa, the reserves could be "pockety," as they had been over the river in Mexican Hat. Or the mesa could be harboring another something big.

Lewis had more than money on his mind, though. He had five children of his own and they too had lived in Cane Valley at times. At their grandparents' place, like everyone else, they had played on the tailings pile. Lewis was proud of his kids. A daughter in the military was a world-class runner. A son studied psychology and lived in Durango. But mixed in with his pride was worry. Another son, Terlando, was also a college graduate. In his early thirties, Terlando had recently been diagnosed with cancer. It was cancer of the lungs.

He feared for his son. And the fear made him focus more on family: the whole family, all of Adakai's kin. One day, I was with Lewis when we ran into Lorissa. They were related but barely recognized each other. "I will not know her kids when I see them," Lewis told me. "Her kids will not know me. That has to be changed. That is one of the things I want to rectify when I move back there."

In October of 2008, an obstacle arose in Lorissa's path back to the valley. Juanita's house, the federal officials told her, appeared to be sitting smack dab over a uranium deposit. So much radiation was coming from under the building that this was the only possible explanation. The EPA could not use Superfund or its emergency powers if the hazard was a natural outcrop. That would come under the heading of dangerous-but-not-our-department. We'll take it down, they told her. But we can't clean up uranium that is part of the earth and we can't build you that log cabin you selected. This has nothing to do with the mine or the mill. You'll have to move somewhere else.

Lorissa was crestfallen, but she did not meekly give in. She asked if anyone else had been asked to relocate and the EPA said no. She tried to explain how much the rise by the rocks meant to her and her brothers and sisters. She told them that she didn't want to leave the area. And if she had to go to another part of Cane Valley for the sake of her health, she insisted that the government put up some kind of structure on the spot where Juanita had lived with *leetso* until she died from it. The family story was tied to their movements and this was where they went to tell the story. Lorissa had contributed money, and so had her brothers, to maintain the old house. It was their lodestone, drawing everyone together when they needed to be with each other to make a big decision, always pointing them to the true path.

Lorissa had a talk with one of the federals and he suggested retesting the soil around the house when it was time to take it down, if only to confirm the agency's judgment.

Juanita's house was forty-three years old on November 13, 2008, the mild, sunny day that the government's heavy equipment rolled in. Lorissa was teaching, so she missed most of it. The EPA took only two hours to undo the months of work that had gone into a place for Juanita Jackson to come back to.

Lorissa missed her moment of vindication, too. The United States had promised to retest the ground underneath the house, and the team got to work to do just that. The family had a witness on hand. The government was paying for a temporary apartment for Eunice at Goulding's—yes, Goulding's owned an apartment complex, too—but she stayed around to watch the drama. An excavator lifted shovelfuls of dirt until it hit rock, all right—but it was crushed rock. The tiny bits of yellow dirt gleamed dully against the surrounding red clay, shining like a distant galaxy.

This was no outcrop. It was obvious that long ago someone had very carefully planted a generous helping of uranium tailings on the spot that would become the house. The EPA officials on hand knew immediately that they did have to take responsibility, after all. They surely owed Lorissa a new dwelling, but the volume of radioactive material was so gigantic that they weren't sure that they would have money, people, or time to get the whole job done. Already, they had spent $6 million on testing and razing uranium houses, their whole year's allotment for the operation, and they were reduced to begging for extra funds from the EPA region based in Denver. In an echo of days gone by, the higher-ups were not interested in asking Congress for more money, though Waxman had encouraged all of the officials to come to him for help if they needed it. The nation's economy was sliding rapidly toward a long and hard recession, the country was at war, a new president had just been elected but had not yet taken office, and the budget taskmasters in the White House had made it clear that they had much more important priorities than an old pollution problem on an Indian reservation.[7]

Only one thing was certain: this house was coming down. It looked like a crime scene, and in a way it was. The federal supervisors wore dark shirts with "EPA" in bright yellow letters on the back, just like the DEA and FBI raiding parties that have become staples of television news. A Coast Guard toxics specialist had flown in, too, to help out with this job. On the right arm of his blue jumpsuit was a "Pacific Strike Team" patch, a strange sight in the middle of the desert.

The workers set up generators, and once those were humming, turned on three air samplers. Everyone wore a plastic name tag, of the type that belongs on a friendly drugstore manager. But they were in fact dosimeters; they kept track of an individual's exposure to radiation. If the icon on the tag turned orange, that meant the limit for the year had been reached. The contractor set up a pressurized spray of water to keep down the radioactive dust. Where a family had spent decades of ordinary life, they took these precautions to keep the crew safe.

Roaring like a *Tyrannosaurus rex,* the excavator moved in, dripping water as it bit into the roof. Mechanical jaws clenched and unclenched. The roof fell in.

Eunice prayed and prayed. In the Navajo Way, a *hooghan* is never torn down, for it is a holy thing, a nurturing center of life. The machinery was killing Juanita's house just as surely as the mining blasts had assaulted the mesa. Eunice tried to suppress her shock at the brutal scene unfolding before her. She kept repeating what she was trying to will into being: "I will come back to a house that is safe and will protect us."[8]

She grew thirsty. But she vowed not to budge as long as the work continued. She thought about her ancestors who were taught to stay still for hours on end when hiding from enemy raiders. She thought about her grandmothers, who suffered for days in the time of drought and livestock reduction. "I can make it for a few hours," she pep-talked herself. Lorissa finally joined her in time to see the walls collapse. The big machines chopped and diced the home of their childhood into a ragged heap of lumber and cement. Wedged against one side of the mound was an old concrete slab marked VCA.

The next morning, I picked Eunice up at her duplex at Goulding's, just down the road from the lodge, and drove her over to Cane Valley so she could feed the horses; there were five of them by then. She didn't have enough money for gas to get there on her own. The government promised a per diem while she was displaced but it hadn't kicked in yet and she was down to her last 54 cents. (Later that day, one of the contractors would peel off $100 from a wad of bills in his pocket and hand it to Eunice to tide her over. He would deduct it from her allowance later.)

As we turned off the valley's main dirt road to rumble up the unpaved drive, Eunice trilled, *"No more hoooouse!"* It was not a happy song. But she was trying hard. "There won't be any radiation in the new house except for what I got inside," she joked.

She hurried over to the paddock, fetching hay from the shed. She spread some of the hay over some rocks and whistled, calling the horses back from their wanderings, and then put the rest in a trough inside the corral. The animals followed to munch contentedly. The white horse, Pearl, was pregnant again, she observed. A red-combed rooster strutted past. Fresh eggs waited in the henhouse.

The background music for this pastoral scene was an industrial hum and clink as the excavator continued to dredge yellow dirt just uphill from the livestock enclosure. So much for the rich, layered quiet of Navajo country. Small triangular flags outlined the grave of the house.

A white truck drove up and parked. Alice Black Tsosie, the youngest and most urbane of Juanita's kids, clambered out. She was a nurse in Blanding, having moved there over the summer from Salt Lake to be closer to the reservation. "Wow. Wow," she said at her first glimpse of the ruins. Her first thought was sentimental (and more than a bit concerned): "This is where we used to sit on the ground and play cards." Her second was practical and forward-looking: "If we get relocated, what will the cows do?" They knew to come back to this place from a day on the range. "They will get confused."

The crowd was growing. Ben Stanley showed up. His mother's house was scheduled to fall next, on this day, and then, on the following week, his own would go. He wanted to see what the fuss would be like. Then the men in the EPA shirts joined the contractor crews. They were mulling the mystery of all that crushed rock.

I eavesdropped with growing frustration as they talked. The builder was standing *right next to them*. They had never tried to find out who constructed the houses, or how. Finally, I couldn't stand it anymore. I was a writer, an observer. I wasn't supposed to get involved. But since my job was to get answers, I could surely pose questions. "Hey, Ben," I said casually, but loudly, "you helped make this house. You brought tailings down for the cement. But how did so much get under the house?" The government men were listening intently by the time I finished asking.

Ben looked embarrassed, a flush visible even on his ruddy face. "I put it there," he said. The surface on the hill had been bumpy and rough. He had brought many extra truckloads of waste from the upgrader. He had worked really hard to make a nice little terrace just for Juanita Jackson.

"How did you even it out?" I asked him.

"Oh," he said. "I drove my truck over it, back and forth, back and forth."

In the new spirit of accommodation, the EPA extended an offer to Lorissa a few months later. The uranium at the family homesite was quite obviously a mining by-product, agency officials acknowledged, but they couldn't find a cost-effective way to remove every bit. They would cart away all that they could, but the radon levels were going to stay too high to build a house on the exact same footprint. They couldn't let her live there. What if the U.S. government erected a replacement a little farther down the hill, closer to the paddock and the road? The view of Comb Ridge would be almost the same.

After some thought, Lorissa agreed that this was fair. She could compromise, too. She would always look back; she was Navajo, after all, and the stories were ceremony, to be told at just the right place and time. Yet she also wanted to move forward. She and her family would still be able to recount the legend of *łeetso* within yards of where Juanita had lived it.

Maybe the blank spot could serve as the marker she'd wanted, like the monolith up on the mesa, a reminder of the yellow days in the tale of Adakai's people. But Lorissa could live in the next world, fresh and clean and safe, to watch over what was and what would come to pass. This should not be a time of sadness, she reminded herself. This was a time of new beginnings.[9]

Epilogue

The Steeple

Lorissa's truck was barreling down the dirt road to Cane Valley in the middle of the night, under a sky so dark that the towering stone sentinels to the west were not visible, even in silhouette. She was in a hurry to get the horses fed and return to the high school campus before the break of day. She had to start work at seven. After school she would hit the road again, heading south on the highway to Kayenta, where she taught an adult keyboarding class once a week for the tribe's Diné College. She wouldn't finish there till 9:00 p.m.

Eunice was at this point biding time in a Farmington hotel, much too far away to do the chores. When Goulding's tourist season kicked in, Eunice had been kicked out because EPA could not afford the higher rates. For the same reason, Ben and Mary were up in Cortez, Colorado, making the two-hour drive every day to care for their own livestock, then heading back north to their motel. By this time, late in September of 2009, they had all spent ten months in limbo.

But the new foundations had been laid and they had set. The new walls, and the promise of a new Cane Valley, were rising.

A panoply of stars spilled across the inky heavens overhead. Their glimmer comforted, but did not show the way. The truck's headlights beamed downward, picking up the mix of gravel, dust, and weeds that the tires would hit next, but nothing more.

I felt groggy but delighted to be sitting in the passenger seat. I'd logged twelve hours behind the wheel the day before, traversing half the reservation with many stops along the way. One was unscheduled. My always precarious off-road driving career had hit a new low. I got stuck. Two strangers and a Navajo EPA staffer pushed my vehicle while I steered in reverse to get it out of a sandy swath of trail.

Like the sun, I had started in the east and worked my way west. That was my usual routine, but this had been a very different trip than all the others. Instead of filling my notebooks with tales of neglect, I was there to watch the EPA honor its promises and redeem the reputation of the United States.

Will Duncan, a tall, doughy man who was the latest EPA coordinator, had inherited the job at a good time. He was looking forward to this mission. I followed him to his first appointment at the Red Valley chapter house, not far from the cemetery where victims of uranium were still being laid into the ground. This was where the worried locals had come together to lead Franz Geiger to the outlying pumps to fill his vials. The building served many purposes: Neighbors could come in from their isolated camps to do laundry for free, or take a shower. The staff dished up meals for the hungry.

It was also a convenient rendezvous point. Daniel Yazzie, yet another of Luke's sons, was waiting in the parking lot, at the wheel of a mud-spattered truck. He had left his home down south in Church Rock at 6:00 a.m. and driven three hours for this meeting. He rolled down his window and the EPA man handed him a U.S. Treasury check for $29,159.45.

Daniel had built a mine-waste *hooghan* near his dad's house, and it had been torn down. He was sharing his compensation payment with one of his sisters, who had succeeded him in the structure for a time. They had figured out themselves how to divvy up the money and EPA had cut them two separate checks. Neither would go back to Cane Valley. He drove off without ever getting out of his truck.

Lillie Lane, from Navajo EPA, joined us and we headed over to Oaksprings. The old condemned houses were no more. The long quest that had begun with Harold Tso's fruitless knocks on so many federal doors was finally winding down. One of the new houses was ready to be turned over for occupancy.

With Lillie as our guide, we drove along unmarked country roads until we pulled up to a prefab unit with tan siding and brown shutters. Mary Jane Russell, a classic Navajo "grandma," was getting the keys to this new place. She had been living with her two daughters in an old *hooghan* next door, waiting for this day.

Mary Jane was a thin, frail woman with a long nose and twinkling eyes. She wore her gray hair pulled back, oversized glasses, a plaid flannel shirt that was also too big and the requisite long cotton skirt. She stepped forward to greet Lillie, who wrapped both arms around her, and hugged her tightly.

Inside were tile floors and high bright walls. An arched cut-out in the living room revealed the modern kitchen beyond. Mary Jane Russell made a beeline for the refrigerator, opening it and closing it, over and over, eyes wide, smile bright. She had reached the age of seventy-six without ever having one before. In this house, electricity flowed at the flick of a switch and water came right out of the taps.

The manufacturer's rep had thrown in a coffeemaker as a housewarming gift; Mary Jane's daughter unboxed it right away and put the power and water to work. Then, after a quick visit to the neighboring *hooghan*, a cast-iron skillet showed up on the gas stove, the daughter was patting a round ball of dough, and in short order a basket of warm frybread was ready. Sliced melon appeared on the counter. So did a pot of stew.

Before feasting, everyone in the family who spoke English had something to say. This excluded the hostess, Mary Jane, but she nodded emphatically throughout. "This new house is nice for my mom to enjoy," said the daughter from the kitchen doorway. Her voice thickened. "She went through a lot." Mary Jane's husband had died of lung disease. "We just want to really thank you."

Will Duncan answered, somewhat formally: "It makes us feel good to do something for your mom, especially after all she went through." He was remembering the first time he met the Russells. This same daughter had angrily asked if he had come to take the radon canister that was left at their old house twenty years before. No one had bothered to come pick up the sample and analyze the results.

———

We spent the rest of the day like that, taking the back trails through the pinyon mountain country and the red sandstone flats, dispensing keys and checks. There was just one bad moment, in Teec Nos Pos, after we turned off a paved highway to travel three tracks, each one rockier and brushier than the one before, all the way to the foot of the Carrizo range. In the shadow of the old uranium mines, the inspectors had found a contaminated place belonging to a man named Chester Yazzie. The uranium in the house had come from material he'd recycled from an older home, a piece of information with frightening implications.[1] How many new shelters were being built with old radioactive rocks and lumber? Chester Yazzie's, at least, was now replaced by an updated version of a traditional *hooghan*, made from clean pine logs, courtesy of the EPA.

Three days before the scheduled walk-through, Mr. Yazzie had passed away. Lillie Lane had heard about it through the grapevine. She didn't know the cause.

Will Duncan peered through the window at the oak cabinets and the oven and refrigerator along one curving wall. Then he stood back. His mouth turned down. He was struggling to hold back tears. "Okay, well, I guess we just needed to peek," he said. This was the problem with "better late than never." It wasn't always true.

The week before I traveled west for Will Duncan's road show, I caught up with half a dozen "grandmas" who had come the opposite way. There they were on Capitol Hill, in their long skirts and turquoise pins, lobbying congressmen and senators for uranium-related health studies. They wanted help for families exposed to radiation even if they didn't work in the mines. They had collected promises and hugs from Ben Ray Lujan, a House freshman, and from Tom Udall, who had won a seat in the Senate. He hurried in from voting, clutching a clear plastic container with a small cafeteria salad, to come see them.

One of the elders on the trip was Helen Nez, who had lost six children, including little Euphemia, to Navajo neuropathy. I was amazed to see her there. She was about Mary Jane Russell's age, leaning on a walker. Her family had raised $238 so she could ride on a big plane for the first time in her life, and she was staring openly at the marble floors and dark suits and rolling briefcases all around her. She also had news.

Through an interpreter, she said that she had joined the others because she was angry. She was angry because a new patient had been diagnosed with Navajo neuropathy and she was angry because that patient was her great-grandson. He died in the spring of 2009. He was three.

I had heard about Laura Neztsosie's death in 2008, at age thirty-eight. She had lived longer than anyone else with the syndrome. But I hadn't known about this. A new case, from a known neuropathy family, this long after mining had ceased?

As always, there was more to the story. The boy's mother, like the rest of the family, still spent lots of time at their summer camp at Tah-chee. According to Helen, the pregnant young woman had been drinking from a catch basin at the foot of the hill, even though the others warned her not to. It was the same reservoir that Helen had used for all the years she gave birth to Navajo neuropathy children. It was the only water supply on hand and it had run through the exposed uranium at the old mine. The Nezes shared it with another family that had its own tragic history: several fatal cases of stomach cancer.[2]

Of course, by that time, the tribe had reclaimed the pit mine at the top and had even come back a few years after Glynn Alsup reported erosion. New gullies allowed rainwater to seep through the clean soil to the irradiated center. He had walked with a scanner up the slope, recording jumps in radiation where scores of tiny springs bubbled to the surface. So the AML had repaired the damage. That was in 1998.

But the patch-up didn't hold. I had gone to Tah-chee with a detector myself in 2005, the year before the boy was born. I found hot chunks of uranium ore along the surface, and an open core hole. I put an ear to the hole and heard running water at the bottom. As I climbed back down, I tested some green liquid trickling in a mini-fall from under the mine; it was radioactive too, four times the natural background.

The exposure was probably there. Was the gene? Helen was accompanied on her trip to D.C. by her daughter, Seraphina. The young mother of the dead boy was her niece. Seraphina told me she had telephoned Dr. Snyder to ask that he test the whole family for the mutation that the

Columbia lab had pinpointed. She said he told her that he would get back to her, but six months had passed and she'd heard nothing. "We just want to know," she said.

We just want to know. The tribal government felt the same way about the dumps. Rejected by DOE, the Navajos hired a consultant to analyze everything in the rectangles in the desert where the radiation surfaced. He discovered carnotite ore of the same chemical composition as the rock from the Cameron pits that had been processed in Tuba City. He also came upon hundreds of tiny ceramic globes, about the size of marbles. They fit the description of the distinctive grinding balls that had been used only at the Tuba City mill.

In the spring of 2009, a team of Navajo and Hopi scientists were scouring the other dump, the old town landfill. They were still hell-bent on finding out what was polluting the water. One of them said, "If anyone finds a marble, I'll buy him lunch." Someone else piped up, "I'll buy him dinner." A third: "I'll pay his mortgage."[3]

A geologist employed by Navajo EPA bent down. "I see something." He picked up a little grinding ball, bagged it and tagged it. The tribe is keeping it as evidence now.[4] The Navajos' lawyers might have to make use of it in court.

The Navajos knew by this time that to purify the *Dinétah* would take many decades of sustained attention. Every time they thought they had a handle on the scope of the problem, a new trouble spot appeared. The first few medical studies of *leetso*'s impact on the health of The People were just getting under way, but already disturbing patterns had emerged: Uranium water in the lab made breast cancer cells grow faster. The levels of kidney disease in the east were higher than the incidence of diabetes. Something else was at work.[5]

They felt like they were wandering down a hallway, opening a door at the end, and finding another corridor beyond.

Yes, it was like that. What would become of it?

But they were energized now. In refusing to accept the Guardian's rebuffs any longer, they were changing the Guardian's perception of them. They had made a stand, were still making a stand, in their holy land. "Hear Our Voices." They were still there. The Night Chant included a passage, repeated and thus made real:

Beautifully my country to me is restored.
Beautifully my fields to me are restored.
Beautifully my house to me is restored.[6]

After all that has happened, Lorissa was saying as she drove, she was glad for a chance to raise her children and grandchildren in health in the special place of their people.

The old mesa still suffered, with *leetso* coming to the fore again and again. The valley floor had poison water coursing through its veins. Ben had the mesa lodged deep in his lungs, and so did Lewis's son, and who knew what else lay in store?

Yet Adakai's family remained and more were coming back. They would atone for betrayal with perseverance. They could transform destruction into rebirth.

Despite the night, Lorissa knew exactly where she was, and at precisely the right moment, she steered the truck onto the dirt path to Juanita's. Just before the paddock, the headlights caught a wall of pine logs, with casings for the windows and door, facing east, of course. Lorissa had seen that much before, but the builders had added something new: an A-frame on top that would someday support the roof. The house was going to have a sleeping loft, so the trestle was pitched long and narrow.

The old dwelling had nestled low into the rocks. The new roof frame reached high; it would be seen for miles around. Streams of light from the truck flowed through the holes for the windows and shot right out the open top. Lorissa really had to rush, but she couldn't help lingering to take in the sight of her steeple, glowing luminous yellow in the dark, a beacon and a prayer for Cane Valley.

ACKNOWLEDGMENTS

One great pleasure of writing a book is the chance to publicly thank those who were crucial to the enterprise. The many Navajo families who shared their stories—their treasure—are first and foremost on that list. Adakai's relations in particular put up with my repeated appearances in their lives, my intrusive questions, and my very *bilagáana* eccentricities, from my pressure for documentation to my annoying inability to find my way around in the absence of street signs (or streets). I'd like to express special gratitude to Lorissa Jackson, Eunice Jackson, Ben and Mary Stanley, and Lewis Yazzie and Mary Lou Yazzie. I also greatly appreciate time spent with elders John Holiday, Anna Adakai Cly, Don Wilson, and Anna Benally.

A number of people helped me forge connections, no small matter in a country where privacy is prized and technology is scarce. To single out a few: Patricia Seltzer, the gracious principal at Monument Valley High School, dispatched messengers on my behalf to people living without telephones in remote locales. Jeff Spitz went to great lengths to put me in touch with Elsie and Sarah Begay. Larry Martinez took me to Oaksprings; Jess King led me around Cove. Lillie Lane shared contact information, recommended books, and rescued my marooned SUV from a sandy back stretch between Dennehotso and Cane Valley. Alexander Thorne and Polly Crank were ace interpreters. The late Cherie Daut Neztsosie, who married her clients' brother, brought me to Laura and Lois Neztsosie in Tuba City. Gilbert Begay answered a message that I left at the Blue Gap Trading Post, leading to my first interview with his grandparents, Leonard and Helen Nez.

Presented with any question about the uranium industry on the Colorado Plateau, Bill Chenoweth's photographic memory instantly retrieves the answer, invariably with paper to back it up. Chris Shuey holds scores of valuable reports about contamination and potential health impacts. Glynn Alsup and his colleagues conducted several deluxe tours of their sampling databases. David Taylor and John Hueston for the tribe, Eric Jantz of the New Mexico Environmental Law Center, and Mark Pelizza of Uranium Resources Inc. all ensured that I never lacked for legal reading material, nor for explanations. Richard I. Kelley and Andrew Sowder offered basic lessons and informed counsel. Perry Charley's devotion to both his people and the scientific method was an inspiration. Phil Schiliro and Jeff Baran, of Representative Henry Waxman's staff, and Harry Allen IV and Will Duncan of the EPA took my incessant phone calls.

I earned my varsity letter in archive diving, coached by Stephanie George and Kevin DeMea of the Center for Oral and Public History at California State University–Fullerton (with a long-distance assist from Gary Shumway), Carol Leadenham of the Hoover Institution Archives, Nik Kendziorski, Jen Pack, and Nick Costa of the Center for Southwest Studies at Fort Lewis College, Crystal White of the National Library of Medicine, and Roger Myers and Carrie Larson at the University of Arizona special collections. Dan Ford granted access to the John Ford papers at Indiana University's Lilly Library.

These trips weren't cheap. For supporting my research, as well as my confidence, thank you so much to the Lukas Prize Project—to Linda Healey and Arthur Gelb, the committee co-chairs, and to Michelle Goldberg, Janet Silver, and Robert Whitaker, judges. The Fund for Investigative Journalism and the University of Arizona also provided grants. Some material in Chapter 15 and the epilogue was adapted in an article for *Smithsonian;* the magazine helped finance my travel to the Navajo Nation in September 2009.

I spent a good chunk of the fall of 2008 at an incredible idea factory, Stanford University's Bill Lane Center for the American West. The Fearsome Foursome writing group (Matthew Morse Booker, Robert M. Wilson, Peter Alagona, and Gregory Simon) kindly made room for a fifth. Tammy Frisby and David M. Kennedy were exceptionally supportive. Brainstorming with Jon Christensen, Glenn Willumson, and Kevin

Hearle was both helpful and delightful. Richard White critiqued a partial draft of the manuscript, improving it immeasurably.

The Hoover Institution generously offered me a perch during the final phase of editing, giving me space and time for revisions and reflection.

As I left my comfort zone to try something new, Jack Farrell, Amy Eisman, Chuck Lewis, Arlene Morgan, David Pasternak, Tom Rosenstiel, and Butch Ward served up sympathy laced with sound advice. David Ferrell, Megan Garvey, and Steve Carney were convivial hosts. Susan Green and Pat Rideout took the trouble to meet up with me when I was lonely on the road. Murrae Haynes, Daniel Kosharek, Colin Crawford, and Michael Riley helped me track down critical photos and articles.

Without the *Los Angeles Times*, there would have been no book. Deborah Nelson was the guiding hand behind the series that launched me down this path. She taught me how to organize a big project and loved the story from the very start. John Carroll gave it his defining stamp and, along with Dean Baquet, carved out time to get it done. The indomitable Karlene Goller and Kelli Sager won release of public documents wrongfully withheld. Marc Duvoisin rode to the rescue at a time of crisis. Gail Fisher took stunning photographs and was a boon companion on several long drives through Navajoland. Two researchers were instrumental: Mark Madden, who retrieved documents from far and wide, and in one case, from a wastebasket, and John Beckham, who kept coming to my aid long after both of us had left the paper. Doyle McManus championed the work and introduced me to Rafe Sagalyn, my literary agent.

Rafe is demanding yet patient, the perfect blend for a writer stretching for the first time from newspaper to book. He and his colleague Shannon O'Neill read an early version of the manuscript, told me it needed retooling, and administered cocktails. Both have been more than generous with their time and their pitch-perfect judgment.

At Free Press, the skillful Hilary Redmon prepared me well in the beginning and made the back-end editing a pleasure. She saw the book in my proposal, and made it better. Sydney Tanigawa and Kathryn Higuchi kept the process running smoothly.

Thank you to my parents, Amy and Joseph Pasternak. My mother cherishes wordplay and story; my dad prizes military history and science. I have kept them both in mind as I worked. I wish I could summon the words to describe all they've done for me.

My son, Isaac Braun, grew to manhood listening to this story. All along, he offered cheerleading, consultation, affection, and understanding. I love that he is proud of me, and I am so proud of him.

And finally, Steve Braun, my husband. With editing pen in hand, he was the first to read every word I wrote. His eye for detail and deep insights were indispensable, as always. He also steered me through precarious times, dispensing comfort in my hours of self-doubt and sharing fully in every heady high. For that, and for our life together, I'm ever grateful.

NOTES

Prologue. S-37, SOM, and SOQ

1. Telephone interview with Clara Mastrovich, December 5, 2009. She is the widow of Anthony Mastrovich, who was the leader of Union Mines Field Party No. 4.
2. Four of the Union Mines maps were provided to the author by William L. Chenoweth, a former Atomic Energy Commission geologist.
3. Clara Mastrovich interview. Her husband turned down the Navajo's invitation.
4. William L. Chenoweth, "Uranium Procurement and Geologic Investigations of the Manhattan Project in Arizona," Arizona Bureau of Geology and Mineral Technology Open-File Report 88-2, January 1988, p. 10.
5. *Bulletin of the American Association of Petroleum Geologists,* Vol. 28, 1944, Item notes, p. 892.
6. Nancy C. Maryboy and David Begay, "The Navajos of Utah," accessed online at http://historytogo.utah.gov/people/ethnic_cultures/the_history_of_utahs_ameri can_indians/chapter7.html
7. William L. Chenoweth, "The Geology, Leasing and Production History of the King Tutt Point Uranium-Vanadium Mines, San Juan County, New Mexico," Open File Report No. 394, New Mexico Bureau of Mines and Mineral Resources, April 1993, p. 8.
8. Chenoweth, "Manhattan Project," p. 13.

Chapter 1. The Special Rocks

1. John Holiday and Robert S. McPherson, *A Navajo Legacy: The Life and Teachings of John Holiday* (Norman: University of Oklahoma Press, 2005), pp. 62–63. Author interview with John Holiday at his home near Train Rock in Monument Valley, UT, June 13, 2009. John Holiday is Adakai's nephew.
2. John Holiday interview. Author interview with Anna Adakai Cly, Blanding, UT, May 27, 2008. Anna Cly is Adakai's daughter.
3. Anna Cly interview.
4. John Holiday interview, Lorissa Jackson translation of the Holiday tape. Holiday and McPherson, *A Navajo Legacy.*
5. John Holiday interview.
6. Author interview with Suzy Taylor, Shiprock, NM, May 28, 2008. Suzy Taylor is

Adakai's granddaughter. Shiprock is the largest town on the Navajo Nation and is located southeast of Cane Valley, close to the reservation border town of Farmington, NM.

7. Author interview with Ben Stanley, Cane Valley, AZ. May 25, 2008. Ben Stanley is Adakai's grandson.

8. Author interview with Don Wilson, Cane Valley, AZ, May 25, 2008. Don Wilson is Adakai's grandson.

9. Don Wilson interview.

10. Ben Stanley interview.

11. Peter Iverson, *Diné: A History of the Navajos* (Albuquerque: University of New Mexico Press, 2002), pp. 55–56. Iverson cites an August 12, 1864, letter from Capt. John Thompson to Julius Shaw, reporting that he'd chopped down more than 4,100 peach trees during a two-week march through the canyon.

12. Hampton Sides, *Blood and Thunder: An Epic of the American West* (New York: Doubleday, 2006), pp. 368–369, and Iverson, *Diné: A History of the Navajos,* p. 59. Iverson notes that syphilis was soon "a significant problem" among the Navajo captives.

13. Sides, *Blood and Thunder,* pp. 338–339.

14. Holiday and McPherson, *A Navajo Legacy,* p. 335, footnote 30.

15. Ibid., p. 332, footnote 14.

16. Holiday and McPherson, *A Navajo Legacy,* p. 268. Death certificate of Adakai's son, Luke Yazzie, lists the name of the deceased man's father as John Adakai.

17. Cly, Wilson, Holiday interviews. Author interviews with Ben Stanley in Kayenta, AZ, on June 12 and 13, 2009.

18. Colleen O'Neill, *Working the Navajo Way: Labor and Culture in the 20th Century* (Lawrence: University Press of Kansas, 2005), p. 23.

19. Holiday and McPherson, *A Navajo Legacy,* pp. 116–120.

20. Author interview with Anna Benally at her home in Shiprock, NM, on June 18, 2009. Benally is Adakai's granddaughter. Born in 1936, she was drafted into Adakai's workforce. Her cousin Juanita was her herding partner.

21. Samuel Moon, *Tall Sheep: Harry Goulding, Monument Valley Trader* (Norman: University of Oklahoma Press, 1992), p. 29.

22. Ibid., p. 36.

23. Ben Stanley interview.

24. Anna Benally interview.

25. Ben Stanley, Anna Cly, Anna Benally interviews.

26. Moon, *Tall Sheep,* p. 177.

Chapter 2. The Secret Quest

1. Adakai's birth date is not known. Before the Treaty of 1868, white officials did not have access to information that would allow them to keep records, and Navajos saw no reason to keep track. Birthdays were not celebrated in Navajo culture. The best

clues to his age come from Adakai's cousin, Navajo Oshley, who was interviewed for several different oral histories. The year of Oshley's birth was given variously as 1882, 1879, 1885, and 1893. He refers to Adakai as his "older brother" (cousins are often addressed as "brother" in Navajo culture; their mothers were sisters). John Holiday, in an interview, said that Adakai was born a few years after the return from the Long Walk, which would mean sometime in the 1870s.

2. Doris Valle, *Looking Back Around the Hat: A Brief History of Mexican Hat* (Mexican Hat, UT: D. Valle, 1986), p. 11. Valle's son, Richard, who runs a pizza restaurant in Mexican Hat, loaned a copy of this self-published booklet to the author.

3. Ibid., p. 12.

4. Ibid., p. 8.

5. Ibid., p. 16.

6. Navajo Tribe v. United States, nos. 69 and 299, U.S. Claims Court.

7. Valle, *Looking Back Around the Hat*, p. 32.

8. Jay Ellis Ransom, "We Followed the Lure of Carnotite," in *The Desert Magazine*, Vol. 13, No. 4, February 1950, p. 14.

9. Preston Redd, *From Horseback to Cadillac, I'm Still a Cowboy: True Tales of the Old West* (Tempe, AZ: Tavas Cash Press, 1988), p. 227.

10. Interview with Luke's son, Herbert Yazzie, at his home in Cow Springs, AZ, November 17, 2008.

11. Holiday and McPherson, *A Navajo Legacy*, pp. 163–164.

12. Papers of Harold L. Ickes, Diaries and Index, Sunday, October 12, 1941, p. 5937. Reviewed in Manuscript Reading Room of the Library of Congress, Washington, DC. Ten leaseholds from the 1920s still existed and the VCA men plotted to get hold of the one belonging to Wetherill's brother-in-law at a bargain-basement price. One of the partners was willing to buy out the others without informing them of VCA's interest, then turn around and sell the whole lease to the big corporation. "I have gone into this with the Indian Office in Washington and there will be no trouble," one of the company managers wrote, according to an antitrust lawsuit later brought against VCA. But the maneuver did not work and the company went on to get leases on its own.

13. Betty Rodgers, interviewed by Brad Cole of Northern Arizona University, for the United Indian Traders Association Oral History Project, July 14, 1999. Betty Rodgers is a Navajo who was raised by the Wetherills.

14. Personal communication from Wetherill family historian Harvey Leake, September 23, 2008.

15. The account of this incident is derived from Chapter 5, "My Foray into Uranium," of Preston Redd's memoir, *From Horseback to Cadillac*.

Chapter 3. Jumping on the King

1. Moon, *Tall Sheep*, p. 46.
2. Ibid., p. 45.
3. Ibid., p. 48.
4. Ibid., pp. 145–150.
5. The figures for *Stage Coach* pay and expenses come from an October 20, 1938, letter to Dan Keefe at Walter Wanger Productions from Ray Heinze, copied to John Ford, Wingate Smith, Lowell Farrell, Jack Kirston, and John Eckert. Ford spoke of his love for the valley in an oral history interview with his grandson, Dan Ford.
6. Moon, *Tall Sheep*, p. 176.
7. Letter, E. D. Bransome to Assistant Interior Secretary Oscar L. Chapman, July 24, 1942.
8. Moon, *Tall Sheep*, p. 176.
9. Author interview with Gary L. Shumway, Blanding, UT, May 27, 2008. Shumway, a retired California State University, Fullerton, historian, knew Viles personally. His father and uncle worked for VCA.
10. Luke's cousin, John Holiday, says that Luke told him that he was looking for the rocks because Goulding was interested. Holiday says that on his own he took a few small stones from the old cave to the trading post and was able to exchange them for food. But his samples apparently weren't big or radioactive enough to arouse the trader's interest further.
11. Anna Cly interview. Interview with Luke's daughter, Mary Lou Yazzie, on November 16, 2008, at Kayenta, AZ.
12. Unpublished transcript of Samuel Moon's full interview with Luke Yazzie on July 23, 1975, with Luke's son Herbert Yazzie translating, p. 6. Reviewed by the author at the Center for Oral and Public History, California State University, Fullerton (CSUF).
13. Anna Cly, Ben Stanley interviews, along with a June 25, 2005, interview for the *Los Angeles Times* with Hoskey Sloan, Oscar's son.
14. The account of Luke Yazzie's interaction with Harry Goulding is drawn from oral histories with both men in Moon's *Tall Sheep*, an article by Goulding titled "Navajo Hunt Big Game: Uranium," in *Popular Mechanics* in June of 1950, author interviews with Anna Cly and Ben Stanley, and a brief interview with Yazzie in Peter Eichstaedt's fine book about the Navajo uranium miners' fight for compensation, *If You Poison Us* (Santa Fe: Red Crane Books, 1994).
15. Anna Benally interview.

Chapter 4. The Power of *Leetso*

1. "The Romance of Uranium," remarks prepared by Jesse C. Johnson, director of the Raw Materials Division of the Atomic Energy Commission, for delivery to the American Institute of Mining and Metallurgical Engineers, February 20, 1956.

2. Letter stamped "Restricted" and "Confidential," from R. H. Allport, District Mining Supervisor, U.S. Geological Survey, Carlsbad, NM, to Allen G. Harper, Navajo Area Director for the Office of Indian Affairs, Window Rock, AZ, July 25, 1950.

3. Union Carbon and Carbide Corporation and Vanadium Corporation of America, appellants, p. 67. *Union Carbide and Carbon Corp. v. Nisley.* Union Carbide and Carbon Corp. Nos. 6319–6320, U.S. Court of Appeals 10th Circuit rehearing denied.

4. The charges for hauling were noted in a transcript of an oral history interview of Robert L. Anderson conducted by Gary L. Shumway and Harry Henslick on August 1, 1970, p. 9. Reviewed by the author at the Center for Oral and Public History, CSUF. A contract with VCA from 1943 specifies payment for both vanadium and uranium content. Contract No. W-7405 eng-267, "Supply Contract, War Department. Contractor: Vanadium Corporation of America." The amount is left blank.

5. William L. Chenoweth, preliminary report, "Early Vanadium-Uranium Mining in Monument Valley, Apache and Navajo Counties, Arizona, and San Juan County, Utah," Arizona Bureau of Geology and Mineral Technology, Open-File Report 85-15, p. 4.

6. Robert L. Anderson interview, CSUF.

7. The guest register at Goulding's Lodge for December 13, 1942, is signed by E. D. Bransome, New York, and D. W. Viles, Monticello, UT.

8. Peter Eichstaedt, *If You Poison Us: Uranium and Native Americans,* (Santa Fe: Red Crane Books, 1994), p. 179.

9. Anna Benally, Eunice Jackson interviews.

10. Transcript of an unpublished portion of Samuel Moon's oral history interviews with Harry Goulding. Tape 103, August 23, 1974, p. 8. Reviewed at CSUF.

11. Transcript of an oral history interview of Robert L. Anderson conducted by Gary L. Shumway and Harry Henslick on August 1, 1970, pp. 55–56. Reviewed at CSUF. Anderson later went to work for VCA. He was not in the business in the early 1940s but was acquainted with a lot of miners and millers when he heard the buzz about the Army's wartime interest in uranium.

12. Transcript of unpublished portion of Moon interviews with Goulding, reviewed at CSUF. Tape 103, August 23, 1974, p. 6.

13. Unpublished transcript of Goulding interviews by Moon, Tape 103, pp. 8–11. The book *Tall Sheep* does not include Goulding's account of his persuasive tactics with reluctant Navajo miners, nor does it make the connection between those conversations and his questioning by the FBI.

14. Moon, *Tall Sheep,* p. 181.

15. Ibid., p. 182. A story about the Eisenhower letter and response, "Navajos Greet Gen. Eisenhower," was also published on the front page of the military newspaper *Stars and Stripes,* August 17, 1943.

16. Dwight D. Eisenhower to Harry Goulding, July 24, 1943. The letter is on display at a small museum in the original trading post building.

17. Chenoweth, "Early Vanadium-Uranium Mining in Monument Valley," p. 6.

18. Ibid., pp. 4 and 6, and personal communication from Chenoweth, November 24,

2009. Bids for Monument No. 1, for instance, were opened twenty-one days after
the tract was advertised.

19. Redd, *From Horseback to Cadillac.*
20. Mining lease I-149-IND-6204. This lease for Monument No. 2 was the standard
    wording in all Navajo tribal mine leases (other than oil and gas).
21. *Tall Sheep,* p. 180.
22. John Holiday interview.
23. Eichstaedt, *If You Poison Us,* p. 25.
24. Telephone interview with Clara Mastrovich, December 5, 2009.
25. Mastrovich interview.
26. *Union Carbon and Carbide Corporation and Vanadium Corporation of Amer-
    ica, Appellants, v. Frank Nisley, Jr., Union Carbon and Carbide Corporation and
    Vanadium Corporation of America, Appellants v. John F. Wade, Union Carbon and
    Carbide Corporation and Vanadium Corporation, Appellants v. Howard Balsley.* U.S.
    Court of Appeals, Tenth Circuit, December 27, 1961, footnote 17.
27. Letter from Page Edwards to Jesse C. Johnson, July 17, 1963.
28. Union Carbon and Carbide Corporation and Vanadium Corporation of America,
    Appellants. p. 69.
29. William L. Chenoweth, "Chenoweth Examines Strategic Procurement for Manhat-
    tan Project," *Paydirt,* Wyoming Mining Association, January 1998.
30. Allport to Harper letter, July 25, 1950. The tonnage was shipped before February 7,
    1944 to the VCA-operated mill at Monticello.
31. Allport to Harper, July 25, 1950. The amount of uranium oxide was calculated
    from Table 2 in Chenoweth, "Uranium Procurement."
32. Tom Zoellner, *Uranium: War, Energy and the Rock That Shaped the World* (New
    York: Viking, 2009), p. 59.
33. Zoellner, *Uranium,* p. 65.
34. Chenoweth, op. cit.
35. Death estimates from "The Manhattan Project: An Interactive History," by the
    U.S. Department of Energy Office of History and Heritage Resources, available on-
    line at http://www.cfo.doe.gov/me70/manhattan/index.htm.

Chapter 5. Cold War

1. Jesse C. Johnson, "The Outlook for Uranium," remarks prepared for delivery to the
   American Mining Congress, San Francisco, September 22, 1954. From the Jesse C.
   Johnson papers, Hoover Institution Archives, Box 3, Folder 6.
2. Atomic Energy Act of 1946, Public Law 585, 79th Congress, Section 5, paragraphs
   2 and 5.
3. Jesse C. Johnson, "The Development of the Uranium Program," speech to the
   Washington section, AIME, May 7, 1957.
4. Ibid.
5. Jesse C. Johnson, "The Uranium Program: The Development of the Industry and

the Future Outlook," remarks upon receipt of the Ambrose Monell Medal Award, Columbia University, May 12, 1961.

6. Chenoweth, in *Paydirt.*

7. April 11, 1948, press release: "U.S. Atomic Energy Commission Announces Program to Stimulate Production of Uranium."

8. Eisenhower Administration Project, Oral History Research Office, Columbia University. Jesse C. Johnson, p. 33. Transcript of a tape-recorded interview by John T. Mason, Jr., with Johnson on September 20, 1967, in Seattle, WA.

9. May 12, 1948, press release: "AEC Announces Price Increase for Uranium Bearing Ores."

10. Jeff Todd Titon, Linda Fujie, David Locke, and David P. McAllester, *Worlds of Music: An Introduction to the Music of the World's Peoples* (Belmont, CA: Thomson Schirmer, 2005), p. 54.

11. Transcript of an unpublished interview by Samuel Moon with Jack Sleeth in Monument Valley on July 15, 1974. Sleeth worked for Harry Goulding at the Monument Valley Trading Post.

12. Edwin R. Junckes, mineral engineer, U.S. Bureau of Mines, "Vanadium," in *Engineering and Mining Journal,* February 1947, p. 88.

13. Viles had gained so much influence within VCA that G. R. Kennedy, an executive at Kerr-McGee, described him as "the one-man corporation Denny Viles of VCA," in a speech to the American Mining Congress in San Francisco on September 23, 1954, about uranium operations during the early days of the Cold War. Johnson kept the text in his files.

14. October 16, 1948, press release: "AEC Announces New Uranium Production Plans."

15. In his 1954 speech, Kennedy described Johnson's negotiation style as "blandishments and genial persuasiveness."

16. Lt. Commander W. L. Stevenson, U.S.N.R.F., to J. C. Johnson, undated. Johnson's Alaska work files are dated 1917 and were reviewed at the Hoover Institution Archives.

17. Kennedy used this term in his 1954 speech. He was involved in the industry as the co-owner of Navajo Uranium Co., which also mined in the Lukachukais. Navajo Uranium was bought out by Kerr-McGee.

18. Union Carbon and Carbide Corporation and Vanadium Corporation of America, Appellants, footnote 23.

19. Lewis Yazzie interview.

20. Andrew Hecht, "The Great Uranium Rush," in *Argosy: The Complete Man's Magazine,* January 1955, pp. 60–61.

21. Brad Cole of Northern Arizona University, interview with Ethel Kennedy in Farmington, NM, March 12, 1998, for the United Indian Traders Association Oral History Project. Transcript of Side 1. Accessed online at http://www.nau.edu/library/speccoll/exhibits/traders/oralhistories/textfiles/kennedy-e.txt.

Chapter 6. The Obstacle

1. Lewis, Robert K., Pennsylvania Department of Environmental Protection, Bureau of Radiation Protection, Radon Division. *A History of Radon—1470 to 1984*, presented at the 2006 National Radon Meeting. The text can be found at http://www.crcpd.org/radon/HistoryOfRadon.rtf, on the website of the Conference of Radiation Control Program Directors, Inc.
2. Ibid.
3. Ibid.
4. Duncan A. Holaday, Wilfred D. David and Henry N. Doyle, *An Interim Report of a Health Study of the Uranium Mines and Mills by the Federal Security Agency, Public Health Service Division of Occupational Health and the Colorado State Department of Public Health,* May 1952, p. 4.
5. Lewis, *A History of Radon.*
6. *Nuclear Terms: A Brief Glossary*, USAEC Division of Technical Information and Division of Public Information. Letter from Robert F. Bell, M.D., to Page Edwards, January 13, 1966.
7. Ralph V. Batie to Stewart L. Udall, December 26, 1979.
8. B. S. Wolf, M.D., Medical Director, New York, to P. C. Leahy, Manager, Colorado Area Office, classified memorandum, "Medical Survey of Colorado Raw Materials Area," July 19, 1948. The copy from Jesse Johnson's files was reviewed by the author at the Hoover Institution of Stanford University in Palo Alto, CA.
9. Stewart L. Udall, Handwritten notes of a conference in Patterson, NY, with retired Public Health Service industrial hygienist Duncan Holaday, March 20, 1980.
10. Henry N. Doyle, *The Federal Industrial Hygiene Agency: A History of the Division of Occupational Health, United States Public Health Service.* Prepared for the History of Industrial Hygiene Committee, American Conference of Governmental Industrial Hygienists. The Smithsonian Libraries catalogue notes that this was probably in 1975.
11. Batie to Udall, December 26, 1979.
12. Deposition of Ralph V. Batie for John N. Begay vs. United States, pp. 10–13.
13. Batie to Udall, December 26, 1979.
14. "AEC press release, "AEC and US Geological Survey to Issue Handbook for Uranium Prospectors," May 8, 1949.
15. Robert Stapp, "Working in Uranium Mine Is Peril to Life," and "Radioactive Particles and Acid Fumes Have Ruined Many Workers' Health," both in the *Denver Post* of July 7, 1949.
16. Batie to Udall, December 26, 1979.
17. Ibid. On pp. 10–13 of a deposition for *John N. Begay v. United States,* Batie gives a more detailed account and says that Viles may have been accompanied by a second VCA executive.
18. Ibid.
19. White Canyon opened in mid-1949 and was shut down in 1953. It was essentially

a pilot project and was considered less than a rousing success. Energy Information Administration, U.S. Department of Energy, "White Canyon Mill Site." Accessible online at http://www.eia.doe.gov/cneaf/nuclear/page/umtra/whitecanyon_title1 .html.

20. Handwritten items in Jesse Johnson's spiral notebook for his 1949 trip.
21. Handwritten list in Jesse Johnson's spiral notebook, "Work Matters to Discuss Re Col trip 8/21-9_."
22. Batie to Udall, December 26, 1979.
23. Advisory Committee on Human Radiation Experiments—Final Report.
24. Henry N. Doyle, memorandum, "Survey of Uranium Mines on Navajo Reservation, November 14–17, 1949, January 11–12, 1950," U.S. Public Health Service, Salt Lake City, UT, as cited in Eichstaedt, *If You Poison Us.*
25. Ibid.
26. Denny Viles to Allen G. Harper, Area Director, Office of Indian Affairs, Navajo Service, April 11, 1950.
27. Charles C. Hedges, Chief Medical Officer, Navajo Service to Sam Ahkeah, Chairman, Navajo Tribal Council, July 7, 1950.
28. Duncan A. Holaday, Office Memorandum to Henry Doyle, Chief, Industrial Hygiene Field Station, USPHS, Salt Lake City, UT, May 29, 1950.
29. Duncan Holaday, to Henry Doyle, copied to Allen Look (the regional Bureau of Mines director). "Subject: Radon Samples in Uranium Mines," February 21, 1950.
30. Batie, deposition for *John N. Begay v. United States.*
31. Batie to Udall, December 26, 1979.
32. Color slides in the collection of Johnson's papers at the Hoover Institution.
33. D. W. Viles, to Jesse Johnson, letter of September 16, 1950. Viles enclosed "a few snaps" as souvenirs.
34. Johnson noted with a pencil mark this passage in his copy of a report from the Joint Committee on Atomic Energy: ". . . if war should come years hence and if the United States did not then possess as many atomic weapons relative to other types of armaments as would have been desirable, there could be no valid exoneration of either the military or higher authority in terms of uranium shortage . . ."
35. Wayne P. Brobeck to Sen. Henry M. Jackson, letter of May 19, 1961. Brobeck, a former staff member of the Joint Committee on Atomic Energy, was reminiscing about Johnson's "calm and confident voice" when everyone else was desperately afraid of a uranium shortfall.
36. Jesse C. Johnson to George G. Gallagher, letter dated January 20, 1951.
37. Deposition of Duncan A. Holaday, *John N. Begay v. United States.*
38. Duncan Holaday to P. W. Jacoe, Director, Divison of Industrial Hygiene, Colorado Board of Health, letter, January 30, 1951, p. 1.
39. Duncan Holaday to Denny Viles, October 20, 1950.
40. Holaday to Jacoe.
41. Transcript of Proceedings, *An Open Hearing in re Uranium Mining on the Navajo Reservation.* Conducted by the Advisory Committee of the Navajo Tribal Council

and Window Rock Area Office, Bureau of Indian Affairs. Window Rock, AZ, February 6 and 7, 1951.

42. Ibid.
43. Ibid.
44. Ibid., p. 21.
45. Ibid., p. 23.
46. Ibid.
47. Ibid., p. 36.

Chapter 7. A Hundred Tons a Day

1. This account is drawn from the transcript of the Robert L. Anderson interview by Shumway and Henslick, reviewed by the author at CSUF, pp. 13–14.
2. Transcript of Anderson interview by Shumway and Henslick; the various workers' escapades are recounted on pp. 19–21.
3. Transcript of Anderson interview by Shumway and Henslick, pp. 46–47. When Anderson describes the percentage of uranium in the ore, Shumway, whose father and uncles were miners, reacts with a single word: "Wow!"
4. Transcript of Anderson interview by Shumway and Henslick, pp. 16–17.
5. Transcript of oral history interview with Dean Shumway by Gary Shumway, August 12, 1970, in Carroll Hall at Brigham Young University, p. 15. Reviewed by the author at CSUF.
6. Ibid.: "In those days, they could get Indians for next to nothing, and they just had thousands of Indians around there."
7. Interview with Anna Benally in Shiprock, NM, on June 18, 2009. She is Adakai's granddaughter.
8. Ibid., p. 14.
9. Nancy Lofholm, "Family of 'Uranium King' Feuds amid the Ruins of Utah Empire," *Denver Post*, January 15, 2004, p. A-1, and www.lucy-desi.com, website of the Lucille Ball–Desi Arnaz Center in Jamestown, NY.
10. Transcript of Anderson interview by Shumway and Henslick, p. 24.
11. Hoskey Sloan interview in Cane Valley on June 25, 2005, for the *Los Angeles Times*; Eunice Jackson interview with the author in Cane Valley, November 13, 2008.
12. Eunice Jackson interview.
13. Ben Stanley interview with the author in Cane Valley, May 25, 2008.
14. Transcript of Anderson interview by Shumway and Henslick, p. 22.
15. Ibid., pp. 17–18.
16. Ibid., p. 26.
17. Transcript of oral history interview with Ned A. Yazzie by Kathy Biel and Harry Henslick, in Cane Valley on August 6, 1970, p. 2. Reviewed by the author at CSUF.
18. Anderson interview by Shumway and Henslick, p. 32. Also: transcript of oral history interview with Elmer Hurst by Dorothy Erick and Kathy Biel, at his Utah home, undated, p. 26. Reviewed by the author at CSUF.

19. Anderson interview by Shumway and Henslick, p. 31.
20. Mary Lou Yazzie interview with the author.
21. Unpublished transcript of Luke Yazzie interview by Samuel Moon, p. 9.
22. Ibid., p. 11.
23. Unpublished transcript of Goulding interview by Samuel Moon, August 23 and 24, 1974, p. 9.
24. Unpublished transcript of Goulding interview with Samuel Moon in Page, AZ, on July 13, 1975, p. 8.
25. Ibid. Goulding is vague in the Moon interviews on the subject of the checks' frequency (weekly, monthly, yearly) and the duration of the period that he got paid. The material, which was not included in *Tall Sheep*, is the first disclosure that he got paid at all.
26. Ibid., p. 9.
27. Ibid.
28. Transcript of Anderson interview with Shumway and Henslick, p. 51.
29. A.T. Steele, "Uranium Finds and Oil Leases Putting Money in Navajo Coffers," *St. Louis Post-Dispatch*, undated. Bill Richardson, "New Mexico, Arizona Indians Reaping Uranium Boom Profit," Associated Press, December 9, 1954.
30. Ibid., p. 52.
31. Unpublished Goulding interview by Moon, August 23, 1974, p. 8.
32. Letter from Jesse C. Johnson to Denny Viles, June 22, 1953.
33. Memorandum to Chief, Division of Industrial Hygiene, Public Health Service, from Lewis J. Cralley, Senior Scientist, March 29, 1951. Subject: Report of Trip, Colorado Plateau Area, to Discuss with the Mine Operators Steps for Reducing the High Radon Concentration Found in the Uranium Mines. Cralley accompanied Holaday.
34. Holaday deposition, *Begay vs. United States*, p. 135. Holaday named Booth Eckman and John Maxwell as VCA executives whom he also talked to "more than once" about dangerous radon levels in the mines.
35. Anderson interview by Shumway and Henslick, p. 35.
36. Duncan A. Holaday, Wilfred D. David, and Henry N. Doyle, An Interim Report of a Health Study of the Uranium Mines and Mills by the Federal Security Agency, Public Health Service, Division of Occupational Health, and the Colorado State Department of Public Health, May 1952, p. 6.
37. "Radiation Problem in Uranium Mines of the Colorado Plateau: Report by the Director of Raw Materials," p. 5. The memo was circulated to commissioners on April 4, 1952.
38. Holaday deposition, *Begay vs. United States*, pp. 39–43.
39. Federal Security Agency, For Release Thursday, June 26, 1952, pp. 1–3.
40. Letter from Holaday to Udall, January 16, 1984.
41. Holaday deposition, *John N. Begay vs. United States*, p. 66. Costs are from "Underground Uranium Mining Costs," a presentation to the National Western Mining Conference, Denver, February 1958, by Gordon B. Peck, chief, ore evaluation sec-

tion, Grand Junction Operations Office, U.S. Atomic Energy Commission. Peck noted "a comfortable mining profit."

42. Holaday deposition, *John N. Begay vs. United States*, p. 176.
43. Ernest R. Rodriguez, Mining Health and Safety Engineer, Bureau of Mines, "Mine Safety Inspection Report, Monument No. 2 Mine, Vanadium Corporation of America, Navajo Indian Reservation, Apache County, Arizona," July 23, 1953. As read into the record of the Holaday deposition in *John N. Begay vs. United States*.
44. James Egan, "The Development and Progress of a Health Study of Uranium Miners with Consideration of Some of the Problems Involved," National Cancer Institute internal report, December 1956, p. 3.
45. The Department of Defense Research and Development Board, "Program Guidance Report, Joint Panel on the Medical Aspects of Atomic Warfare," September 12, 1952, p. 15. Declassified. Reviewed by the author at the National Security Archive, Washington DC.
46. The full story of the injections is revealed in Eileen Welsome's excellent book *The Plutonium Files: America's Secret Medicine Experiments in the Cold War* (New York: The Dial Press, 1999).
47. Letter from Joseph G. Hamilton, M.D., to Shields Warren, Director, Division of Biology and Medicine, U.S. Atomic Energy Commission, November 28, 1950, p. 3.
48. Undated memo from William F. Bale to "The Files." Reviewed by the author at the University of Arizona special collections, Tucson, AZ.
49. The miners' study did give the AEC something to work with. ". . . rightly or wrongly the USAEC evaluated the biological effects of plutonium based at least partly on the human data from the uranium miners," wrote a Department of Energy researcher decades later. Sidney Marks, M.D., Analysis and Assessment Program, Division of Biomedical and Environmental Research, U.S. Energy Research and Development Administration, "A Trip Report for the Energy Research and Development Administration to Dr. Geno Saccomano in Grand Junction, Colorado," p. 9. The report is undated but according to the memo, the trip occurred in August of 1975; a response from another ERDA official, Walter Weyzen, was written on November 20, 1975. Reviewed at the National Security Archive, George Washington University, Washington DC.
50. Egan, p. 5.
51. Pope A. Lawrence, "Uranium Miners Field Notes," 1954, reviewed by the author at the National Library of Medicine, History of Medicine Collection, Bethesda, MD.
52. Pope Lawrence, field notes, April 16, 1954.
53. Drawn from Pope Lawrence field notes in June and July 1954.
54. Egan, p. 8.
55. Letter from James Egan to Dr. William Baum, Field Investigations and Demonstrations Branch, National Cancer Institute. August 15, 1954.
56. Holaday deposition, *John N. Begay vs. United States*, p. 101.
57. Lawrence field journal.
58. Lawrence field journal, August 2, 1954.

Chapter 8. Endings

1. Mary Lou Yazzie interview.
2. Herbert Yazzie interview.
3. Anna Benally interview.
4. John Holiday interview.
5. Ibid.
6. Eunice Jackson interview.
7. Anna Benally, John Holiday interviews.
8. Letter from Allen D. Look, Arizona Section Chief, U.S. Bureau of Mines, to D. W. Viles, July 31, 1953. The note was stiffly, painfully polite: "It was the impression of our engineer that it was a policy to give no consideration to the recommendations which would be made in our report although we could make our mine visits as a courtesy. It would be sincerely regretted if this were indeed true . . ." He sent a copy to the tribal chairman and another to the Commissioner of Indian Affairs. From headquarters in DC, the letter made its way back west to Interior's area director on the scene, Allan Harper. Just as he had assured the tribal council that health studies would protect the miners, Harper promised his distant superiors that "sound safety practices will be demanded" of VCA. But he sent all of the material back and the Bureau of Mines inspectors kept making the same complaints over and over through the following year.
9. Letter, William Wade Head, Gallup area director, Bureau of Indian Affairs, to Glenn L. Emmons, Commissioner of Indian Affairs, October 29, 1954. Bill Richardson, "New Mexico, Arizona Indians Reaping Uranium Boom Profit," Associated Press, Albuquerque, December 9, 1954.
10. Dorothy L. Pillsbury, "Indians Inventory Tribal Problems," *Christian Science Monitor,* September 1, 1955.
11. Gary Shumway, unpublished doctoral dissertation, "A History of the Uranium Industry on the Colorado Plateau," University of Southern California, 1970, p. 126, with additional details from author's interview with Shumway, in which he said that five different miners told him about this gambit. He wrote that two miners, relatives of his named Harris and Lee Shumway, discovered that VCA kept two sets of logs.
12. Head letter to Emmons, October 29, 1954.
13. Robert S. Bird, New York Herald Tribune News Service, "Indians Mine Uranium Ore," reprinted in the *Columbus Dispatch,* November 19, 1954.
14. "Girl About Town" column and various articles from the *Durango Herald-News,* saved by Viles in the collection of his papers at the Center for Southwest Studies, Ft. Lewis College, Durango, CO. True to form, Viles attempted to turn his political connections to his business advantage. He persuaded a state legislator, Tom Kimball, to campaign for the nonexistent job of federal on-site supervisor for uranium exploration and leasing for the Interior Department's Indian Office. This would have given VCA the inside track on all matters Navajo. A powerful congressman,

Wayne Aspinall, was persuaded to suggest the position be added for Kimball, but the Commissioner of Indian Affairs, Glenn Emmons, politely rejected the idea. Aspinall and Emmons exchanged letters on November 23, 1953, and January 14, 1954.

15. "Monument Valley Upgrader Site (Monument 2 Mine)," Remediation of Mill Sites, Energy Information Administration, accessed online at http://www.eia.doe.gov/cneaf/nuclear/page/umtra/monument_valley_title1.html.

16. Ben Stanley interview.

17. Gordon Dean to Jesse Johnson, December 21, 1951. USAF Brig. Gen. James Mc-Cormack Jr. to Jesse Johnson, undated. This was a farewell note from McCormack, who retired in 1955.

18. "Time Clock," *Time* magazine, July 9, 1956.

19. Memorandum from James W. Egan, senior assistant surgeon, Public Health Service, Salt Lake City, to Samuel C. Ingraham II, head, general field studies section, National Cancer Institute, March 2, 1956.

20. *Mining World,* March 1963, p. 25.

21. U.S. Department of Energy Germantown Site History, accessed online at http://www.er.doe.gov/sc-80/trail/history.htm.

22. Minutes of the Uranium Advisory Committee Meeting, Salt Lake City, UT, July 21–22, 1959; memorandum from Pope A. Lawrence, head, Environmental Field Studies Section, Field Investigations and Demonstration Branch, National Cancer Institute to Chief, FIDB, NCI, July 30, 1959.

23. Holaday deposition in *John N. Begay vs. United States*, pp. 72–73 and p. 158.

24. Wyoming Mining Association, April, 1959, Riverton, WY. (Uranium was found in Wyoming, too.) Leslie Johnson, supervising engineer, Bureau of Mines. "Mine Radiation Studies."

25. Remarks Prepared by Jesse C. Johnson, director, Division of Raw Materials, United States Atomic Energy Commission, For Delivery Before the American Mining Congress, Denver, Colorado, September 16, 1959. "Radiation Hazards in Uranium Mines and Mills." Letter from Johnson to Edward J. Bauser, executive director, Joint Committee on Atomic Energy, November 19, 1971: "I am enclosing a copy of a talk . . . which I gave on September 16, 1959 . . . I am not proud of my effort . . ."

26. Press release, "USAEC Raw Materials Activities Described in AEC Annual Report for 1960," January 30, 1961, p. 5.

27. Holaday deposition, *John N. Begay vs. United States*, p. 100.

28. Memo from J. G. Terrill, Jr., to B. W. Harwell, Public Health Service, Division of Radiological Health, Re: Uranium Miners Study, March 4, 1962.

29. Letter, Head to Emmons.

30. Author's unpublished telephone interview for the *Los Angeles Times* with Howard B. Nickelson, a former USGS inspector based in Carlsbad, NM, who was sent to the reservation to help out with the uranium mines, October 17, 2005.

31. Eichstaedt, *If You Poison Us,* p. 76.

32. John Lewis Gaddis, *The Cold War: A New History* (New York: Penguin Books, 2007), p. 78.

33. Undated letter from Jesse C. Johnson to T. C. Runion, vice president, W. R. Grace and Company.

34. Ibid.

35. Factory communication, Vanadium Corporation of America, unsigned to Page Edwards, October 20, 1961, offers assurances that the radiation level in the Durango mill is much lower than a dose that was found to kill donkeys. Edwards's handwritten reminder note of May 3, 1963, about physical exams and X-rays includes one underlined phrase: "Cases in Dgo."

36. Page Edwards, spiral notebook, handwritten entries from May 3, 1963; August 28, 1963; October 1, 1963; and August 31, 1964.

37. Letter from Victor Archer, U.S. Public Health Service, to Page Edwards, September 13, 1965.

38. Unsigned internal VCA memo. "Additional Sources of Uranium Available to VCA at the Mining Level but Not From Mines," June 21, 1963. The memo said 1 million tons of tailings were piled up at Monument No. 2, and these could produce 380,000 pounds of uranium. As the upgrader continued work, an additional 680,000 tons of tailings over the next forty months would produce 176,800 pounds of uranium.

39. Energy Information Administration, U.S. Department of Energy, Nuclear Decommissioning, "Monument Valley Upgrader (Monument 2 Mine), Apache County, Arizona." Available online at http://www.eia.doe.gov/cneaf/nuclear/page/umtra/monument_valley_title1.html

40. Mark Madden, unpublished spreadsheet summarizing inspection reports of Navajo mines, 2005. According to a memo titled "Recap" in Page Edwards's papers at the Center for Southwest Studies, Ft. Lewis College, Durango, CO, the Monument No. 2 mine had employed 125 Navajos and 26 white men ten years previously, in 1956–57.

41. Judson MacLaury, U.S. Department of Labor historian, "Tragedy in the Uranium Mines: Catalyst for National Workers' Safety and Health Legislation," paper delivered at "Lyndon Baines Johnson's Legacy," a symposium at Miami University, Oxford, OH, April 27, 1998. Additional details from Eichstaedt, *If You Poison Us*, p. 79.

42. Vacation schedule, 1967, for VCA Navajo mines.

43. This account of the end days of Monument No. 2 comes from a company interoffice memo from R. L. Anderson to William Howard/Monument #2, August 1, 1968, copied to Page Edwards; the EIA Monument Valley Upgrader website, established by the Energy Department during the 1990s cleanup; and unpublished notes from the author's interview for the *Los Angeles Times* with Cecil Blackmountain at his home in Cane Valley, June 24, 2005.

44. Nickelson interview.

45. Howard B. Nickelson, Memorandum to files, "Abandonment of Uranium Mines on the Navajo Reservation in Arizona, Foote Mineral Company (Vanadium Corporation of America)," October 29, 1969, p. 3.

46. Navajo production figures compiled for the author by William Chenoweth, a former Atomic Energy Commission geologist and uranium consultant for companies, museums, and the government. Chenoweth wrote that 1,375,198 tons of ore came from Monument Valley from 1944 to 1986. All Navajo mines together produced 3,915,920 tons of ore during this period.

Chapter 9. Fallout

1. Lorissa Jackson interview, June 14, 2009.
2. Eunice Jackson interview, June 14, 2009, Farmington NM.
3. Eunice Jackson and Lorissa Jackson interviews.
4. Ben Stanley interview.
5. Author viewings of the house in 2005 and 2008.
6. Energy Information Administration, Monument Valley Upgrader (Monument 2).
7. W. B. Harris, A. J. Breslin, H. Glauberman, and M. S. Weinstein, Health and Safety Laboratory, Atomic Energy Commission, New York, "Environmental Hazards Associated with the Milling of Uranium Ore," *AMA Archives of Industrial Health,* November, 1959, p. 380.
8. Interviews with Lorissa Jackson, Eunice Jackson, Lewis Yazzie, Herbert Yazzie, Mary Lou Yazzie, Timothy McThias, Terrance McThias, Della McThias.
9. Interviews with Lewis Yazzie, Herbert Yazzie, Mary Lou Yazzie.
10. Ben Stanley interview.
11. Unpublished interview with Bernice Roe for the *Los Angeles Times,* June 22, 2005, at the Red Valley chapter house in Arizona.
12. Judy Pasternak, "A Peril That Dwelt Among the Navajos," *Los Angeles Times,* November 19, 2006, p. A-1.
13. H. Peter Metzger, Off the Beat syndicated column, "AEC vs. the Public: The Case of the Uranium Tailings," July 13, 1974. Metzger, who held a doctorate in biochemistry, was science editor of the *Rocky Mountain News.*
14. Office diary of Glenn Seaborg, Atomic Energy Commission, June 30, 1971.
15. Pasternak, "A Peril That Dwelt Among the Navajos," *Los Angeles Times,* and unpublished telephone interview for the *Times* with John Elmer, an engineer at Department of Energy contractor S.M. Stoller Corp., July 18, 2005. Elmer worked on the Grand Junction tailings removal project.
16. Testimony of Roy L. Cleere, Colorado health director, "Use of Uranium Mill Tailings for Construction Purposes," Hearing Before the Subcommittee on Raw Materials of the Joint Committee on Atomic Energy, Congress of the United States, October 28 and 29, 1971, pp. 102–103.
17. Judy Pasternak, "Oases in Navajo Desert Contained a 'Witch's Brew,'" *Los Angeles Times,* November 20, 2006.
18. Lorissa Jackson interview.
19. Ibid.

20. Author interview with Ben and Mary Stanley at their home in Cane Valley, May 25, 2008. The missionary from Montana was Calvin Sandlin, who worked for many years among Navajos in southern Utah (Cane Valley straddles the Arizona-Utah line).
21. Author interviews with Lorissa Jackson at Monument Valley High School, Monument Valley, UT, on May 24, 2008; Suzy Taylor and Anna Jean Tsosie in Shiprock, NM, on May 27, 2008, and telephone interviews with Timothy McThias and Terrance McThias in August of 2009.
22. Lorissa Jackson interview.

Chapter 10. Avalanche of Suspicion

1. U.S. Department of Health, Education and Welfare, Federal Water Pollution Control Administration, Region VIII, Denver, CO, and Colorado River Basin Water Quality Control Board, "Disposition and Control of Uranium Tailings Piles in the Colorado River Basin," March 1966, p. 24.
2. Letter from Donald C. Gilbert, executive director of the Arizona Atomic Energy Commission, to Rep. Wayne Aspinall, October 18, 1971. Letter from Louis C. Kossuth, Arizona Health Commissioner, to Aspinall, October 13, 1971.
3. Peter MacDonald, "Indian Groups Coordinate Vast US Energy Holdings," Christian Science Monitor News Service, January 13, 1980. The joint venture was set up, but low uranium prices prevented a launch.
4. Author telephone interviews with Joseph M. Hans, Jr., in 2005 and 2006.
5. Pasternak, "A Peril That Dwelt Among the Navajos."
6. Hans interviews. Hans named William Mills, who headed EPA's division of air and radiation, as the official who rejected his proposal. Mills, reached in 2006 by the author in Olney, M.D., said in a telephone interview that he couldn't remember Hans's specific request, but was certain that he would have said no because he believed that the best defense against lung cancer was not to lower radon, but to quit smoking (most Navajos did not smoke habitually). Hans couldn't remember the names of his contacts at the IHS.
7. Interviews for the *Los Angeles Times* by telephone with Nina Bennett, Queenie Greenstone, and Sharon Black, and in Cane Valley with Hoskey Sloan.
8. Berlinda Cly interview. The author scanned the debris pile with a radiation detector in 2005. The reading on contact was 4.2 times the background level.
9. Joseph M. Hans, Jr., and Richard L. Douglas, Office of Radiation Programs, Environmental Protection Agency, Las Vegas, NV, "Radiation Survey of Dwellings in Cane Valley, Arizona and Utah, for Use of Uranium Mill Tailings," August 1975, and Hans interview.
10. Ford, Davis & Bacon Utah, Inc.
11. Author telephone interview with Hans. The EPA could not find the letter in its files, but Hans had saved the list. A Department of Energy contractor in Grand Junction

provided corroborating documents. Craig Little, a radiation consultant, also confirmed in an interview that a request had been made to examine these houses and Harold Tso was told by Hans about his efforts at the time.

12. Eichstaedt, *If You Poison Us,* p. 96.

13. Unpublished interview with Fannie Yazzie for the *Los Angeles Times,* June 23, 2004, in the Red Valley chapter house and at her home in Oaksprings, Ariz.

14. Eichstaedt, *If You Poison Us,* p. 96.

15. Fannie Yazzie interview.

16. Pasternak, "A Peril That Dwelt Among the Navajos."

17. Eichstaedt, *If You Poison Us,* pp. 96–97, 101.

18. Notes, Stewart L. Udall, December 7, 1960, "Log on Interior Job," viewed at University of Arizona Special Collections, AZ.

19. Eichstaedt, *If You Poison Us,* pp. 100–102.

20. Unpublished interview for the *Los Angeles Times* with Mae John at her home in Cove, AZ, June 21, 2005.

21. Deposition of Harold Tso in *The Navajo Tribe vs. United States of America,* in the United States Claims Court, taken at the United States Courthouse in Albuquerque, pp. 530–532.

22. Pasternak, "A Peril That Dwelt Among the Navajos." Unpublished telephone interviews for the *Los Angeles Times* with Harold Tso, July 29 and 30, 2004, and February 2005. The house belonged to Carl Thomas.

23. Harold Tso interviews.

24. Staff to Navajo Environmental Protection Commission, The Navajo Tribe, "Briefing Paper: Radiation Uranium Mining Houses," April 28, 1980, pp. 2–5.

25. Pasternak, "A Peril That Dwelt Among the Navajos."

26. Molly Ivins, "Uranium Mines Leaving Indians a Legacy of Death," *New York Times,* May 20, 1979.

27. William H. Weise, M.D., editor, Birth Defects in the Four Corners Area: Transcript of Meeting Held February 27, 1981, Albuquerque, NM, p. 70.

28. Ibid., pp. 76–77.

29. Ibid., p. 77.

30. "Uranium Mining Cited as Stomach Ca [*sic*] Cause in Southwest Indians," *Family Practice News,* August 15–31, 1987, p. 26.

31. R. M. Auld, Jr., and W. S. Haubrich, Department of Gastroenterology, Scripps Clinic and Research Foundation, La Jolla, CA. "Rapidly Rising Incidence of Gastric Carcinoma in Navajo Indians and Its Relationship to Uranium Mining," Abstracts of Papers, *Gastroenterology,* May 1987, p. 1301.

32. Unpublished telephone interview for the *Los Angeles Times* with Richard Auld, from his office in Santa Rosa, CA, June 24, 2004.

33. Unpublished telephone interview for the *Los Angeles Times* with Steve Cinnamon, 2004.

34. Don Payne, for the Department of Water Management, Division of Water Resources, The Navajo Nation (he was on loan to the tribe from the IHS), "A Pre-

liminary Assessment of the Extent of Radionuclide Contamination of Surface and Groundwater in the Cameron Uranium Mining Belt," July 10, 1986, and "An Assessment of the Extent of Radionuclide Contamination of Surface and Groundwater in the Cameron Uranium Mining Belt," April 1987.

35. Ibid.

36. Pasternak. "Oases in Navajo Desert Contained a 'Witch's Brew.' "

37. Ibid. The mother was Helen Nez, who gave the same account through two different translators a year apart. Snyder declined to comment, but in notes on the Nez family that he wrote in 1990, after treating six siblings with the disease, he included this observation: "A uranium mine was within one mile of the home where all these children lived, and uranium tailings were closer."

38. Pasternak, "Oases in Navajo Desert Contained a 'Witch's Brew.' "

Chapter 11. A Blind Eye and a Deaf Ear

1. Interview with former Indian Health Service official who asked to remain anonymous because he did not have authority to speak publicly.

2. Notation with filing instructions scrawled on copy of *Family Practice News* article received as part of a response to Freedom of Information Act request PHS2K5-A-076.

3. Department of Health and Human Services, Public Health Service, Health Resources and Services Administration, Indian Health Service and Office of Environmental Health, "Health Hazards Related to Nuclear Resource Development on Indian Land: A Report," November 1982. Congress requested this study and authorized $300,000 for it, but never gave HHS the money. The department said it didn't need to do it, anyway, because "the adverse health effects of radiation exposure have been extensively studied," p. 3.

4. Memo from Ward B. Hurlburt, Deputy Director, Navajo Area Indian Health Service, to Marlene E. Haffner, Area Director, Navajo Area Indian Health Service, "Dr. Gottlieb's Proposal," June 11, 1980. Letter from Emery A. Johnson, Director, Indian Health Service to Leon S. Gottlieb, M.D., June 19, 1980.

5. Memorandum from Charles A. Reaux to the director, chief medical officer, and director of environmental health, Navajo Area Indian Health Service, December 15, 1986, p. 1.

6. According to Tso, they were Levon Benally and the late Arlene Luther. In his deposition, he refers to a document about this meeting dated April 1981.

7. Unpublished Tso interview for the *Los Angeles Times,* July 30, 2004.

8. The History of Nuclear Energy, Dept. of Energy, DOE/NE-0088, accessed at http://www.ne.doe.gov/pdfFiles/History.pdf, p. 12.

9. Unpublished interview for the *Los Angeles Times* with Glenn and Lorene Livingston in Church Rock, NM, June 2004.

10. Larry King, a Navajo rancher who worked as a surveyor for United Nuclear at the Church Rock mine, said in an unpublished interview in Church Rock for the *Los*

Angeles Times on June 27, 2004, that he was one of a group summoned to inspect the dam earlier in the summer of 1979. He said he saw many six-inch cracks at that time, but figured the dam was just drying out, reported his observations, and went back to work mapping tunnels underground over at the mine. He believes now that the cracks presaged the spill.

11. Telegram from Chester Yazzie, Chairman, Emergency Services Coordinating Committee, Navajo Nation, Window Rock, to New Mexico governor Bruce King, U.S. representative Manuel Lujan, and U.S. senator Pete Domenici, August 3, 1979.

12. Memo, Robert Young, field engineer, Gallup District to William Ryan, director, Office of Environmental Health, "Church Rock School Well, Radiological Water Analysis," July 5, 1979.

13. Letter from Gordon Denipah, assistant chief, Area Environmental Health Services Branch, IHS, to Anson C. Damon, Jr., director, Division of Water and Sanitation, Navajo Nation, July 26, 1979, and memo from Don Payne, Gallup Service Unit Sanitarian, Office of Environmental Health and Engineering, to Wilmer Benalley, director, Gallup Community Health Representative Program, July 19, 1979.

14. Tso interview, July 30, 2004.

15. Interviews with the Livingstons, who said their charts were marked with American flag stickers, and with Douglas Peter, chief medical officer for the Navajo Area Indian Health Service, who said he was not aware of any effort to track the health of those exposed to contamination of the Puerco.

16. Unpublished telephone interview for the *Los Angeles Times* with Chris Shuey, director, Uranium Impact Assessment Program, Southwest Research and Information Center, Albuquerque, 2005.

17. Tso deposition, p. 564.

18. Unpublished telephone interview for the *Los Angeles Times* in September 2005, with New Orleans attorney Allan Kanner, who was the tribe's legal consultant.

19. Stewart L. Udall radiation cases journal, Monday, January 8, 1979.

20. Stewart L. Udall, "Memorandum of phone conversation with Duncan Holaday 3/4/80," and handwritten "Notes Re Patterson, NY, Conference with Duncan Holaday 3/20/1980."

21. Stewart Udall interview on "Capitol Notebook," air date June 26, 1994. Author telephone interview with Udall, 2005.

22. Kathleen Stanton, "Uranium Miner Left Family Nothing, Widow Says During Radiation Trial." *Arizona Republic,* August 10, 1983.

23. Author interview with Tom Udall, October 30, 2009.

24. The eleven claims included at trial were those of widows Lucy W. Benally, Priscilla Ben, Lucy Coty, Minnie Frank, Daisy Garnenez, Elizabeth Gray, Grace B. Tuni, and Betty Jo Yazzie (one claim for each husband), along with miners Roy Bekis and Don T. Benally.

25. Kathleen Stanton, "Mine Radiation in '50s Called Worse Than at Hiroshima; U.S. Failed to Address Hazards, Court Also Told," *Arizona Republic,* August 18, 1983, page B1.

26. Associated Press story carried in *Deseret News,* March 21–22, 1984.
27. *Arizona Republic,* April 15, 1984, p. AA10.
28. Kathleen Stanton, "U.S. Freed of Liability for Cancer Among Navajo Uranium Miners," *Arizona Republic,* July 11, 1984.
29. Letter, Duncan Holaday to Stewart Udall, July 20, 1984.
30. Stewart Udall, *The Myths of August: A Personal Exploration of Our Tragic Cold War Affair with the Atom* (New York: Pantheon, 1994), p. 201.
31. Naryani P. Singh, David D. Bennett, and McDonald E. Wrenn, University of Utah, and Geno Saccomano, St. Mary's Hospital, Grand Junction, CO, "Concentrations of (alpha)-emitting Isotopes of U and Th in Uranium Miners' and Millers' Tissues," *Health Physics,* September, 1987, pp. 261–265.
32. Collaborative research between the Office of Navajo Uranium Workers and Gary Weglarz, MSW candidate, "An Examination of Cultural Bias in the Radiation Exposure Compensation Act (PL 101–426) and in Its Implementation," May 1994, p. 29. The author reviewed a copy from the files of the Navajo Area Indian Health Service obtained through the Freedom of Information Act and it carried the notation: "Must Reading!!" Weglarz, the author, urged more studies of the relationship of uranium and by-products from its mining on these cancers.
33. Memo from Douglas Peter, chief medical officer, Navajo Area Indian Health Service, to "all concerned," "Minutes of Uranium Miner's Conference Call, 1/27/95."
34. L. M. Shields, et al., "Navajo Birth Outcomes in the Shiprock Uranium Mining District," *Health Physics,* November 1992, pp. 542–551.
35. R. Singleton, M.D., et al., "Neuropathy in Navajo children: Clinical and epidemiological features," in Brief Communications, *Neurology,* February 1990, p. 363.
36. Pasternak, "Oases in Navajo Desert Contained a 'Witch's Brew.' "
37. Uranium Mill Tailings Remedial Action Project, U.S. Dept. of Energy, "Environmental Assessment of Remedial Action at the Monument Valley Uranium Mill Tailings Site, Monument Valley, Arizona, Final," June 1989, p. 19; personal communication from Bob Darr, SM Stoller Corp., DOE Legacy Management Support, September 9, 2009.
38. Author interview with Roy Hathale, Roger's son, at the family house atop Comb Ridge on June 13, 2009. Lorissa Jackson interview.
39. Eichstaedt, *If You Poison Us,* p. 145.
40. Ibid.
41. "Monument Valley Upgrader Site (Monument 2 Mine)," Remediation of Mill Sites, Energy Information Administration, accessed online at http://www.eia.doe.gov/cneaf/nuclear/page/umtra/monument_valley_title1.html.
42. Telephone interview with Sharon Black, 2006. The daughter of Jesse Black, she worked for two years as a truck driver hauling tailings out of Cane Valley.
43. At Shiprock, DOE cleaned up fifteen commercial buildings, residences, and open tracts; at Mexican Hat, eleven; at Tuba City, seven, all of which were attributed to wind dispersal rather than use in construction.

44. Unpublished telephone interview for the *Los Angeles Times* with Craig Little, who was employed by Oak Ridge National Laboratory when he worked as a DOE subcontractor on vicinity properties, July 18, 2005.
45. Letter, John G. Themelis, project manager, Uranium Mill Tailings Project Office, Department of Energy, Albuquerque, to Louise Linkin, executive director, Navajo Environmental Protection Administration, "Vicinity Property MV013, Juanita Black, Tenant," July 9, 1985. Similar letters were sent regarding the other tribal members whose homes were evaluated and are available from the DOE's Legacy Management Office in Grand Junction, CO.

Chapter 12. "Hear Our Voices"

1. Lorissa Jackson interviews, May 24, 2008.
2. Unpublished telephone interview for the *Los Angeles Times* with Peterson Zah, May 4, 2005.
3. Unpublished interviews for the *Los Angeles Times* at Haystack with Brown Vandever in 2004; Gary Vandever, Sam Long, James Largo, and Albert Largo on June 20, 2005. "ATSDR Activities in New Mexico," accessed online at http://www.atsdr.cdc .gov/statefactsheets/sfs-nm.html.
4. Vandever, Largo interviews.
5. Zah interview.
6. Judy Pasternak, "Navajos' Desert Cleanup No More Than a Mirage: Through a Federal Program, Decontamination Seemed Possible. But Delays and Disputes Thwarted the Effort," *Los Angeles Times*, November 21, 2006.
7. Ibid.
8. Ibid.
9. Ibid.
10. By this time, the Navajo president was Albert Hale, the lawyer who had assisted Stewart Udall in the miners' suit.
11. Telephone interview for the *Los Angeles Times* with Sadie Hoskie, May 5, 2005. "I wished I had shut up," she said.
12. Pasternak, "Navajos' Desert Cleanup No More Than a Mirage."
13. Pasternak, "Oases in Navajo Desert Contained a 'Witch's Brew.' "
14. Ibid.
15. Ibid. Additional details from unpublished interview for the *Los Angeles Times* with John F. Rosen at his office at the lead clinic at The Children's Hospital at Montefiore in the Bronx, NY, February 10, 2004.
16. Lorissa Jackson, typed notes on the "Hear Our Voices" project. November 4, 1998.
17. Lorissa Jackson interview
18. Author telephone interview with Trent Harris, September 3, 2009.
19. Leontine R. Oliver, "Uranium Among the Navajos," unpublished Monument Valley High School paper.
20. Eichstaedt, *If You Poison Us*, p. 181.

21. Author interview with Mary Lou Yazzie, who was present and served as translator.
22. Mary Lou Yazzie interview.
23. Mary Lou Yazzie, Lewis Yazzie interviews.
24. "Hear Our Voices" documentary, Monument Valley High School, Monument Valley, UT, 1998, 13 minutes, 22 seconds.
25. Lorissa Jackson interview. The man's name was Billy Martin.

Chapter 13. Under Scrutiny from Every Angle

1. Esther Yazzie-Lewis and Jim Zion, "*Leetso:* The Powerful Yellow Monster," *Indigenous Woman* magazine, Vol. II, No. 1, p. 24, 1994. This essay was republished as Chapter 1 in *The Navajo People and Uranium Mining*, a collection of essays and oral histories edited by Doug Brugge, Timothy Benally, and Esther Yazzie-Lewis. University of New Mexico Press, 2006.
2. Interview with Valentina Smith, June 13, 2009. She was part of the student crew.
3. Larry King interview.
4. Author interview with Patricia Seltzer at Monument Valley High School, September 23, 2009.
5. Elsie's parents were Willy and Happy Cly. Interviews for the *Los Angeles Times* with Jeff Spitz on the telephone and in Chicago, 2005, 2006, and 2007, and with Elsie Begay in Farmington, NM, June 21, 2005 and, along with her brother, John Wayne Cly, in Los Angeles, March 27, 2006.
6. Office of Surface Mining Reclamation and Enforcement, Department of Interior, "Annual Evaluation Report for the Abandoned Mine Land Reclamation Program Administered by the Navajo Nation, Evaluation Year 1999 (Oct. 1, 1998, through Sept. 30, 1999)," p. 14.
7. Unpublished interview in 2006 for the *Los Angeles Times* with a mining consultant who asked to remain anonymous so that he could discuss his conclusions candidly without offending potential clients.
8. Ben Stanley interview for the *Los Angeles Times,* June 23, 2005.
9. AML Reclamation, Appendix A, EY-2002, p. 1. A photo on this page has a caption discussing the waste pile next to this Cane Valley house. The house in the photograph was identified as Jesse Black's by Lorissa Jackson.
10. Press release, Department of Interior, Office of the Secretary, "Secretary Babbitt Announces Winners of 1999 Abandoned Mine Land Reclamation Awards," August 24, 1999.
11. Unpublished telephone interview for the *Los Angeles Times* with Nina Bennett, November 2006.
12. Pasternak, "Navajos' Desert Cleanup No More Than a Mirage."
13. *People v. Tuthill and Neztsosie*, No. BC9G95, Attorney Regulation, Supreme Court of Colorado. Cherie Daut fell in love with the Neztsosie girls' older brother, David, and had married him by this time. Her Colorado license was suspended for ninety

days, with a two-year probationary period. In interviews, she said the reason for her missed deadlines was her lupus, and files in tribal court cases show requests for extensions because of her illness.

14. Pasternak, "Oases in Navajo Desert Contained a 'Witch's Brew.' "
15. Unpublished interview with Glynn Alsup for the *Los Angeles Times*, Washington, September 22, 2004.
16. Pasternak, "Navajos' Desert Cleanup No More Than a Mirage."
17. The account of the testing and demolition of the Holiday *hooghan* and of Leonard Begay's illness and death is from Pasternak, "A Peril That Dwelt Among the Navajos."

Chapter 14. Resistance

1. Judy Pasternak, "Bush's Energy Plan Bares Industry Clout," *Los Angeles Times*, August 26, 2001.
2. Ibid.
3. Interview for the *Los Angeles Times* with Franz Geiger, June 23, 2004, in Farmington, NM.
4. Pasternak, "Navajos' Desert Cleanup No More Than a Mirage."
5. Ibid.
6. Resolution of the Navajo Nation Tribal Council, "Diné Natural Resources Protection Act of 2005," p. 5.
7. Kathy Helms, "Shirley Will Ink Uranium Mining Ban: President to Sign Agreement Today," *Gallup Independent*, April 29, 2005. Navajo Nation press release, "Navajo Nation President Joe Shirley, Jr., Signs Diné Natural Resources Act of 2005," April 30, 2005.
8. Telephone interviews for the *Los Angeles Times* with Juan Velasquez and John DeJoia of Strathmore Minerals and Mark Pelizza of Uranium Resources Inc.
9. Judy Pasternak, "Mining Firms Again Eyeing Navajo Land: Demand for Uranium Is Soaring. But the Tribe Vows a 'Knockdown, Drag-out Legal Battle,' " *Los Angeles Times*, November 22, 2006.
10. Interviews for the *Los Angeles Times* with Robert McNair and Derrith Watchman-Moore.
11. The lunch was held on May 15, 2006.
12. Pasternak, "Mining Firms Again Eyeing Navajo Land."
13. Navajo Nation press release, "Federal EPA Reaches Determination on 'Indian Country,' Upholds Navajo Sovereignty, Uranium Mining Prohibition," February 8, 2007.
14. Correspondence between URI Chairman Paul K. Wilmott and BIA officials, obtained from the Bureau of Indian Affairs under the Freedom of Information Act. Interviews in 2006 for the *Los Angeles Times* with URI's Mark Pelizza and with BIA spokeswoman Nedra Darling.

Chapter 15. Ghosts

1. Interviews for the *Los Angeles Times* with Hoskey Sloan in Cane Valley, June 25, 2005, and by telephone with Carl Holiday.
2. Craig Little interview.
3. U.S. Department of Energy, Grand Junction Office, Grand Junction, CO. "Final Site Observational Work Plan for the UMTRA Project Site at Monument Valley, Arizona," pp. 4–48 and 6–9, and Energy Information Administration, Monument Valley Upgrader Site (Monument 2 Mine) accessed online at http://www.eia.doe .gov/cneaf/nuclear/page/umtra/monument_valley_title1.html.
4. DOE Grand Junction, "Final Site Observational Work Plan," pp. 6-3 to 6-6.
5. Ibid., pp. 8–41.
6. Ibid., pp. 8–24 and 8–41.
7. Their names are Susie Taylor, now living in Shiprock, and Anna Jean Tsosie, now living in Farmington.
8. Susie Taylor interview.
9. Interview for the *Los Angeles Times* with Perry Charley, director of the Uranium Education Program at Diné College, Shiprock, NM, on April 7, 2005. Charley was in charge of the eastern section of AML before joining the tribal college staff.
10. TLI Solutions, Appendix D, Interview Summaries, from "Tuba City Open Dump, Uranium Mills, and Uranium Mill Waste Disposal Sites, PRP Search Final Report," Interview 8, p. D-12. A redacted version of this privileged and confidential report for the Department of the Interior is in possession of the author.
11. The woman's name was Lucille Saganitso-Krause. Interviews with Cassandra Bloedel, September 23, 2004, in Washington and September 24, 2009, in Tuba City. Navajo Nation EPA video testimony of Saganitso-Krause and Manygoats, obtained in November 2004 from Arlene Luther, who was Bloedel's supervisor. Ray Manygoats testimony to the House Committee on Oversight and Government Reform, October 23, 2007.
12. Interview with Mark Merchant, EPA Press Office.
13. The author was permitted to observe this meeting. It took place on September 23, 2004, in Room 1334, Longworth House Office Building, Washington.
14. The chiropractor's name was Ronald Berg.
15. The translator asked not to be identified because of her current job in the legal profession.
16. Telephone interview for the *Los Angeles Times* with Steve Helgerson, May 19, 2005.
17. The IHS also refused for more than a year to provide public documents I had sought under the Freedom of Information Act. I was left hanging with no response and no explanation for the delay until my editor and I contacted the assistant director of the agency. He finally gave a reply: a total rejection of my request. *Los Angeles Times* lawyers appealed the decision to an assistant secretary of the Department of Health and Human Services, of which IHS is a part. The assistant secretary instructed IHS to release the information.

18. Collins was nominated by President Barack Obama to be director of the National Institutes of Health in July 2009.

19. The colleague was Darryl De Vivo, a pediatric neurologist who also participated in the Navajo neuropathy research.

20. Charalampos L. Karadimas, Tuan H. Vu, Stephen A. Holve, Penelope Chronopoulou, Catarina Quinzii, Stanley D. Johnsen, Janice Kurth, Elizabeth Eggers, Lluis Palenzuela, Kurenai Tanji, Eduardo Bonilla, Darryl C. De Vivo, Salvatore DiMauro, and Michio Hirano, "Navajo Neurohepatopathy Is Caused by a Mutation in the MPV17 Gene," *American Journal of Human Genetics,* September 2006, pp. 544–548. Posted online June 28, 2006.

21. E-mail to the author from Richard I. Kelly, August 10, 2006.

22. E-mail to the author from Salvatore DiMauro, November 13, 2006.

23. Ruth Ottman, a Columbia colleague of DiMauro's and an epidemiologist, had analyzed Justice's paper for the Neztsosie legal team. Like Kelly, she remained convinced after news of the mutation was published that it told only part of the story. Someone, she suggested, should conduct experiments to see how the gene interacts with uranium or other heavy metals in the lab. "It's a way to bring the two lines of reasoning together," she said.

24. Author interview with Henry Waxman, May 13, 2008, in his office in Washington, DC.

25. Tom Udall interview.

26. Ibid.

27. Author notes from the hearing were buttressed by a preliminary transcript, which can be accessed at http://oversight.house.gov/documents/20071127163605.pdf.

Chapter 16. Beginnings

1. Clancy Tenley, associate director of the communities and ecosystems division at EPA Region 9 in San Francisco, told me that after the first meeting following the committee hearing, the change in attitude among the agencies, and the tribe as well, was clear. By this time it was obvious that Waxman wasn't going to let up. He characterized the new thinking as, "Hey, you know what? We have to do this, so let's do it together." Author telephone call with Tenley, Mike Montgomery, and Harry Allen IV on June 16, 2008.

2. Telephone interview with Harry Allen IV, chief, emergency response section at EPA Region 9, October 1, 2009.

3. E-mail from Milton Yazzie to Deb Misra, Navajo Department of Water Resources, July 19, 2006, "Re: sympathies." Yazzie forwarded a copy to the author.

4. Author interview with Roy Hathale, son of Roger and Dina Hathale, outside the family home on Comb Ridge, June 12, 2009.

5. Eunice Jackson interview.

6. Clancy Tenley, Harry Allen IV, and Will Duncan of the EPA showed me the invention in San Francisco on October 20, 2008.

7. Author interview with Harry Allen IV, an EPA emergency coordinator, at the Hampton Inn in Kayenta, AZ, November 13, 2009.
8. Eunice Jackson interview in Cane Valley, November 14, 2008.
9. Lorissa Jackson interview.

Epilogue. The Steeple

1. Interview with Stanley Edison of the Navajo Nation EPA, May 22, 2008, in Washington, DC.
2. E-mails from D. Y. Begay, of Scottsdale and Tselani, AZ, whose father was one of the neighbor family's cancer victims, September 20, 2005; September 30, 2005; and November 8, 2005.
3. Interview with Sharon Masek Lopez, Hopi Water Resources Dept., September 24, 2009, in Tuba City, AZ.
4. Henry W. Haven, Jr., "Summary of Findings: Discovery and Recovery of Uranium Ceramic Ball from the Tuba City Open Dump, Tuba City, Arizona," July 21, 2009, pp. 2 and 8.
5. The breast cancer work was conducted by Cheryl Dyer, a biologist at Northern Arizona University. The kidney work is being done by a consortium that includes Johnnye Lewis, of the University of New Mexico, and Chris Shuey.
6. George W. Cronyn, editor. "For Second Day of the Night Chant," *American Indian Poetry: An Anthology of Songs and Chants* (New York: Ballantine Books, 1918), p. 77.

SELECTED BIBLIOGRAPHY

A NOTE ON SOURCES

Getting to the heart of events over a ninety-year span in an isolated valley at the foot of a ruined mesa required extensive travels around the Navajo Nation and journeys from one end of the United States to the other. To piece together the story of Adakai's family and, more broadly, of uranium and the *Diné*, I conducted more than two hundred interviews. For the voices of mining executives and federal officials from the Manhattan Project and Cold War eras, I depended heavily on oral histories and papers at widely scattered archives. Briefs, arguments, depositions, and exhibits from several lawsuits filed at every level of the judicial system—from tribal court to federal claims court to the U.S. Supreme Court—also proved invaluable. I learned about contemporary government thinking from interviews, but also from thousands of internal memos and reports requested under the Freedom of Information Act. The Indian Health Service provided documents only after *Los Angeles Times* lawyers filed an appeal with the Department of Health and Human Services. The most important Environmental Protection Agency papers are housed in the Navajo Nation Uranium Mines collection at the Region 9 office in San Francisco. It took attorney action to secure release of these as well. Historical mining inspection records came from the U.S. Bureau of Land Management. Recent correspondence with uranium companies about mineral rights came from the Bureau of Indian Affairs.

Though most of my work was based on original research, I would like to highlight some of the most helpful secondary sources. Peter H. Eichstaedt's *If You Poison Us* is an exhaustive account of the Navajo uranium miners' fight for justice. In the mold of Walter Dyk, who recorded a Navajo man's amazingly unvarnished memoir in 1938, Robert S. McPherson has collected and published oral histories of individual Navajos. As it happens, at least two McPherson subjects were related to Adakai; the footnotes yielded particularly helpful gleanings. Two documentaries, "Hear Our Voices" and *The Return of Navajo Boy*, helped me better understand those who were featured in them.

ARCHIVAL COLLECTIONS

Jesse C. Johnson Papers: Hoover Institution Archives, Stanford, CA.

Sen. Clinton Anderson Papers and Papers of Harold L. Ickes: Manuscript Division, Library of Congress, Washington, DC.

Pope Lawrence Papers: History of Medicine Division, National Library of Medicine, Bethesda, MD.

Uranium History Collection: Center for Oral and Public History, California State University–Fullerton. The full transcripts of Samuel Moon's interviews with Harry Goulding, Luke Yazzie, and others conducted between 1973 and 1979 also surfaced in a back room here. Many unpublished passages illuminate key parts of the Monument No. 2 story.

Denny Viles Papers and Page Edwards Papers: Center for Southwest Studies, Fort Lewis College, Durango, CO.

Stewart Udall Papers: University of Arizona Special Collections, Tucson, AZ.

John Ford Papers: Lilly Library, Indiana University, Bloomington, IN.

Human Radiation Experiments collection, including duplicates from the Department of Energy of documents from the Advisory Committee on Human Radiation Experiments: National Security Archive, George Washington University, Washington, DC.

Federal Radiation Council Records Group 412, and records of litigation brought by the Navajo tribe in U.S. Claims Court, NRG-434-99-200: National Archives, Washington, DC.

Work papers for "Uranium Development in the San Juan Basin Region," U.S. GPO 1980/778/177/177 Office of Trust Responsibilities, Bureau of Indian Affairs Region 8, Albuquerque: U.S. Department of Interior Library, Washington, DC.

Correspondence files for the Board on Radiation Effects Research: National Research Council, National Academy of Science, Washington, DC.

PRIVATE COLLECTIONS

Many families provided personal documents, including birth and death certificates, Navajo census records, pay stubs, correspondence, and photographs. Other sources include:

Medical files for nine Navajo neuropathy patients (obtained with signed release papers from patients or next of kin).

Southwest Research and Information Center, Albuquerque. This anti-mining advocacy group catalogues its document collection online at http://www .sric.org/uranium/rirf.html.

William L. Chenoweth, a consulting engineer and former Atomic Energy Commission geologist, Grand Junction, CO, has a wide-ranging library of geologic studies, maps, and reports.

BOOKS

Brugge, Doug, Timothy Benally, and Esther Yazzie-Lewis, editors. *The Navajo People and Uranium Mining*. Albuquerque: University of New Mexico Press, 2006.

Cronyn, George W. *American Indian Poetry: An Anthology of Songs and Chants*. New York: Fawcett Columbine, 1962.

Dyk, Walter. *Son of Old Man Hat*. Lincoln: University of Nebraska Press, 1967.

Eichstaedt, Peter H. *If You Poison Us*. Santa Fe: Red Crane Books, 1994.

Evans, Will. *Along Navajo Trails: Recollections of a Trader 1898–1948*, edited by Susan E. Woods and Robert S. McPherson. Logan: Utah State University Press, 2005.

Gaddis, John Lewis. *The Cold War: A New History*. New York: Penguin Books, 2005.

Gillmor, Francis and Louise Wade Wetherill. *Traders to the Navajos: The Story of the Wetherills of Kayenta*. Albuquerque: University of New Mexico Press, 1965.

Groueff, Stephane. *Manhattan Project: The Untold Story of the Making of the Atomic Bomb*. London: Collins, 1962.

Groves, Leslie R. *Now It Can Be Told: The Story of the Manhattan Project*. New York: Harper and Bros., 1962.

Hintze, Lehi F. *Guidebook to the Geology of Utah, No. 21: Uranium Districts of Southeastern Utah*. Salt Lake City: Utah Geological Society, 1967.

Holiday, John, and Robert S. McPherson. *A Navajo Legacy: The Life and Teachings of John Holiday*. Norman: University of Oklahoma Press, 2005.

Hungate, Adam B. *Let Them Eat Yellowcake: Navajo Uranium and American*

Marginalization. Unpublished dissertion, University of California, Riverside, June 2005.

Iverson, Peter. *The Navajo Nation*. Albuquerque: University of New Mexico Press, 1983.

Iverson, Peter, and Monty Roessel. *Diné: A History of the Navajos*. Albuquerque: University of New Mexico Press, 2002.

Iverson, Peter, editor, and Monty Roessel, photo editor. *For Our Navajo People: Diné Letters, Speeches & Petitions, 1900–1960*. Albuquerque: University of New Mexico Press, 2002.

Left Handed, Walter Dyk, and Edward Sapir. *Left Handed, Son of Old Man Hat: A Navajo Autobiography*. Lincoln: University of Nebraska Press, 1995.

Locke, Raymond Friday. *The Book of the Navajo*. Los Angeles: Mankind Publishing Company, 6th edition, 2005.

McAllester, David P. *Enemy Way Music: A Study of Social and Esthetic Values as Seen in Navaho Music*. Milwood, NY: Kraus Reprint Co., 1973.

McPherson, Robert S. *Navajo Land, Navajo Culture: The Utah Experience in the 20th Century*. Norman: University of Oklahoma Press, 2001.

Memories Come to Us in the Wind and the Rain: Oral Histories and Photographs of Navajo Uranium Miners & Their Families. Boston: Navajo Uranium Miner Oral History and Photography Project, 1997.

Moon, Samuel. *Tall Sheep: Harry Goulding, Monument Valley Trader*. Norman: University of Oklahoma Press, 1992.

Nabokov, Peter. *Native American Testimony*, revised edition. New York: Penguin Books, 1999.

O'Neill, Colleen. *Working the Navajo Way: Labor and Culture in the 20th Century*. Lawrence: University of Kansas Press, 2005.

Oshley, Navajo. *The Journey of Navajo Oshley: An Autobiography and Life History*, edited by Robert S. McPherson. Logan: Utah State University Press, 2000.

Redd, Preston. *From Horseback to Cadillac, I'm Still a Cowboy: True Tales of the Old West*. Tempe: Tavas Cash Press, 1988.

Rhodes, Richard. *The Making of the Atomic Bomb*. New York: Simon & Schuster, 1986.

Robinson, Ruth Shumway, and Gary Lee Shumway. *The Family of Peter and Mary Johnson Shumway*. Fullerton: The Oral History Program, California State University, Fullerton, 1976.

Roussel, Ruth. *Navajo Stories of the Long Walk Period*. Tsaile, AZ: Navajo Community College Press, 1973.

Schwartz, Stephen I., editor. *Atomic Audit: The Costs and Consequences of U.S. Nuclear Weapons Since 1940*. Washington, DC: Brookings Institution Press, 1998.

Shumway, Gary. *The Development of the Uranium Industry in San Juan County, Utah,* Master's thesis, Brigham Young University, July 1964.

————, *A History of the Uranium Industry on the Colorado Plateau.* Unpublished dissertation, University of Southern California, January 1970.

Sides, Hampton. *Blood and Thunder.* New York: Doubleday. 2006.

Trennert, Robert A. *White Man's Medicine: Government Doctors and the Navajo, 1863–1955.* Albuquerque: University of New Mexico Press, 1998.

Udall, Stewart L. *The Myths of August: A Personal Exploration of Our Tragic Cold War Affair with the Atom.* New York: Pantheon, 1994.

United States Congress, House Committee on Interior and Insular Affairs, Subcommittee on Energy and the Environment. *Mill Tailings Dam Break at Church Rock, New Mexico. October 22, 1979.* Washington: U.S. Government Printing Office, 1980.

————, Senate Committee on Labor and Human Resources. *Health Effects of Radiation Exposure Caused by Open Air Atomic Testing and Uranium Mining. February 8, 1990.* Washington: Government Printing Office, 1990.

————, House Committee onNatural Resources. Subcommittee on Oversight and Investigations and Subcommittee on Native American Affairs. *Uranium Mine Waste on the Navajo Reservation, November 4, 1993.* Washington: U.S. Government Printing Office, 1994.

————, House Committee on Oversight and Government Reform. *The Health and Environmental Impacts of Uranium Contamination in the Navajo Nation, October 23, 2007.* Washington: U.S. Government Printing Office, 2008.

Valle, Doris. *Looking Back Around the Hat: A Brief History of Mexican Hat.* Mexican Hat, UT: D. Valle, 1986.

Welsome, Eileen. *The Plutonium Files: America's Secret Medical Experiments in the Cold War.* New York: The Dial Press, 1999.

White, Richard. *The Roots of Dependency: Subsistence, Environment and Social Change Among the Choctaws, Pawnees and Navajos.* Lincoln: University of Nebraska Press, 1983.

Williams, Aubrey W. *Navajo Political Process.* Washington, DC: Smithsonian Institution Press, 1970.

Zoellner, Tom. *Uranium: War, Energy, and the Rock That Shaped the World.* New York: Viking Penguin, 2009.

AUTHOR INTERVIEWS

The interview list does not include speakers observed at public meetings, hearings, or roundtables. Only a few people asked to remain anonymous. Among those who spoke on the record, many of them multiple times, are:

Academics and researchers—Temashio Anderson, Richard Auld, Sharon Austin, Fred Begay, Doug Brugge, Karletta Chief, Teresa Coons, Darryl De Vivo, Salvatore DiMauro, Cheryl Dyer, Franz Geiger, Joseph Hoover, Jani Ingram, James W. Justice, Richard I. Kelley, Charles R. Key, R. Clark Lantz, Elliott D. Lesses, Johnnye Lewis, Robert S. McPherson, Paul Mushak, Mansel Nelson, Ruth Ottman, John F. Rosen, Steve Semken, Ken Silver, Andrew Sowder, Gary Shumway, Diane Stearns, Bernadette Tsosie, William Walker, Gary Weglarz, Charles L. Wiggins, Tuan Vu.

Blackfalls/Cameron/Tuba City/Bodaway Gap—Nez Bencroft, Lisa Deel, Cherie Daut Neztsosie, David Neztsosie Jr., David Neztsosie Sr., Laura Neztsosie, Lois Neztsosie, Nora Neztsosie, Blanche Taho, Leland and Irene Yazzie, Milton Yazzie, Louise Yellowman, Raymond Yellowman.

Blue Gap/Tah-chee—D. Y. Begay, Gilbert Begay, Sadie Bill, Raymond Joe, Christopher Nez, Leonard and Helen Nez, Seraphina Nez, Susan Nez.

Cane Valley—Starlite Begay, Anna Benally, Nina Bennett, Sharon Black, Cecil Blackmountain, Anna Adakai Cly, Berlinda Cly, Queenie Greenstone, Roy Hathale, John Holiday, Eunice Jackson, Joe Jackson, Lorissa Jackson, Paul "Tim" Jackson, Mary Kinney, Bert Manheimer, Della McThias, Luke McThias, Terrance McThias, Timothy McThias, Hoskey Sloan, Ben and Mary Stanley, John and Huberta Stanley, Susie Taylor, Anna Jean Tsosie, Alice Black Tsosie, Daniel Yazzie, Herbert and Daisy Yazzie, Lewis Yazzie, Mary Lou Yazzie, Don and Rose B. Wilson.

Church Rock/Crownpoint/Haystack—Leonard Arviso, Tom Arviso, Peterson Bell, Gerald Brown, Mitchell Capitan, Ed Carlisle, Tony Hood, Marie Johnson, Wanda Johnson, Larry King, Albert Largo, Bessie Largo, James Largo, Sam Long, Melton Martinez, Teddy and Bertha Nez, Lynnea Smith, Brown Vandever, Gary Vandever.

U.S. Congress—Jeff Baran, Cynthia Cook, Karen Lightfoot, Jeanette Lyman, Ben Miller, Marissa Padilla, Rick Renzi, Phil Schiliro, Andrew Schneider, Tom Udall, Henry Waxman.

Navajo government officials and contractors (current and former)—George Arthur, Tommy K. Begay, Jr., Cassandra Bloedel, Perry Charley, Stanley Edison, Eugene Esplain, Stephen B. Etsitty, Albert Hale, George Hardeen, Carl Holiday, John Hueston, Sadie Hoskie, Rex Kontz, Arlene Luther, Cora Maxx-Phillips,

Diane Malone, Satya D. Misra, John Plummer, Joe Shirley Jr., David Taylor, Harold Tso, William Walker, Derrith Watchman-Moore, Peterson Zah.

Oljato—James Adakai, Elsie Begay, Sarah Begay, Daisy Haycock, Frank Haycock, Mary Holiday, Mary Holiday Parrish.

Red Valley/Cove/Oaksprings—Crystal Begay, J. C. Begay, Mary Alice Begaye, Mary Frank, James George, Phil Harrison Jr., Davin Joe, Dorothy Joe, Mae John, Jess King, Rex Kinsel, Leroy Light Sr., Albert Litson Jackson, Gloria Manning, Bernice Roe, Betty Russell, Lorraine Russell, Larry Martinez, Marshall Tome, Nellie Tsosie, George Tutt, Dolores Yazzie, Fannie Yazzie, Donald Yellowhorse.

U.S. Environmental Protection Agency—Harry Allen III, Harry Allen IV, Andrew Bain, Wendy Chavez, Will Duncan, Peter Guria, Joseph Hans, Clancy Tenley, Luis M. Garcia-Bakarich, Harrison Karr, Mark Merchant, William Mills, John Millett, Michael Montgomery, Wayne Nastri, Margot Perez-Sullivan.

Additional U.S. officials and contractors—Glynn Alsup, Victor Archer, Lucy Boulanger, Bruce Chelikowski, Steve Cinnamon, John Elmer, Mike Everett, John Fogarty, Steve Helgerson, John T. Hull, Brian Jordan, Margaret Knight, Craig Little, Robert Meyer, Judy Miller, Howard B. Nickelson, Jeffrey Nolte, Douglas Peter, Don Payne, Charles Reaux, Sydney Sewall.

Uranium mining industry—John DeJoia, Benjamin House, Jon Indall, Robert McNair, Mark Pelizza, David Miller, Thomas Sansonetti, Kenneth Vaughn, Juan Velasquez, Richard Wheatley.

Others—Tandie Askan, Thomas Atcitty, Gilbert Badonie, Dan Barber, Ronald Berg, Susan Black, Diane Curran, Michael Demangone, Geoffrey Fettus, Trent Harris, John Hueston, Homer and Sylvia Jackson, Eric Jantz, Harvey Leake, Sharon Masek Lopez, Bob, J. D. and Vonnie Mueller, Steve Passmore, Ann Phillips, Blanche and Richard Redhouse, George Rice, Earl Saltwater Jr., Patricia Seltzer, Chris Shuey, Valentina Smith, Jeff Spitz, Tully Stanley, Stewart Udall, Enrique Valdivia, Richard Valle.

ARTICLES

American Metal Market, "Isbell and Edwards Assume New Posts at Vanadium Corp," March 19, 1966.

Atomic Age Magazine (Official Publication of the Uranium Institute of America), "An open letter to Jess Johnson," July 1961.

Engineering and Mining Journal, "In the News and in the Mines," September 1954.

Daily Sentinel (Grand Junction, CO). "AEC Orders Cutback in Ore Buying at Monticello, Moab Buying Stations." February 6, 1955.

———. "Uranium Hunters Learning How to Get Rich on Plateau," and "Khrushchev Wields Iron Fist." February 8, 1955.

———. "Verbal Donnybrook Erupts at Uranium Troubles Meet," October 11, 1959.

———. "Bothersome UIA Problems Explained by AEC Official" and "Independent U Miners Unload Troubles on Senator Allott," October 10, 1959.

Durango Herald-News, Girl About Town column, September 5, 1956, and October 25, 1957.

Goodbody and Company Weekly Market Letter, July 7, 1954.

Mining World, "Johnson Retiring from AEC," March 1963.

Nucleonics Magazine, "Nuclear Industries Assn. Forming a Lobby," June 1958.

PAYDIRT (a Publication Devoted to the Interests of the Arizona Small Mine Operators), "Radiation Not High Enough to Cause Immediate Ill Health," March 18, 1955.

San Francisco Call-Bulletin, "Airplanes Prospect for Uranium Ore," September 23, 1954.

Time, "New Luster for Vanadium," August 20, 1945.

———, "Time Clock," July 9, 1956.

Times Independent (Moab, UT). "Colorado Plateau: Fabulous Treasure House of Energy," 1955, special edition.

Wall Street Journal, "Nuclear Test Ban Treaty Signed in Moscow," August 15, 1963.

Adler, Elissa. "Navajos Mined Cancer." *In These Times,* February 25–March 3, 1983.

Begay, Sararesa. "Forgotten at Black Falls? Family Says Health Problems Caused by Exposure to Uranium from Abandoned Mines Is Overlooked." *Navajo Times,* February 27, 2003.

Bird, Robert S. "Indians Mine Uranium Ore." *New York Herald Tribune News Service,* as published in the *Columbus Dispatch,* November 19, 1954.

Bissinger, Buzz. "Inventing Ford Country." *Vanity Fair,* March 2009.

Bragg, Rick. "The Valley of Broken Hearts." *St. Petersburg Times,* August 1, 1993.

Davis, Tony. "Uranium Has Decimated Navajo Miners." *High Country News,* June 18, 1990.

Drury, Allen. "Ample Uranium for Decade Seen. AEC Tells Congress U.S. Is Strong 'Competitively' and in 'Total Reserves.'" *New York Times,* March 6, 1957.

Guccione, Eugene. "Fuel Shortages Trigger New Uranium Rush in NM." *Mining Engineering,* August 1974.

Hastings, Deborah. "Uranium's Legacy for Navajo Miners Is a Painful Death." *Associated Press,* July 30, 2000.

Hecht, Andrew. "The Great Uranium Rush." *Argosy: The Complete Man's Magazine,* January 1955.

Helms, Kathy. "Shirley Will Ink Uranium Mining Ban: President to Sign Agreement Today." *Gallup Independent,* April 29, 2005.

———. "Navajo requests largely ignored in clean-up plan," *Gallup Independent,* August 17, 2008.

———. "I.H.S. to monitor Uranium Exposure." *Gallup Independent,* December 10, 2009.

Ivins, Molly. "Uranium Mines Leaving Indians a Legacy of Death." *New York Times,* May 20, 1979.

———. "'50s Uranium Miners Tell of Disease and Fight for Aid," *New York Times,* September 1, 1979.

Jennings, Trip. "A Big, Dirty Mess: The Federal Government Is Only Beginning to Clean Up Decades of Uranium Contamination Across the Navajo Nation," *New Mexico Independent,* June 27, 2008.

Lang, Daniel. "The Coming Thing," *New Yorker,* March 21, 1953.

Levy, Jerrold E. "Who Benefits from Energy Resource Development: The Special Case of Navajo Indians," *The Social Science Journal,* January 1980.

Pillsbury, Dorothy L. "Indians Inventory Tribal Problems." *Christian Science Monitor,* September 1, 1955.

Proty, Dick. "Nuclear Firm Given Clean Bill of Health." *Denver Post,* October 8, 1967.

Ransom, Jay. "We Followed the Lure of Carnotite," *Desert Magazine,* February 1950.

Richardson, Bill. "New Mexico, Arizona Indians Reaping Uranium Boom Profit," *Associated Press,* Albuquerque, December 9, 1954.

Ritchie, Jim. "AEC Promises to Hike Buying of Uranium," *Denver Post,* February 7, 1959.

Russell, Christine. "U.S. Failed to Protect Uranium Miners from Cancer Risk, Panel Is Told," *Washington Star,* June 20, 1979.

Ruffing, Lorraine Turner. "Navajo Mineral Development," *The Indian Historian,* Spring 1978.

Sabo, Pat. "Radiation Hazards Not Explained, Miner Testifies," *Phoenix Gazette,* August 19, 1983.

———. "Official Recalls Closing 2 Mines," *Phoenix Gazette,* August 19, 1983.

———. "Judge Denies Dismissal Bid in Damage Suit by Miners," *Phoenix Gazette,* August 20, 1983.

Scher, Zeke. "Stewart Udall Pioneering Toxic Chemical Litigation," *Denver Post,* January 8, 1984.

———. "Udall accuses U.S. of evading toxic liability," *Denver Post,* January 14, 1984.

Schmidt, William E. "Federal Judge Says U.S. Deceived Him in Fallout Case." *New York Times,* August 5, 1982.

Schneider, Keith. "Uranium Miners Inherit Dispute's Sad Legacy." *New York Times,* January 9, 1990.

Senia, Al. "Navajo N-Miners, Kin File Contamination Suit," *Albuquerque Journal,* December 15, 1979.

Shebala, Marley. "Anti-Uranium Forces Cheer Signing of Law," *Navajo Times,* May 6, 2005.

———. "Shirley Calls for Complete Cleanup of Uranium Wastes," *Navajo Times,* July 23, 2009.

Smith, Grant E. "Navajo Cancer Rate Linked to Uranium," *Arizona Republic,* July 22, 1979.

———. "29 Claims Filed Against U.S. for U-Miners' Lung Disorders," *Arizona Republic,* July 21, 1979.

———. "Navajo Families Sue Uranium Firms for Work Hazards," *Arizona Republic,* December 15, 1979.

Stanton, Kathleen. "Trial Nears on Navajo Miners' Claims Against U.S.," *Arizona Republic,* July 31, 1983.

———. "Uranium Perils Ignored, Suit Claims," *Arizona Republic,* August 3, 1983.

———. "U.S. Agencies Blamed for Uranium-Mine Peril," *Arizona Republic,* August 4, 1983.

———. "Mine Radiation 'Almost Certainly' Killed Worker," *Arizona Republic,* August 5, 1983.

———. "Uranium Miner Left Family Nothing, Widow Says During Radiation Trial," *Arizona Republic,* August 10, 1983.

———. "Mine Radiation in '50s Called Worse Than at Hiroshima: U.S. Failed to Address Hazards, Court Also Told," *Arizona Republic,* August 18, 1983.

———. "U.S. Freed of Liability for Cancer Among Navajo Uranium Miners," *Arizona Republic,* July 11, 1984.

Stapp, Robert. "Working in Uranium Mine Is Peril to Life" and "Radioactive Particles and Acid Fumes Have Ruined Many Workers' Health," *Denver Post,* July 7, 1949.

Steele, A.T. "Uranium Finds and Oil Leases Putting Money in Navajo Coffers," *St. Louis Post-Dispatch.* Undated copy in Stewart Udall Congressional papers.

Unna, Warren. "Uranium's Running Out of Nation's Ears," *Washington Post* and *Times Herald,* April 8, 1956.

White, Gordon Eliot. "First Claims on U-Mine Cancer Are Filed," *Deseret News,* July 21, 1979.

Yurth, Cindy. "Uranium Miners, Widows Get Warm Reception," *Navajo Times,* November 5, 2009.

———. "Protesters Picket URI Speaker in Gallup." *Navajo Times,* November 19, 2009.

MEDICAL JOURNALS

Appenzeller, Otto, Mario Kornfeld, and Russell Snyder. "Accromutilating, paralyzing neuropathy with corneal ulceration in Navajo children." *Archives of Neurology* 33, 11 (1976), pp. 733–738.

Archer V. E. "Health concerns in uranium mining and milling." *Journal of Occupational Medicine* 23, 7 (1981), pp. 502–5.

Auld, R. M. Jr. and W. S. Haubrich. "Rapidly rising incidence of gastric carcinoma in Navajo Indians and its relationship to uranium mining." *Gastroenterology* 92, 5 Part 2 (1987).

Gilliland, Frank D., William C. Hunt, Marla Pardilla, and Charles R. Key. "Uranium mining and lung cancer among Navajo men in New Mexico and Arizona, 1969 to 1993." *Journal of Occupational and Environmental Medicine* 42, 3 (March 2000), pp. 278–283.

Gottlieb, L. S., and L. A. Husen. "Lung cancer among Navajo uranium miners." *Chest* 81, 4, pp. 449–452.

Holve, S., D. Hu, M. Shub, R. Tyson and R. Sokol, "Liver disease in Navajo neuropathy," *The Journal of Pediatrics* 135, 4, pp. 482–493.

Karadimas, Charalampos L., Tuan H. Vu, Stephen A. Hove, Penelope Chronopoulu, Catarina Quinzii, Stanley D. Johnsen, Janice Kurth, Elizabeth Eggers, Lluis Palenzuela, Kurenai Tanji, Eduardo Bonilla, Darryl C. De Vivo, Salvatore DiMauro, and Michio Hirano. "Navajo neurohepatopathy is caused by a mutation in the MPV17 gene." *The American Journal of Genetics* 79 (September 2006).

Kurtiio, Paivi, Hannu Komulainen, Aila Leino, Laina Salonen, Aussi Auvinen, and Heikki Saha. "Bone as a possible target of chemical toxicity of natural uranium in drinking water." *Environmental Health Perspectives* 113, 1 (January 2005).

Moure-Eraso, Rafael. "Uranium mining in the Navajo nation (1947–1966): A case of undesigned human experimentation." *International Congress Series: The History of Occupational and Environmental Prevention,* 1999.

Raymond-Whish, Stefanie, Loretta P. Mayer, Tamara O'Neal, Alisyn Martinez, Marilee A. Sellers, Patricia J. Christian, Samuel L. Marion, Carlyle Begay, Catherine R. Propper, Patricia B. Hoyer, and Cheryl A. Dyer. "Drinking water with uranium below the U.S. EPA water standard causes estrogen receptor-dependent responses in female mice." *Environmental Health Perspectives* 115, 12 (December 2007).

Rosen, John F., and Mushak Paul. "Metal and radiation-induced toxic neuropathy in two Navajo sisters." *Pediatric Research* 45, 4 part 2 (April 1999) p. 346A.

Ruttenber, A. J., Jr., K. Kreiss, R. L. Douglas, T. E. Buhl, and J. Millard. "The assessment of human exposure to radionuclides from a uranium mill tailings release and mine dewatering effluent." *Health Physics* 47, 1 (1984), pp. 21–36.

Salsbury, C. G. "Cancer Immunity in the Navajo." *Arizona Medicine* 13, August 8, 1956, pp. 309–10.

Shields, L. M., W. H. Wiese, B. J. Skipper, B. Charley and L. Benally. "Navajo birth outcomes in the Shiprock uranium mining area." *Health Physics* 63, 5 (1992), pp. 542–551.

Singleton, R., S. D. Helgerson, R. D. Snyder, P. J. O'Conner, S. Nelson, S. D. Johnsen, and J. E. Allanson. "Neuropathy in Navajo children: Clinical and epidemiological features." In Brief Communications, *Neurology* (February 1990), p. 363.

Vu, Tuan H., Kurenai Tanji, Stephen A. Holve, Eduardo Bonilla, Ronald J. Sokol, Russell D. Snyder, Stephany Fiore, Gail H. Deutsch, Salvatore DiMauro, and Darryl De Vivo. "Navajo neurohepatopathy: a mitochondrial DNA depletion syndrome?" *Hepatology* 34: 1 (July 2001), pp. 116–120.

Wagoner, J. K., V. E. Archer, F. E. Lundin, D. A. Holaday, and J. W. Lloyd. "Radiation as the cause of lung cancer among uranium miners." *New England Journal of Medicine* 273, 4 (1965), pp. 181–188.

Yazzie, M., G. Reuss, S. L. Gamble, E. R. Civitello, and D. Stearns. "DNA damage induced by reactions of uranyl acetate with ascorbate." *Environmental and Molecular Mutagenesis* 39, Supplement 33 (2002), p. 69.

INDEX

Pages beginning with 265 refer to notes.

ABOUT THE AUTHOR

Judy Pasternak has written for a wide range of media outlets, including the *Daily Beast, Smithsonian* magazine, the Investigative Reporting Workshop, and the *Nonproliferation Review*. Previously, she reported for the *Los Angeles Times,* in Los Angeles, Chicago, and Washington, D.C., where she tackled subjects as varied as al Qaeda's private airline, a band of right-wing bank robbers, backstage maneuvering at Dick Cheney's energy task force, and the giant black hole at the center of the Milky Way. She has won numerous awards for environmental and investigative journalism. She lives near Washington, D.C., with her husband and son.